DATE DUE

MAR 1 1 1998	
DEC 1 5 1998	
SEP 2 8 2001	

Education for Democratic Citizenship

**DECISION MAKING
IN THE SOCIAL STUDIES**

Education for Democratic Citizenship

**DECISION MAKING
IN THE SOCIAL STUDIES**

Shirley H. Engle

&

Anna S. Ochoa

TEACHERS
COLLEGE
PRESS

Teachers College, Columbia University
New York and London

Published by Teachers College Press, 1234 Amsterdam Avenue,
New York, NY 10027

Library of Congress Cataloging-in-Publication Data

Engle, Shirley H.
  Education for democratic citizenship.

  Bibliography: p.
  Includes index.
  1. Civics—Study and teaching—United States.
2. Social sciences—Study and teaching—United States.
I. Ochoa, Anna. II. Title.
H62.5.U5E54   1988   300'.7'1073   87-26721

ISBN 0-8077-2889-6
ISBN 0-8077-2888-8 (pbk.)

Manufactured in the United States of America

93 92 91 90 89 88   1 2 3 4 5 6

Contents

Part I

**RATIONALE FOR A CURRICULUM
DESIGNED TO PROMOTE
DEMOCRATIC CITIZENSHIP**

1

Implications of the Democratic Ideal for the Social Studies

In this book the social studies are linked incontrovertibly with the democratic ideal. Social studies is taken to be that part of general and liberal education that specializes in the education of an effective democratic citizen. The democratic citizen is not to be understood merely in the classic "good citizenship" sense of one who is patriotic, loyal, and obedient to the state; rather, the good citizen is also a critic of the state, one who is able and willing to participate in its improvement. The characteristics of such a citizen will be spelled out in Chapter 2, and the education necessary to develop these characteristics will be laid out in succeeding chapters. Whatever the particular forms that social studies may take—the disciplines to be studied, social problems to be resolved, and school and community activities to be engaged in—these forms must be continually verified in terms of their service to democracy. Therefore, we believe an elaboration of democratic principles provides guidance in developing social studies programs.

We are perfectly aware that democracy is an imprecise and continuously developing social form. As Harry Broudy (1981) puts it in a recent book, "At the moment, it is difficult to formulate a definition of democracy that would not be as divisive as the diversity it is intended to unify" (p. 149). To paraphrase Broudy further, the term democracy is invoked by Marxists and by free enterprise capitalists alike, by terrorist groups in the Middle East and by so-called freedom fighters almost everywhere. It is invoked by conservatives who say they want freedom from governmental interference and by liberals who see governmental interference as the guarantor of social justice.

That the democratic ideal is so pervasive as to invade the thinking of so wide a spectrum of conflicting groups is in itself a telling fact about

3

democracy. Called by Thomas Jefferson "the great experiment," democracy clearly may take varied forms, but its appeal is to basic beliefs that transcend these differences.

Gunnar Myrdahl, the distinguished Swedish economist, in his book *An American Dilemma* (1944) identified the essential ideas of what he called "The American Creed" as being respect for the dignity of the individual human being and a belief in human perfectibility, in the fundamental equality of all people, and in certain inalienable rights to freedom, justice, and a fair opportunity for all. From these ideas flow still others, such as government based on the consent of the governed, respect for decisions made by the majority, freedom of speech and the press, tolerance of racial and religious differences, and the value of decisions arrived at by common counsel rather than by violence and brutality. Myrdahl sees these ideas as deeply rooted in the English Common Law and the Enlightenment. He sees them as the driving force in our war for independence and as being celebrated in the Declaration of Independence, in the Preamble to the Constitution, in the Bill of Rights, and in the constitutions of the various states. He sees them as continuously being called into play in the law-making process, in Supreme Court decisions, and in politics.

However, despite this seeming unity of purpose, there have always been disharmonies as the Creed was applied to particulars. Just as recent debates in Congress over tax simplification and reform have revolved around the question of fairness and equality of treatment, so throughout our history has there been a continuous discussion over the meaning of democracy when applied to specific cases. Particularly bothersome has been the conflict between two of the most basic ideas of democracy: that of freedom and that of equality. The exercise of one person's freedom may well mean the denial of equality to another. The debates between conservatives and liberals, both professing democratic ideals, have tended to rage along this uncertain line, as described by Reinhold Niebuhr (1971):

> A democratic society is distinguished from the traditional societies of the ancient and medieval periods by at least three characteristics. First, it invites the free play of political opinion and social forces and arms its citizens with ultimate authority over the government by giving them the right to vote. . . . Second, democratic societies do not, and cannot, compel cultural and religious uniformity. . . . Third, Western democracies allow free competition between economic forces on the theory that justice can be achieved through the free market. . . .
>
> We are thus brought to the real issue of the problem on consensus in a democratic community. That problem concerns the measure of consensus operating within the very differences of opinion and interest that are allowed free play within society. Here is the core of the problem. For if

the differences are too wide, the party conflict may become so acrimonious that each side will accuse the other of disloyalty to the common good. And if there is no consensus below the level of political conflict, contradictory moral and religious convictions may also destroy the unity of the community. (pp. 1–4)

It is our position that the best hope for democracy lies not in indoctrination of shaky truths or in painting over the problems that plague us, but rather with the cultivation of citizens who, with open eyes and awareness of democratic values, have the facility to make intelligent political judgments related to controversial issues in our society. John Courtney Murray (1964) has put his finger on the problem and the solution that we have chosen to embrace:

There is the problem of the relationship between power and freedom; the problem of rethinking the whole principle of "consent"; the problem of rethinking the principle of representation. There is the issue of the respective functions of executive and legislative. There is the problem of the structure of our machinery, especially for foreign policymaking. Finally, there is the role of the people in government, the ancient problem of participation. I think, here, that the big principle we must not get rid of is the one that is rooted in our tradition, in our real tradition—namely, that it is the right and the duty of the people to judge, direct, and correct the actions of the kings. That is what they said in the Middle Ages. Today we would say not "king" but "government." This is a basic principle that one must never go back on. The problem is clear. It is to cultivate among the people the faculty of political judgment, and this means, above all, to lay down standards for right political judgment. This is a problem of ideas. (p. 89)

We are perfectly aware that democracy in this country and in the West generally has had its problems. In a highly urbanized, industrial society, the town meeting form of democracy that suited an agrarian society has broken down. It is discouraging to democratic ideologues that the "majority" is frequently a minority, simply because citizens do not bother to vote. The citizen is not always well informed and is frequently misled by the media. Well-heeled special interests wield inordinately more power than do ordinary citizens. The rights of individuals and minorities have been unevenly protected, to say the least. International affairs are not really subject to the will of the people and frequently are conducted in opposition to the interests of democracy. Democratic institutions have faltered badly under the stress of war. But even the harshest critics of democracy, such as Harry Elmer Barnes (1942) and Lord James Bryce (1921), have concluded that democracy, with all its problems, is still the

best hope for human beings on the earth. This book accepts that judgment. It is premised on the belief that if democracy has its problems, and
it does, the solution lies not in authoritarianism but in more effectively
conceived democratic institutions. For the sake of all peoples, democracy
must be made to work better and education must be enlisted in developing the kind of citizens who will promote its welfare.

All of this must be done with a clear realization that the conditions
under which democracy must work today are vastly changed from those
prevailing in the days of the founders and that these conditions will continue to change. The responsibility that the citizen is called upon to
shoulder is vastly more complicated than it was 200 years ago, or even 75
years ago, when the social studies were first conceived. Technology has
produced an upheaval in the ways that people live and consequently in
the ways that individuals relate to one another. The wars into which democracies have been drawn and the economic displacement which has
followed them have placed a tremendous strain on the maintenance of free
democratic institutions.[1] Many older democratic institutions simply do not
fit the circumstances of postindustrial society. Many of our contemporary
problems, such as protection of the environment from toxic waste, did not
exist—or were not yet recognized as problems—as recently as fifty years
ago. Individual civic responsibilities have not only vastly increased in
number over just a few years ago but they have changed in kind as well.
In today's world our closest relationships may well be with people whom
we may never see rather than with those in our immediate communities.
The traditional face-to-face community to which most problems were addressed in the context of intimate community relationships hardly exists
anymore. Furthermore, traditional democratic values such as freedom,
equality, and justice have taken on new meanings in a world of instant
communication and huge and economically powerful multinational con-
glomerates. For instance, labor unions, which came into existence barely
a hundred years ago, were until very recently bulwarks of power and influence in our society. They are now in headlong retreat in the face of the
high-tech revolution. The two-party system that has dominated the process of political decision making in the United States for well over 200
years is now in sad disarray because of special interest voting. Political
party discipline is rapidly becoming unenforceable. Old word-of-mouth and
face-to-face relationships and old party loyalties, through which decisions were made in earlier times, are now seriously compromised by the
mass media. Furthermore, the credibility of leaders in education and of
the clergy, the professions, and the press has been badly compromised by
the growth of a special interest morality over that of the common good.[2]

Democracy must not only persist in its ancient values, but it must at the same time develop new institutions and new values compatible with the old if it is to survive and prosper in a postindustrial world. The extent to which such changes affect the nature of civic responsibility has been well stated by Father Robert O. Johann, S.J., (1965), a distinguished Catholic intellectual:

> First of all there is the increased sense of time and history. Institutions and formulations that were formerly considered to be absolute are now seen to be relative, the product of history. Traditional patterns and conventions which were once thought of as presuppositions, part of the given and set up by God, are now viewed as human accomplishments. However much they may embody absolute values, they are still only limited and contingent expressions of those values and must be measured for their shortcomings against the very values they try to express. Thus norms and behaviors which were once beyond discussion are now considered as proper matters for discussion.
>
> Secondly, there is the tremendous growth of this area of communication. The individual is no longer able to be reared in his formative years within the context of a single world view that gives him the truth about his place in the universe. From infancy he is bombarded by a plurality of traditions. The result has been to weaken the authority of any one of them as normative for his life. The individual must decide the stand he will take and do on his own responsibility. . . .
>
> The scope of personal responsibility has been immeasurably broadened. The person is no longer responsible merely for the conduct of life and for bringing it into conformity with pre-existing patterns. He now sees himself responsible for the very patterns themselves. For contemporary man nothing finite and determinate is final or incapable of improvement. The person today sees himself in the role of a perpetual and wholesale renovator. (pp. 142–143)

Father Johann's statement, when applied to the problem of the education of citizens, tells us that in present-day democracy, it is of far greater importance to focus on helping young people make intelligent and responsible decisions for themselves than it is to tell them what to think. Blind indoctrination is futile, if not immoral, and is wholly out of character with democracy. We must stop exhorting students to be "good citizens" according to our own unquestioned view of good and help them instead to ask "good questions" about their own values and those of others. We must engage ourselves, teachers and students alike, actively and directly in the difficult task of reconsidering our behavior as individuals and as a community in light of the traditional values that we may have taken for granted or even ignored in the past. The ultimate training ground for civic competence is engagement in the resolution of the issues and problems that confront our society. It is an evasion of our responsibility as educators to stop short of this engagement.

It has been the unique contribution of the United States along with other democracies to keep the debate over justice, freedom, and equality open and free of the violence and brutality that characterize autocracies whether of the right or the left, even those which profess to be democratic. It stretches credibility to the breaking point to conceive of democracy being imposed upon people by armies, secret police, and death squads, or for that matter by indoctrination, propaganda, intellectual harrassment, secrecy, and deceit. It is naïve to believe that anyone except the wielders of such power will be better off in the long run from the exercise of such authority. It is in this conception of democracy and its problems that we see the purpose of social studies in the education of citizens. Its purpose is not to impose any particular form of democracy on young people or to intrude itself in such a way as to preclude the consideration of any other point of view, however abhorrent it may be. Rather, its purpose is to keep the dialogue open. Its role is to help children and youth acquire the knowledge and the intellectual skills needed to keep the discussion open and to enable the young citizen to participate in the process of improving the society. Citizens in a democracy must be able to judge the credibility of various claims to truth. They must be able to exercise independent judgment about social and personal affairs. We therefore applaud the following statement from Robert Hutchins (1982) on the aim of a democratic society. In our view the education of citizens is to be achieved by seizing every opportunity to keep talking about questions worth talking about and with as much intelligence as can be mustered. It follows logically from this statement of purpose that controversies, rather than fixed knowledge and values, will play a central role in the structuring of social studies instruction. As Hutchins explained:

> I think that the only thing it is possible to do in a democratic country on any subject is to keep talking and to seize every opportunity to talk. I recently ran across a letter from Thomas Jefferson to John Adams. Jefferson, at the age of 70, wrote to John Adams, aged 78. Jefferson said, more or less in these words, "I state my difference with you not because I wish to begin a controversy when we are both too old to change opinions arrived at over a long life of experience and reflection. I state my difference with you only because I believe that we ought before we die to explain ourselves to one another." This in a sentence or two is the aim of a democratic society.

Having recognized both the potential and the problems of democracy, having staked out a position which argues for an open curriculum, and having charted the central role of the social studies as aiding and abetting a continuing dialogue, we offer a survey of democratic values. The listing is admittedly idealistic, and there will be those who will be incensed because it lacks realism or even because it is in conflict with their own private beliefs—those, for example, who for ideological or selfish reasons, may argue that people are not really equal after all. Nonetheless, this list will afford a basis for argument in thinking about a curriculum more responsive to the needs of democracy.

The most basic value of democracy is respect for the dignity of the individual. This value includes the protection by the state of the life and general well-being of the individual as well as the protection of individuals in their right to dissent from the group. The right of dissent includes the right to exercise influence as a member of a minority group.

A prominent feature of democracy in the United States is the upward mobility of its people and their constant striving to improve, to spread everything—culture, economic well-being, and understanding—upward and onward. Improvement comes about through the exchange of ideas which democracy not only allows but protects. In a democracy it is theoretically possible for one individual or one small group to persuade the whole nation to change its course. Thus it is impossible to think of democracy as existing at all without the protection of the right to dissent. In fact, the strength of democracy lies in the exercise of this right.

Respect for the individual also implies acceptance of the differences between individuals and groups and, most importantly, respect for the feelings and opinions of others. In schools such respect would mean that the experiences and questions of children are never to be ignored. More generally, respect for the individual runs counter to discrimination because of race, religion, sex, cultural differences, and the like. Respect for the individual works to lessen the use of compulsion and force in human affairs and to increase the use of reason and dialogue together as the better way to make decisions.

A second important tenet of democracy is the right of individuals and groups to participate in decisions within the society as a whole. Without such participation, respect for the individual is meaningless and democracy becomes unworkable. In a modern, populous, and pluralistic society participation has been extended to mean the right to vote and to have one's vote count. This also includes the right to be fairly represented through the mechanisms provided by the political system (committees, councils, legislatures, executive officials, and the like). Implied also in the right of participation is equality of opportunity to participate in all of the organizations by which the social system is controlled. This would include not only the educational system and the workplace but social and political organizations of all kinds which engage, directly or indirectly, in the political process. Important in this respect is the right of individuals and groups to be represented by spokespersons in the halls of government. The bottom line is that all citizens within the society must have a fair chance to be heard and to influence decisions.

A third tenet of democracy is the right of all citizens to be informed, that is, to have knowledge. Participation in a democracy is meaningless unless citizens have full access to information. The widest and freest distribution of information to all of the people is a democratic necessity, and therefore the education of the masses is a central concern of a democracy.

Yet dependable knowledge is not achieved merely by having information disseminated in the schools, the media, or the arts. Individuals must make information meaningful for themselves, using their own intellectual capabilities. Equally important is the development of the intellectual skills needed to collect, sort, verify, and apply meaningful knowledge to problems and issues in the society. Dependable and meaningful knowledge seldom comes full-blown out of books or lectures or television programs. It must be worked over in the mind and utilized in life situations never before seen and in some measure unique to every individual. Consequently, a large responsibility of education in a democracy is the development of the intellectual skills whereby information is rendered meaningful.

Fourth, democracy assumes an open society in the sense that change and improvement are taken for granted. Democracy is never completed. There are no final solutions, no unquestioned answers. Instead democracy is characterized by a constant striving for improvement, a belief that it is possible to improve the quality of life for all. In this respect democracy is to be contrasted with authoritarian systems that allow no variations except those that suit the ruling elite at the top and that discourage questioning, depreciate the importance of new information, and insist on the strict obedience of the citizen to the governing class. The strength of democracy lies in its openness, its responsiveness to new information and new conditions, and its fostering of questioning and of dissent.

Lastly, democracy assumes some independence of the individual from the group. Because democratic citizens are expected to exercise independent judgment, their education cannot be looked upon as merely a matter of being socialized or conditioned to accept unquestioningly the ways of the group, as might be true among the citizens of a dictatorship. An open society requires that individuals achieve some autonomy from their own group. This requires some understanding of the origins and reasons for group differences and the nature of cultural biases, including those of one's own group. Such understanding requires a broadening of experience and perspective beyond the local, the common, and the immediate. Citizens of a democracy must be allowed room for doubt, even of their own most cherished beliefs. They must be encouraged to question. They must be able to withstand the socializing process. An important responsibility of education in a democracy is the countersocialization of youth. Countersocialization serves as the very crux of liberal education and the lifeblood of democratic education. Students are taught how to be skilled critics of the society rather than unquestioning citizen-soldiers who obey whoever is in power without raising a question. It is the tolerance of democracy for the countersocialization process that sets it apart from authoritarian systems. It is the tolerance of democracy for questioning and critical citizenship that makes the system work.

If this be democracy, then it is important for those of us who are engaged in the education of citizens for a democracy to understand that the democratic citizen is a new and different breed, very unlike the obedient, unquestioning citizen-soldiers who have inhabited most societies down through history. We cannot hope to advance the development of democratic citizenship by imitating educational models based on autocracy. On the contrary, we must develop educational methods that are consistent with the freedom and rationality upon which democracy thrives.

In the matter of cultural transmission and habit formation the contrast between autocracy and democracy shows clearly. In an autocracy habit formation through blind conditioning and with little if any reflection on the part of the learner is almost the totality of citizenship education. Citizens are expected to be unquestioning creatures of habit and blindly loyal to authority. In stark contrast, in a democracy habits are only a part, and a minor part at that, of the citizen's accoutrement, and habit formation is tempered with reason. Habits are held with more flexibility and greater tentativeness and, once learned, may even be questioned and modified.

This does not mean that democratic citizens are less committed to democracy than are their counterparts to autocracy. Their commitment may even be stronger because it has reason on its side. Citizens in a democracy are more likely to stand by their commitment in times of crisis, for theirs is a commitment to broad principles that they have accepted voluntarily. Under democracy adjustments can be made for new conditions without threatening the underlying democratic foundations of the society. Citizens of a dictatorship are more likely to become disoriented in times of social crises, for there is no room under dictatorship for reasoned adjustment.

While democratic citizens are characterized by habits friendly to democracy and by commitment to democracy, they also are expected, somewhat paradoxically, to possess countersocializing characteristics such as the willingness to criticize and the ability to question social norms. Citizens are expected, for good reasons, to stand out against the crowd. They are expected to be able to see a social problem in its broadest perspective and be inclined to seek rational and political, as opposed to arbitrary and military, solutions to problems.

In all societies, the education of the very young is almost totally a process of socialization. From parents, peers, and teachers, young children learn how to behave, what to believe, what to honor and respect, what to fear—indeed almost everything they need to know to fit into the society. This is learned almost as if by osmosis, without the child's really doing any thinking about it. The pressure of society on young children is to conform to the folkways of the society. Even such important matters as political bias and the social attitudes of a particular social class are learned by small children without their having substantive reasons for holding to these beliefs.

In an autocracy, this process of socialization is continued throughout adulthood. Citizens are expected to be loyal, patriotic, and unquestioning. Those in absolute authority continue the socializing process into adult life through such means as controlling or censoring the media and prescribing the content of education, both of which are used to spread propaganda favorable to the rulers. Citizens who persist in raising questions are suppressed or even killed.

In sharp contrast to the life-long socialization that characterizes the education of citizens under dictatorships, citizens in a democracy should be exposed as they grow in mental maturity to educational experiences which will liberate them from the dead weight of socialization. At an early age, citizens should be helped to develop substantive reasons for beliefs which they earlier accepted on faith. As they reach the age when rational thought is possible, certainly by the time they are in middle school, they should be encouraged and helped to develop the intellectual capacity for independence of thought, social criticism, and problem solving.

Thus we see that citizenship education appropriate to a democracy will be both socializing and countersocializing at one and the same time. It will prepare citizens who possess the habits and commitments necessary to democratic survival, such as a deep respect for others, but who hold these habits and commitments in a reasoned way. It will also prepare citizens who willingly and skillfully engage in the process of criticizing and improving the democratic society of which they strongly feel a part. The optimum development of each of those characteristics is the task of citizenship education in a democracy.

Because socialization may be merged almost imperceptibly into and overlap with countersocialization, especially at lower grade levels, there is a danger that those in charge of citizenship education will not distinguish sufficiently between the two processes. Educators may continue to socialize youngsters far beyond the period in their development when they are fully capable of critical thinking. They may use content—as, for instance, the social sciences—in such a way as to further socialize youngsters, when this content would be more appropriately used as an instrument of countersocialization. Or, for example, elementary teachers may be carried away with transmitting to children the oversimple and sometimes purely fictional versions of reality, including democracy. In such cases, teachers may be insensitive to the opportunities for developing questioning skills in children even at an early age. For instance, the question might be asked, "Are there other versions of the same event?" A second version could then be read to students, followed by the questions: "How does it happen that there is more than one version of the same event? How can we know which version is correct?" Such a line of questioning may lead to the more general question, "What is the nature of evidence and of proof?" Or, to take another instance, children who have been reading in poetry or in historical prose about wars for freedom might be directed toward some further analysis of the meaning of freedom by being asked, "What is freedom? How can we know when we have freedom?"

We are now ready to offer a definition of the social studies consistent with the nature of citizenship in a democracy as set out above.

The social studies are concerned exclusively with the education of citizens. In a democracy, citizenship education consists of two related but somewhat disparate parts: the first socialization, the second countersocialization.

Socialization, which occurs primarily but not exclusively at lower grade levels, is concerned with transmitting a reasoned attitude and understanding of democratic culture and with developing the basic habits necessary to make democracy work in an unreflective manner. The democratic behavior of young children is heavily influenced by the examples set by adults and by simple narratives based on history, as well as by the social sciences and even by works of fiction that describe and celebrate democratic institutions.

Countersocialization, which occurs primarily but not exclusively at higher grades when socialization is no longer necessary or appropriate, is concerned with developing the ability for independent critical thinking and with fostering individual responsibility in citizens. The focus here is on questioning the validity of alternative truth claims and on resolving social problems. The social sciences and history, along with literature, journalism, the arts, and—not unimportantly—the firsthand experience of students, may be used as the data base for the study of important questions and problems. Critical attention is paid to the credibility of each part of the data base as a source of reliable information.

Having described the democratic ideal, we should hasten to reiterate that democracy has never worked perfectly in real life, nor has the democratic ideal been yet achieved, if indeed it ever can be. Yet one advantage claimed for democracy is that it makes it possible to recognize freely the problems of society and to work for their resolution.

We need to recognize that there have been throughout its existence and continue to be even now major disharmonies within democracy. For instance, the freedom under democracy to pursue private or corporate gain frequently runs counter to civic justice and the general welfare. As Robert Reich (1983), has documented, American democracy has operated throughout its history with two cultures: the one, the private, later corporate, business culture that claimed for itself responsibility for investment, productivity, and economic growth; the other, the civic culture that claimed for itself responsibility for the equitable distribution of welfare among our citizens, including health, education, public services, environmental protection, and the like. The two cultures are frequently in conflict. The government has tended to throw its weight to first one and then to the other of these interests. The challenge to democracy is in the provision of both economic growth and social justice.

A related issue is the disharmony between the possession of great wealth by some and equality or equity for all. By whatever means, whether through individual initiative, political advantage, or just luck, some people grow much richer than others. Once achieved, riches give to those who possess them an advantage in gaining still greater wealth. With wealth go power and influence, over the economy and over government, as well as easier access to culture and education. The wealthy may come to control the very production and distribution of knowledge. By financing and hence controlling research, by owning and hence controlling the media, and by exerting inordinate influence on government, the wealthy may come to control the schools and what they teach. Democracy has always undertaken to restrain the owners of wealth by such measures as progressive taxation and free public education. Just how to do this and to what extent are perennial problems that confront democracy.

Lastly, the promise of democracy for individual growth and improvement and for openness and dynamism in dealing with the problems of society conflicts with the tendency of culture to reproduce itself with all its rigidities, inconsistencies, and inequities intact. The problem is exacerbated by the fact that the socialization process is to a great extent a silent process. It lies in the things taken for granted, in the habits of the culture, including many no longer appropriate but never questioned. It may be transmitted easily by example and by gesture, even by the raising of the eyebrow. Conformity is a comfortable state even when it glosses over gross inequities and disfunctions.

Schools, enmeshed in the timeless web of the culture, tend naturally to be conservative institutions, since it is more comfortable to pass along conventional wisdom than to question the assumptions of society. There is a body of evidence showing that schools do more to stamp in the status quo than to foster the questing spirit and the creativity so essential to democracy and that they do more to maintain the class structure of society than to open up the opportunities that every individual in a democracy rightly deserves (Bowles, 1972; Apple, 1982). The challenge to democracy is to achieve both conservation and reform at one and the same time. The challenge to democratic education is to reach a reasonable accommodation between socialization of youth and the development of their critical capabilities.

In all of these matters we recognize that democracy is faced with grievous problems and disharmonies. Nonetheless, we believe that democracy is the best possible vehicle for overcoming these problems. However, social studies education which ignores these problems is not only unreal and without credibility with students or citizens, but hypocritical and immoral as well. The only sensible solution is to take an approach that recognizes our problems for what they are and treats them with reason and compassion as key elements in democratic development.

2

The Citizen We Need
in a Democracy

This chapter assumes that the purpose of the social studies is the development of good citizens in a democracy. In planning the social studies curriculum, it is necessary, therefore, to inquire: What is it that good citizens in a democracy are required to do? What attitudes, what knowledge, and what skills do they need if they are to be effective citizens?

WHO IS A CITIZEN?

Citizenship is conferred on an individual by a state or nation. A citizen is a legally recognized member of a state or nation. Within this strict sense citizenship is the set of relationships that exist between an individual and a state. These relationships include both rights and responsibilities. In the case of democracy the rights of individuals include the right to be heard and to participate in their own governance, the right to equal protection of the law, and the right to basic freedoms such as those of religion, speech, and the press. The responsibilities of the citizen include respect for the law and the responsibility to participate in the governance of the state by voting, holding office, joining political parties and interest groups, and the like. The citizen's responsibilities also include the responsibility to be informed, for participation in a democracy is irresponsible if it is not informed.

In a broader sense, citizenship may be seen as extending to almost the whole of life. In this sense, whenever individuals make a decision or act in any way that affects others, directly or indirectly, knowingly or unknowingly, they are acting as citizens. Thus the individual who independently decides, out of a concern for the world's supply of dwindling natural resources, to buy a smaller car without being required to do so by law, is performing an act of citizenship; some would say an act of good citizenship. This decision, along with those of others, could be as powerful as any law intended to compel the same behavior. Significantly, the behavior of such citizens could profoundly affect the welfare of people outside their own state and throughout the world. Thus, the self-imposed conservation of gasoline by people in numerous countries during the oil crisis of the 1970s was an unexpected turn of events of great importance. It is clear that the private decisions and acts of citizens are an important, if not a critical, part of the fabric of citizenship in a democracy.

In still another sense citizenship transcends the affairs of the state. Individuals are members of many groups that extend beyond the strict purview of the state. In this sense individuals are citizens of their families, their religious institutions, the workplace, the school, and of the world. Indeed, in today's world, recognition that the largest group to which we belong is the human species is essential. In a context where human beings are capable of destroying civilization and where individuals as well as nations can have world-wide effects, the question of responsibility to the species is no longer an academic issue. The democratic ideal is equally as applicable to all of those groups as it is to the affairs of the state. It is doubtful whether democratic government would be able to survive were not democratic behavior widely protected in every walk of life within the nation. It is also doubtful that a democratic nation can long survive if adherence to democratic principles were to stop at its own borders. The basic strength of democracy seems to lie in the respect it affords to the rights of human beings everywhere. To the extent that this is true, our own democracy at home becomes more plausible and workable.[1]

THE EDUCATIONAL NEEDS OF DEMOCRATIC CITIZENS

It should be clear from the above that citizenship education must include far more than merely knowledge of the mechanics of government. It must include a reasoned commitment to democratic principles and an understanding of how these principles apply in every aspect of life from the most local of social groups to the peoples of the entire world.

Most important of all, the democratic citizen must be a skilled and responsible decision maker. The strength of democracy lies in the broad and intelligent participation of citizens in the affairs of the society at all levels and in all walks of life. In contrast to autocracy, participation in a democracy is not a matter of subservience to power or blind loyalty to the state but is a willingness to be responsible for the state and to engage at all levels in the decisions that chart its course. Decision-making skills and all of the knowledge and attitudes that go into the making of intelligent decisions are at the heart of democratic citizenship. The nature of the education needed by such citizens is discussed below under the following headings: Basic Knowledge, Commitment to the Democratic Ideal, Basic Intellectual Skills, and Political Skills.[2]

Basic Knowledge

What basic knowledge does the citizen in a democracy need? It should be fairly obvious from the above analysis that citizens in a democracy need a broad liberal education. No education that is confined merely to vocational ends will do. Nor are piecemeal excursions into a few academic areas unrelated to the problems that confront society likely to provide the broad liberal education needed. In today's interdependent world, piecemeal treatment of the problems confronting citizens will certainly fail. It is imperative that citizens gain the widest possible perspective on world affairs if they are really to participate in the ordering of these affairs.

First of all, democratic citizens should be able to see their nation, state, and locality in terms of their physical and social relationship to the world and to the universe. Environmental, resource, and population problems with which citizens must deal are poorly understood and dealt with, except in such a broad context. Such an understanding would draw on materials from a wide range of fields, such as geography, geology, and astronomy for an understanding of the earth and its development, and biology, climatology, ecology, and physical anthropology for an understanding of the development of living things on the earth. Obviously, science teaching in the school might share in the study of earth-people problems, but it is important that these subjects be pursued not with the object of making a scientist of the citizen, a proper objective at another time and place in the curriculum, but broadly with the purpose of understanding the relationship between humans and their environment. It is of paramount importance that the study focus at all times on giving the young citizen the opportunity to understand and think about the problems related to this area of study. These include problems in optimally developing natural resources, population distribution and control, and in controlling pollution and protecting the environment, as well as problems with the institutions related to such issues. A continuous and immediate, rather than a delayed, examination of such problems should be an integral part of the study of the earth and its environment at every point in the study and at every grade level. The goal is that the young citizen shall become progressively more involved in actually dealing with problems concerned with earth-human relationships.

Secondly, democratic citizens need to understand how social institutions—including economic, governmental, and legal systems, the family, religious institutions, and most importantly, the institutions and ideas that characterize democracy, such as separation of church and state, the free press, and freedom of speech—have come about. Along with the study of present institutions, the young citizen should be given the opportunity to understand and to think about the problems that have been confronted and overcome in the past as present-day institutions have developed, as well as the problems which attend the further development of these institutions. Present-day democracy, for instance, should be seen not as an end product but as a stage in development, one that has been hotly contested and fought over and even died for at earlier stages and one that is still in the process of development. Democracy, probably the last best hope for humanity on earth, is not without its problems and young people should be involved in the process of its criticism and improvement.

Such an understanding and involvement would draw on content from a wide range of sources, some as far afield as poetry, fiction, and philosophy, but primarily from history. The history to be studied should cover the whole range of institutional history and should include as well the history of economic and political institutions and their impact on less powerful groups such as women, minorities, and the handicapped.

The historical study needed by citizens in this connection is markedly different from that which ordinarily passes for the study of history. Historical study, which usually stops short of the real study of events in depth, is little more than the memorization of the chronology of events. Instead the study indicated here is analytical in nature. It goes broader and deeper in the search for reasons and interrelationships. It focuses on the study of particular institutions or groups of institutions and on the problems, past and present, which relate to their development. Moreover, it looks at the value choices and value problems embodied in these institutions and their effect on less powerful groups and individuals. Investigations into such choices and problems are in many cases more effectively expressed in fiction, art, and music, which should be consulted along with history. Such studies will be described in more detail in Chapter 8, The Framework for the Curriculum.

Thirdly, democratic citizens need to understand the nature of culture differences over time and throughout the world as well as within the United States. They must not confuse differences merely with right or wrong, superior or inferior, friend or enemy. This need is dictated by the increased interaction among people of differing cultures in the contemporary world. As long as people of different cultures lived in relative isolation from each other, with little opportunity for significant commerce, mutual understanding was not a pressing need. Today, people of very different cultures may live as close as next door. They may be our most important trade partners. Democracy, once confined primarily to Western Europe and the Middle East, is now an issue over the entire world. It has therefore become imperative to understand and to appreciate these people of differing cultures both within the United States and abroad.

That democratic citizens need to understand the nature of how cultural differences throughout the world and even within their own country have come about is virtually self-evident. Citizens need to understand that every culture in the world came to its present state through forces that operated in its own history and that these forces have differed from those that operated in our history. The Soviet Union, for instance, is not an accident or the strange machination of some evil force, but a perfectly understandable result of its own history. Similarly, the world is almost certain to look different to the Scandinavians than it does to us. It is even possible that we could learn more about ourselves by reading the foreign press than from reading our own.

Hopefully, citizens will come to see cultural differences as explainable and reasonable. They will accommodate to cultural differences and apply their understanding of these differences to enrich life on the earth and within the United States. They will reject secular fanaticism, which looks upon all who are different as enemies to be destroyed.

To fulfill the need to understand cultural differences the study of the history of world cultures is indicated. Such study should be carried out with breadth, depth, and focus and, as has been suggested earlier, requires the thoughtful examination of democratic institutions. An analytical look at cultural differences as seen by anthropologists and sociologists should be brought to the aid of history in this respect. Such study will also be described in more detail in Chapter 8.

Fourthly, democratic citizens need to understand something of the striving of human beings throughout time for reliable knowledge, how after many false starts we have gradually developed canons of objectivity and rationality and achieved fuller access to information, which are the hallmarks of democracy. Democratic citizens need to see science not only as a technology with great potential for material gain, but as a way of thinking and verifying conclusions, a way of distinguishing between the true and the false. Science should be seen not only as undergirding all modern scholarship but as affording the means for utilizing the human mind and vastly improving the lot of all people everywhere. Democratic citizens embrace science as a more useful way of thinking about problems. They understand the nature of proof and the role of evidence in deciding a public question. They respect facts and distinguish between hard facts and conjecture. At the same time, they understand the limitations of science. They understand that moral and ethical questions do not fit neatly into the scientific mold. They understand how religion, philosophy, and aesthetics contribute to knowledge. They understand how the reliability of knowledge is judged in each of these fields. In short, they need to understand the difference between scientific truth and religious, aesthetic, or ethical truth.

The complex nature of knowledge and the useful relationships between different ways of knowing should be repeatedly exemplified for students while they thoughtfully study the subjects suggested above. However, the problem of dependable knowledge is so central to democracy that it demands special treatment. Meaningful study of history, the social sciences, and the humanities should be supplemented by special units in applied epistemology. This emphasis would help young citizens understand the complexity of the problem of knowing and help them to correctly apply these understandings to their own appraisals of knowledge as applied to citizenship.

But knowing is not only a matter of understanding the canons of proof but of having access to knowledge. Reliable knowledge is of little use in a democracy unless access to it is open to all. Censorship in any form is anathema to democracy. Citizens need to understand how central to the development of democracy has been the struggle for such principles as the freedom of the press to investigate and report its findings, the freedom of speech to spread one's opinions among others even when these opinions are contrary to the opinions held by those in power, and resistance to the withholding of information by those who are privy to it. The citizen needs to understand all of the subtleties by which full knowledge may be denied to the people. These include withholding of knowledge by those in power; censoring books to be studied in school; control of what the press may investigate and publish, either by government censorship or by those rich enough to own the newspapers and television stations; manipulating television coverage to supply only sensational and entertaining content over hard news in order to increase profits; and stonewalling by government officials when requests are made for information. In short, young citizens should grow in the ability to determine when they are getting the full facts and when they are being shortchanged.

As with the problem of the nature of knowledge noted above, the problem of access to knowledge is served in part by continual attention to it when history and other subjects are studied. Accounts of the battles fought for the rights of the people to know have special merit here. Here again the problem is so central to democracy and the required skills of judgment so technical in nature that periodic special treatment is required. Such special units or courses could well be offered in coordination with the language arts program of the school, for language teaching too should be concerned that young citizens are intelligent readers, listeners, viewers, and communicators. Such special study will also be described in more detail in Chapter 8.

Fifthly, and most importantly, democratic citizens need to appreciate the struggle of people throughout time to be just and good in their behavior toward one another. They need to understand the central importance of such values as justice, fairness, equality, and freedom in democracy. They need to understand how such values came into being and what problems of choice between values they entail. They need to understand how values relate to the welfare of individuals and society as a whole and how values play the central role in the resolution of social problems. They need to understand that problems of what to value are the central problems in a democracy. In a democracy, these are questions whose answers cannot be handed down unquestioned from some high authority. Democratic citizens must be responsible for their own morality and they must continually refine and justify the moral and ethical principles they are using in the process of decision making.

Studied as suggested above, the history of democratic institutions affords many examples of value issues over which citizens have taken issue and in some cases fought and died. In addition, many value exemplars are afforded by the humanities. Persuasive cases are made for particular values in literature, in religious writings, in art, and in music. Such literary and artistic works holistically and poignantly dramatize the human condition. Picasso's "Guernica" was inspired by the Spanish Civil War and the German destruction of the city of Guernica. Predominantly an anti-fascist statement, "Guernica" raises fundamental questions about the use of violence. Similarly, Arthur Miller's play, *The Crucible*, serves as a forcefully dramatic presentation of issues that juxtapose individual freedom and social conformity. While young citizens may have been exposed to value analyses courses in literature, art, and music, the problem of what to value and of what to value *most* is of such overwhelming importance that a special capstone effort is needed, a course or unit in several courses, possibly provided in coordination with other programs in the school in which the young citizen is confronted centrally with the questions, "What shall I value? What shall I value more? How shall I decide what to value more?" Such a program will likewise be detailed later in Chapter 8.

Finally, democratic citizens need to be fully aware of the major problems that confront society and be knowledgeable about them. They need to know why people are concerned about these problems and to be familiar with bodies of information that relate to these problems. They need to know what the issues are, including issues over values that block solutions to these problems. They need to have done some orderly thinking about possible solutions to these problems and about where they stand with respect to them.[3]

As we have indicated above, the study of history should contribute importantly to providing a background for understanding our important social problems. History teaching would continually focus on problems in our history. The depth of understanding required for intelligent decision making and the need for involvement of the citizen in decision making suggest that special units are needed throughout the curriculum and/ or that a special capstone course is needed which would focus on at least a few of our most bothersome and persistent social problems, for example, protection of the environment, underemployment of human resources, and fear of nuclear war. All of the resources in the school and in the community might be brought together for a time in such a deep and concentrated study. Such special treatment will be detailed later in Chapter 8.

Commitment to the Democratic Ideal

Basic among the characteristics of the democratic citizen is commitment to the democratic ideal. Democracy is best among social systems if one accepts the idea that respect for the worth of the individual human being is the most highly valued of all human attributes. Respect for the worth of the individual means not only that human beings are to be treated with understanding, generosity, kindness, and compassion but that they have the right to be knowledgeable and to participate with others in making the decisions that concern them and all of society.

Hopefully, children will have learned early to respect these principles through the example set by adults and from stories and simple histories that are read to them celebrating these ideals. Later they should come to have a more reasoned understanding of democracy, including such ideas as freedom of choice, openness to new ideas, and the opportunity for improvement; the protection of minority rights and opinions; freedom of the press, freedom of religion, freedom to speak one's mind, and academic freedom; and democracy's penchant for settling differences through political rather than military means. In contrast to various kinds of autocracies, democracy depends on the participation of individuals in making the decisions that control their lives. In autocracies, these decisions are made by self-appointed and sometimes tyrannical leaders, who enforce these decisions arbitrarily. If individuals, having tasted freedom, value being treated as partners in the affairs of the state, they must choose democracy, whatever its shortcomings, over any other form of social organization and governance. This choice the democratic citizen must understand and freely embrace.

Schools can contribute to the development of a commitment to democracy on the part of young citizens in two ways. First, they can help students to understand democracy as a reasonable outgrowth of human experience, as the study of history as conceived above would do. Second, schools can set a good example of respect for democracy. The most obvious way to is that the governance of a school should be a reasonable facsimile of a democracy rather than a dictatorship. School rules, as with laws, should be fair and reasonable and young people should be helped to understand the reasons for them. Students should also have a voice in the enactment of the rules. Governance should never be coercive or arbitrary. The school should never underestimate the willingness of students to participate in their own governance. As with the adult society, the rights of the minority should be faithfully respected.

The second way in which democracy can be exemplified in schools is by the respect shown by teachers for intellectual honesty. Democratic teaching must be carried on with full respect for the canons of objectivity suggested above. Furthermore, full respect must be given to the intelligence of young children to think for themselves. Skirting the issue, talking down to children, or pressuring the young citizen through propaganda tactics are completely out of character with democracy and must never be employed if commitment to democracy is to be achieved. Teachers must have faith that young citizens will discover useful and productive answers.

Basic Intellectual Skills

The skills needed by citizens in a democracy considerably exceed those frequently listed for the social studies, such as map-reading skills, library skills, communication skills, group work skills, and the like. Such skills are concerned primarily with retrieving and remembering information, skills that are important if the emphasis is to be placed on the remembering of information as from a textbook. By contrast, the skills needed by the citizen in a democracy are more complex in nature and the focus is on utilization of knowledge in making decisions and in implementing one's decision in the social and political arena. The skills thus involved need to be exercised in a more holistic manner and are most usefully learned in the context of problems as broad as those characteristically dealt with in the real world.

Important among such skills are the following:

1. Being able to size up a problem and identify the real point of conflict or the real issue, including the underlying values that are at stake.
2. Being able to select the information which is relevant to the problem and to relate it logically to proposed solutions; being able to judge the reliability of various sources of information, including firsthand experience as well as research-based information. .
3. Being able to see a problem in its broadest possible context, including the value considerations involved.
4. Being able to build a scenario of likely consequences regarding any proposed solution to a problem.
5. Being able to make reasoned judgments where the evidence is conflicting or where there is conflict between desired values.
6. Being able to empathize with people whose points of view with respect to the problem differ from yours.
7. Being able to choose a solution which, though less than ideal, is politically viable and makes progress toward resolving an impasse possible.
8. Being able to exercise political influence toward implementing justifiable decisions; being able to organize others and to work in organizations to achieve justifiable political goals.[4]

Obviously, these intellectual skills have as necessary components many of the lesser skills ordinarily appearing in lists of social studies skills. Yet in real life such skills do not operate in isolation but rather as clusters of skills, as indicated above. It is suggested here that any significant use of these lesser skills for anything more important than preparing secondary research papers, oral reports, and the like, depends on their use in clusters to tackle real-life problems. In this context, such skills as library skills will take on new significance and usefulness.

Political Skills

A central responsibility of the citizen in a democracy is that of voting in elections in which government officials are chosen or in which referendums are held. This is the citizen's most direct avenue to participation in public affairs. Citizens cannot hope to have a voice in the conduct of their government if they neglect to vote or if they do so shoddily. In fact, those who chronically vote blind or fail to vote at all make it more possible for a few, frequently unscrupulous individuals to run public affairs in their own rather than in the public interest.

But the responsibility to vote is not a simple matter. It is not enough merely to know how to mark a ballot. Issues in an election are seldom clear-cut. There may be some good on both sides of any single issue, and elections themselves usually involve numerous issues. Many of these issues may have no clear-cut answers, and many may entail responses that conflict with other issues in the same election.

Citizens need to know how to check the reliability of their sources. Am I being told the truth? Do I have the real facts? Am I being swayed by clever manipulation of the media? Is my vote in effect being bought by those who have the most money to spend on advertising?

Citizens who are socially responsible and vote intelligently must somehow weigh these competing factors and reach a decision, sorting out the true from the false, identifying the salient issue, even suppressing at times the temptation to vote in line with their own more immediate self-interest. The central importance of voting and the complexity of issues makes it fairly obvious that the study of issues, elections, and politics must be a continuous focus of social studies education. There is no piecemeal approach or substitute for this experience. Sophistication in political activity will likely come about only as students engage in it and as their activity is examined critically by their peers and teachers.

In a highly populated democracy such as that of the United States, composed of an almost uncountable number of differing ethnicities, religions, and social and economic interests, the organized interest group has come to be a vehicle, second only to voting itself, for influencing public affairs. Active citizens belong to one or possibly several interest groups, including political parties, and through these they make their voice heard in the public arena. This is in some ways an awful responsibility, for the danger is ever present that in the too-zealous pursuit of group self-interest, the common good, the greater good, and the long-run good will be lost from sight. Voting in elections, en bloc, on the basis of a single issue may result in untold and even unintended damage to other issues of equal or even greater importance to the whole society. Thus, while democratic citizens must work with and through interest groups of all kinds, they must also learn to weigh, balance, and temper their behavior in this respect in keeping with responsibility to others and to society in general. They must have accepted the idea that democracy fails unless all of the people are fairly and equally taken under its mantle.

SUMMARY

The thrust of this chapter has been to emphasize that the unique characteristic of good citizens in a democracy is the knowledge and skills which they are able to bring to the problem-solving process. The survival of democracy depends on citizens who are not only well informed and knowledgeable but who can bring this knowledge appropriately to bear in resolving the social problems that confront people and nations. In this view problem-solving skill is more than mastery of specific bits of information and specific intellectual skills. It is the skill of putting all of these elements together and applying them appropriately in the solution of broad social problems.

Democracy is not only an enlightened way of governing and being governed; it is also a system based on ethical and moral principles that requires continual attention to what is right and just. Every social problem has an ethical and moral dimension, and learning to deal with this dimension is as important as learning to deal with facts.

We believe that citizen problem-solvers in a democracy are best educated by the continuous inclusion in their schooling of real-life situations that require the making of informed and morally responsible decisions. The continued welfare and growth of democracy itself as practiced by students in their classrooms and in school generally are the central ingredients of citizenship education in a democracy.

3

Socialization and Countersocialization of Youth in a Democracy

The task of educating citizens for a democracy presents a challenging and persistent dilemma. On the one hand, a democratic society is dedicated to promoting the exercise of liberty, which entails respect for diversity—politically, culturally, and intellectually. On the other hand, all societies, whether democratic or not, need to establish some degree of consensus and conformity among their citizens. This tension, between the competing goals of political freedom and diversity on the one hand and social conformity on the other, creates the context for debate and controversy about how citizens in a democracy should be educated.

Unlike totalitarian societies, democracies are much more limited in the methods that can be used to influence the views of their citizens. To the greatest extent possible, democracies must avoid the use of manipulation and indoctrination. Such practices are routinely used by totalitarian systems to coerce the loyalty of citizens. Indoctrination denies individuals the right to develop their own attitudes and violates such democratic values as freedom of thought and expression. It disregards human dignity by virtually reducing individuals to mindless robots in service of the state. In a democracy educators must make certain that the content and methods they use to prepare democratic citizens are as consistent as possible with democratic values. It is critical that every educator involved in citizenship education—and here we refer to social studies educators in particular—be acutely aware of the significance of this challenge, for it is social studies educators who influence the nature, ideals, and realities of citizenship education for young people in this nation's schools. If these teachers are not concerned with the consistency between their teaching methods and democratic ideals, if they do not expose young people to controversy, to contrasting interpretations, and to diverse perspectives—in short, if they do not provide every opportunity for students to think for themselves and to make decisions on their own, then there is little hope for developing a reasoned commitment to democratic ideals among the citizenry at large. To put the matter more forcefully—for it cannot be stated forcefully enough—if these educators conduct their classes as if there is only one view of the truth, one set of values to support, or if they promote a blindly patriotic view of this nation, they are indeed breaking faith with the democratic tradition and, concomitantly, are making this society less safe for democracy.

Since a democratic society, due to its very nature, is restricted from the use of coercive, doctrinaire methods, how can it achieve sufficient consensus and conformity to create a socially cohesive society? Our considered response to this question is that a democratic society must place its faith in *reason* and on the capacity of people to think for themselves and to reach reasoned conclusions. This faith in reason is consistent with that demonstrated by those who wrote this nation's fundamental documents, the Declaration of Independence and the Constitution, which express an unwavering belief in the capacity of common people to participate rationally in the process of governing. This faith in reason is at the heart of the democratic experiment. Further, it is our belief that people who have fully developed their capacities to reason independently are more likely to serve as dedicated guardians of democratic principles and that they are least likely to be mindless victims of authority or emotion. In effect, citizenship educators in a democracy have no logical alternative other than to embrace reason as the hallmark of all that they do. Consensus in a democracy needs to be negotiated by people who have a willingness to reason together. It cannot be imposed. Consequently, educators must avoid doctrinaire practices and promote the development of reasoning abilities because the exercise of these abilities represents the very fiber of democratic citizenship.

SOCIALIZATION AND COUNTERSOCIALIZATION

In this chapter, we will explore two concepts that are central to the education of citizens in a democracy. The first concept is *socialization*—the process of learning the existing customs, traditions, rules, and practices of a society. The second is *countersocialization*—the process of expanding the individual's ability to be a rational, thoughtful, and independent citizen of a democracy.

Socialization

Every society inducts young children into its customs, values, and behaviors as a way of continuing existing traditions and practices. The manner by which children learn these traditions constitutes the process of socialization, whose goal is to encourage conformity and thus ensure the continuity of the society. Parents, teachers, peers, and the media serve as the major agents of socialization.

It needs to be emphasized that socialization is, in essence, a conserving process. It transmits traditions and values that are grounded in the past experience of the society. It does not explicitly attend to preparing the next generation for future changes in societal values and practices. With its emphasis on tradition, the practices related to socialization foster conformity to existing ideals. In and of itself, socialization seeks to preserve these prevailing practices and values and to strengthen social cohesiveness.

While socialization is the means by which children are taught to fit into the existing social order, it is not concerned with developing individuals on their own terms by emphasizing their intellect, creativity, or their independence. Yet it is these qualities that deserve special attention in a changing, pluralistic society where controversy and social change call for continuing negotiation by thoughtful and reasonable citizens.

Socialization is not reflective. It does not encourage individuals to think, to analyze, or to support their views with reason and evidence. Rather, it tends to be doctrinaire. It relies upon emotion and authority to gain its ends. Young children, who are still prereflective in their intellectual orientation, are especially influenced by the process of socialization. By offering children rewards or recognition, socialization practices manipulate their behavior so that they comply with adult or societal standards.

Countersocialization

Socialization is an inescapable dimension of citizenship education in a democracy and is the means by which young citizens initially learn the traditions of their society. However, in a democracy the socialization process must be balanced by *countersocialization*, which emphasizes independent thinking and responsible social criticism. These abilities are fundamental to improving the quality of democratic life in a changing pluralistic nation whose interdependence with the rest of the world creates a future of continuing challenges. In this context we suggest that in a democracy, the socialization process must be balanced with countersocialization.

Countersocialization is a learning process designed to foster the independent thought and social criticism that is crucial to political freedom. It promotes active and vigorous reasoning. It includes a reappraisal of what has been learned through the process of socialization so that adolescents can independently and reflectively assess the worth of what they have learned as young children. We wish to emphasize that countersocialization does not necessarily imply a rejection of what has been learned early in life. Rather, it calls for a thoughtful assessment through which individuals can reach their own conclusions as they face an unknown future where traditional values will undoubtedly warrant reexamination. Citizens who have engaged in a thoughtful and critical analysis of their beliefs and who recognize the complexity of public issues and public opinion are, in our view, more likely to contribute effectively to the negotiated consensus required for meaningful and active democratic life.

The Relationship Between Socialization and Countersocialization

In selecting appropriate content and methods for educating democratic citizens, the ability and maturity of the learner are persistent and significant concerns. At young ages children are most manipulable and are easily influenced both by the use of emotion and by the application of rewards and punishments under the control of teachers and other authority figures. From one perspective, young children can be seen as victims of those who attempt to influence them. Due to their susceptibility to authority and to their limited intellectual capability, the manner in which they are socialized deserves especially thoughtful attention. Since children cannot escape the process of socialization, their teachers need to be especially careful in making both the content and the methods for learning as consistent as possible with democratic values.

Even in a democracy, socialization is the dominant learning process during the early years of schooling. For the most part, children will accept what they are told quite unthinkingly. Consequently, the goals that provide direction for this socialization process are all-important. From our perspective, if a democracy is to endure, the goal is to socialize young children by selecting the appropriate content and methods that foster commitment to a nation guided by democratic ideals.

While young children have limited intellectual abilities that necessitate the use of socialization practices, it should also be emphasized that some effort at countersocialization can begin at the elementary level. Young children can develop the initial skills for thinking and decision making when these are exercised in the context of specific and concrete situations that are drawn from their experiences. Opportunities for developing these skills must also be part of the early years of schooling. Yet in spite of the fact that some efforts at countersocialization can take place during the early grades, the socialization process will prevail in shaping the early values, attitudes, and behavior of young children.

As children approach early adolescence, their intellectual abilities enable them to test ideas, to raise questions, to examine evidence, and to reach conclusions. Therefore, countersocialization needs to become the dominant mode of learning during this period. At this point, the intellectual abilities of students permit them to examine alternative points of view, generate explanations for social phenomena, and support their views with reasons and evidence. In short, their abilities are consistent with those needed by effective democratic citizens. It is critical to a democracy that these abilities be fully nurtured.

In sum, we are emphasizing that even in a democratic system, students should be socialized to democratic attitudes and behaviors during the early years of schooling. We urge citizenship educators to guide those early learning experiences in terms of democratic ideals. At the same time, we also urge that the process of countersocialization be applied to the extent that the intellectual abilities of young children permit. However, before the end of the elementary school years and the beginning of the middle school years, efforts at countersocialization should begin in earnest. Every effort must be made to develop these abilities that are so crucial to thoughtful, democratic citizenship. Due to the increasing maturity and intellectual capability of students, there can be no justification for the continuation of socialization practices during the adolescent years.

It is our observation that current practices of citizenship education in both elementary and secondary schools place undue emphasis on content and methods that foster rote memory and unreasoned loyalty. In part, reports that have been issued by the National Science Foundation confirm this observation when they point out that social studies instruction is overwhelmingly based on the textbook and predominantly employs a lecture-recitation mode that ignores or sidesteps intellectual development. The following examples are presented to illustrate existing socialization practices.

EXAMPLE #1. In most, if not all, elementary schools national holidays become an important focal point of classroom activity at virtually every grade level. Columbus Day, Halloween, Thanksgiving, Christmas, the birthdays of Washington and Lincoln, Valentine's Day, and Easter are evident on bulletin boards and in arts and crafts projects, parties, gift exchanges, and the like. In effect, celebration of these holidays constitutes some considerable portion of the social studies curriculum in the elementary grades. Beyond celebrating these events, little explanation of these holidays is typically provided. At the elementary school level, Lincoln and Washington are often cast as unmitigated heroes who have no human failings. Christopher Columbus is noted for his "discovery" of America—a "fact" that totally ignores the Native Americans who were here to meet him when he arrived. While the proportion of classroom time spent on holidays has not been estimated, it is substantial. These holidays are celebrated annually in each of the elementary grades where children are repetitively engaged in activities that encourage unthinking national loyalty and patriotism. These socializing efforts perpetuate myths about the glories of the nation's heritage. They are unreflective and make overt use of children's emotions as well as of rewards in the form of parties and special fun activities that manipulate the minds of the young. While we are not suggesting that national holidays be ignored, we do take issue with instruction that is not balanced or representative of diversity, as well as with instruction that ignores contributions made by members of various cultural groups. Such practices, which distort or avoid certain kinds of content, are, inadvertently or not, manipulative. They promote a blind and unreasoning patriotism to the nation and at the same time present a self-serving and biased version of the truth that denies democratic values.

EXAMPLE #2.   United States history is taught at both the eighth and eleventh grade level in virtually every school system in the nation. In almost all cases, the textbook is the dominant source of knowledge. It is fair to say that whatever information students acquire about this nation's history is, in large measure, derived from that single textbook. Yet, textbooks are usually watered down, simplistic descriptions of historical events. Furthermore, they are not without bias. Before a textbook is published many decisions have been made about what to include and, even more importantly, what to exclude.

The following passage from a current eighth grade textbook has been selected to illustrate how a textbook can socialize young people by subtly manipulating the perceptions they gain of historical events.

WHAT WAS LIFE LIKE FOR THE PILGRIMS AT PLYMOUTH?

The Pilgrims had many hardships during their first winter at Plymouth. More than half of them died from cold and sickness. The rest of the colonists worked hard to clear the land and build homes. They also made friends with the Indians. One Indian, Squanto, learned to speak English. He taught the Pilgrims to grow corn, to fish, and to trap animals for fur.

In the fall of 1621, the Pilgrims held the first Thanksgiving. They invited their Indian friends to dinner. The Pilgrims thanked God for their good crops. Now they would have food for the winter ahead. (Bidna et al., 1982, p. 79)

From this passage, students would easily conclude that the Pilgrims endured severe hardships—a condition that is well substantiated by historical research. However, they would also conclude that the Pilgrims and the Indians became friends. This conclusion is much more questionable. While some Indians, like Squanto, developed strong ties with the English, many others did not. In addition, this passage makes no mention of other accounts that suggest that some of the settlers sold Indians to Spain as slaves or that some Pilgrims were known to have dug up Indian graves for the corn, wheat and beans that had been buried with the dead. Furthermore, no mention is made of the fact that Squanto's collaboration with the Pilgrims is seen as an act of disloyalty by some Native Americans who view Thanksgiving not as a celebration but as a day of mourning.

In sum, the fact that important information is excluded from this passage creates a distorted view of history. It fails to present the perspective of Native Americans regarding the Pilgrim settlement. It paints an overly generous picture of the Pilgrims and ignores the tragic manner in which their settlement affected the lives of original Native peoples. Inadvertently or not, such textbooks present simplistic and questionable generalizations as if they were indisputable. Students who are asked to learn such information acquire a distorted and unrealistic view of historical events. Since alternative accounts are not provided, the student cannot possibly know that what they have read is distorted and incomplete. Instruction that is dependent on this kind of material asks the student to accept these conclusions blindly and without reflection. Indeed, relying on such limited and distorted information is doctrinaire in that it emphasizes information that casts the Pilgrims in a favorable light and excludes information that would have the learner recognize that the treatment the Native Americans received at the hands of the Pilgrims was also characterized by indignities that historians have also recorded.

Both of these examples of traditional socialization practices bias the learner's understanding. They foster blindly patriotic affiliations by avoiding or ignoring alternative information that is critical to a more comprehensive and balanced view of history. Furthermore, these examples do not make any attempt to stimulate intellectual activity on the part of the learner. Students are not asked to compare alternative accounts of history, to question the grounding for each, and subsequently to draw their own conclusions. Such learning may be fitting in a dictatorship where only one view of history is advanced, but it flagrantly contradicts values that must guide democratic education. Furthermore, instruction related to this nation's heritage can be studied in a much more honest and less distorted manner without eroding the respect students have toward their nation. Unlike totalitarian systems that are prone to rewrite history to fit their needs, democracies need not perpetuate myths or half-truths to cultivate a loyal citizenry. Students of all ages can learn that key historical figures recorded significant accomplishments yet, at the same time, had their limitations. They can learn that the Pilgrims represent a significant part of our nation's heritage but that they were not flawless. The point here is that if reason is to be nurtured, the substance of democratic education must be supported by content and methods that involve students in an honest, intellectual search for the truth grounded in evidence and reason. In this way, future citizens are more likely to develop a balanced, comprehensive, and honest view of their heritage. To continue the practices illustrated in the preceding examples is both dishonest and inconsistent with democratic ideals.

To this point, we have addressed the concepts of socialization and countersocialization and their relationship to democratic education. For educational purposes, we feel compelled to discuss their implications for both the content and the methods that are used for the social studies curriculum at the elementary and secondary levels.

ELEMENTARY LEVEL

We have emphasized that socialization is the dominant process during the elementary grades. However, we have also urged that some efforts to lay the foundation for countersocialization can also begin during this period.

Content

Selecting content requires an identification of topics and subject matter that are appropriate for young children. However, in terms of democratic education, specific topics, such as the family (a common topic in the first grade) or the history of a given state (standard fare at the fourth grade), can be subject to different perspectives. For example, children may learn about the family in a monolithic and narrow fashion. That is, they may learn that a family consists of a mother, father, and one or more children. As a result, they are likely to learn that alternative family arrangements (a single parent with a child, an older sister with a young child, etc.) are somewhat peculiar and are not seen as "real" families. In contrast, from a more diverse and broader perspective, children can also learn that families can and do take many viable forms. The point here is that the perspective that influences the treatment given to a specific topic is more crucial to fostering democratic citizens than the topic itself. This is not to say that topics should be selected for elementary social studies in a casual manner. Quite the contrary. However, the selection of topics does represent only the starting point. It is the perspective teachers bring to these topics that creates images of the world in children's minds.

To foster socialization that is consistent with democratic goals, the content needs to meet the following characteristics:

- It needs to emphasize such persistent democratic values as freedom and equality.
- It needs to incorporate the idea of diversity wherever possible—diverse ideas about history, about the family, about cultures.
- It needs to be presented in honest, unbiased, and balanced ways.
- It needs to be treated in ways that develop thinking and decision-making skills.

Traditionally, social studies content that is selected for elementary school use revolves around the following sequence of topics:

Grade 1   Home and School, Families
Grade 2   Community Helpers
Grade 3   Local Community
Grade 4   State
Grade 5   U.S. History
Grade 6   Old World, Western Hemisphere, Eastern Hemisphere

These traditional topics can be handled in a way that meets the characteristics identified above. They can serve as a basis for developing thinking skills consistent with a reflective decision-making curriculum. Within these topics opportunities exist for children to understand diversity, to develop thinking skills, to explain, to generalize, and to make decisions. Persistent questioning represents one method teachers can use even with young children to foster both thinking and the understanding of diversity. The following illustrative questions were designed to accompany a children's story about two families—one Japanese, the other American.

- Which of these groups of people is a family?
- How are families in the U.S. and Japan alike?

○ Can you think of reasons why they are alike?
○ How are they quite different?
○ Can you think of reasons why they are different?
○ What are some of the ways you could solve the problem this family (in the story) is facing?
○ Which solution would you choose? Why?

Within limits young children can respond to these kind of questions. In doing so, they begin to experience diversity and gain experience in those thinking skills that are central to democratic citizenship. In this way even conventional topics typically reflected in the elementary social studies curriculum can be turned into problematic situations and can serve the ends of reflective decision making.

Problem-oriented topics that are especially suitable to preparing democratic citizens can also be incorporated into the elementary social studies curriculum. Young children can begin to learn about pollution, energy use, diverse cultures, and about such world-wide issues as food and hunger. They can explore unit topics such as *What is Fairness?* or *Making Rules*. Both of these topics are well suited to deepening students' recognition of diversity and the dynamics of a democracy. Further, these topics and issues do not have single, simple answers. By examining such topics, children can gain an early foundation for dealing with issues that citizens face.

Method

At the outset, we wish to emphasize that the teaching methods used with elementary school children need to minimize the use of authority and emphasize the use of reason. The more children are rewarded for parroting ideas because the teacher or the textbook says they are true, the more likely it is that children will depend on external authorities rather than their own reasoning abilities for answers. While neither teachers nor students will be able to avoid the use of authoritative frameworks entirely, democratic education requires that the use of reason be encouraged at every possible turn and that, where possible, children should be encouraged to provide their own reasons for their conclusions.

The above emphasis on the use of reason at elementary grade levels leads to the following considerations regarding the teaching methods that are used.

THE TEACHER AS ROLE MODEL. The most important consideration regarding teaching methods resides in the example set by the teacher. The attitudes and behavior exhibited by teachers serve as powerful guides for young children. To enhance democratic socialization, the teacher's behavior needs to reflect respect for reason and diversity, commitment to democratic values, and openness to alternative points of view in every possible way. In contrast to more authoritarian teachers, such teachers will encourage children to ask questions, to think about "why" questions, to generate their own reasons, and to defend their points of view. Furthermore, if teachers regularly provide students with reasons, whether for the behavior they expect of children or the content they want children to learn, these young people are more likely to accept "reason-giving" as an appropriate way of thinking and behaving. Teachers who are willing to admit that they do not know a particular answer or that they are not sure that their answer or that of the textbook is correct are serving as models of democratic behavior. Such behavior challenges the arbitrary acceptance of authority. As we advance these ideas about teachers setting democratic examples, we recognize that young children are likely to blindly accept examples set by their teachers. Nonetheless, from our point of view, it is more fitting in a democracy to socialize in the direction of democratic behavior rather than the authoritarian behavior that invites unthinking compliance.

No textbook, specific technique, or classroom activity can compete with the personal influence teachers have over young children. Nonetheless, there are additional methods that support the democratic socialization of children.

QUESTIONING. Probing questions represent an essential dimension of the democratic classroom. Questions that ask children to probe the meanings of terms ("Is that what 'being fair' *really* means?") and to provide reasons for claims that they make ("How do you know that is true?") all serve to stimulate the child's thinking. Continued experience with these kinds of questions lays the foundation for a more analytical and questioning orientation on the part of young children.

CHILDREN'S LITERATURE. Children's literature can serve as another resource for the democratic socialization of young children. Reading children stories of people from diverse backgrounds who rose above challenges or who serve as examples of democratic ideas can strengthen their acceptance of diversity and expand their views of democratic ideals such as freedom and equality. Of the many examples of children's literature available, two are noted here. *Annie and the Old One* by Miska Miles (1971) portrays a young Navaho child coming to grips with the death of her grandmother. In the hands of a sensitive teacher, this book can help children identify with the young girl's grief and present them with a different view of how people perceive the relationship between life and death. *Giants for Justice: Bethune, Randolph and King* by Beth P. Wilson (Harcourt, 1978) presents short biographies of three American black leaders and their struggle for civil liberties. Plentiful examples of children's literature exist for the purpose of democratic socialization.

OPEN-ENDED DILEMMAS. Still another useful teaching tool is the open-ended dilemma, which can serve as the basis for involving children in decision making. Open-ended dilemmas are very short stories that involve a conflict to which children are asked to supply the ending. While the content of the dilemma can vary to match the interests of children, these dilemmas permit children to assess the worth of multiple solutions. By raising thoughtful questions, teachers can encourage children to identify alternatives, predict consequences, and evaluate alternative solutions before arriving at a defensible decision. These dilemmas need to be specific enough in detail to be manageable for young children. Given these conditions, the open-ended dilemma is a useful way to initiate decision making with elementary school students. The following example is illustrative (Martorella, 1976, p. 380).

> Here are two stories about some little girls. One little girl named Ellen wanted to surprise her mother while her mother was away. She decided to wash and dry the dishes. While she was drying the dishes, she accidentally knocked over the dish rack and broke ten of the dishes.
> Another little girl, Regina, stayed home while her mother went out. Regina got bored watching television, so she decided to play around in the kitchen. She was fooling around with some dishes on the counter, and one fell on the floor and broke.
> Who was naughtier, Ellen or Regina? Why do you think so?

ROLE PLAYING. Finally, the use of role playing offers still another opportunity for children to engage in decision making on their own level. Given a problem that is relevant to their experience, groups of children can be asked to enact alternative solutions. Open-ended dilemmas can provide the setting for the conflict the children are trying to solve. Role playing provides opportunities to empathize with the roles of other individuals and can thus broaden children's understandings as they approach problems.

The methods briefly described above have been emphasized because they are consistent with democratic socialization. They are illustrative and do not exhaust the full range of possibilities. They stimulate the intellect and expand children's awareness of democratic ideas such as diversity, freedom, and equality and can promote the initial development of decision-making skills in young children.

SECONDARY LEVEL: MIDDLE SCHOOL, JUNIOR HIGH, AND HIGH SCHOOLS

Increasingly, with the onset of adolescence, practices that support socialization need to be replaced with countersocialization practices. As the intellectual abilities of young people expand and their experiences take on a more adult-like quality, the teacher's major responsibility lies in developing these abilities to the fullest. Increasingly, the goal of countersocialization needs to guide the selection of content and methods appropriate for the social studies curriculum in a democracy.

Content

The central and critical goals of countersocialization are to develop the ability of students to use reason and to expand their capacity to engage in social criticism, both of which are essential to democratic citizenship. Consequently, the content selected for the secondary social studies curriculum must be tightly tied to that goal. Citizens are continually bombarded by information about contemporary affairs—from television, from newspapers, from magazines and books, from politicians, from their friends and neighbors. The information they acquire from these sources may be self-serving, superficial, sensational, incomplete, and/or biased. Appraising the worth and significance of information is a persistent task of democratic citizenship. In our society the quality of citizen participation increases in direct proportion to the number of informed citizens who can fully exercise their intellectual capacities in addressing public issues. It is here that the social studies curriculum can make its most meaningful contribution to the fabric of democratic life.

Two kinds of content serve the purposes of countersocialization. The first and most important kind is represented by the study of significant social problems. It is our position that *at every grade level* students should study at least one major social problem with as much depth as their intellectual abilities allow. Social problems most closely approximate the real world of citizenship. By studying world hunger or crime in the United States, for example, students encounter the same challenges that are faced by citizens as they search for information, appraise its worth, and try to decide what measures need to be taken. By studying social problems, students will be inescapably involved in an experience that expands their awareness of human diversity, of wide-ranging and competing opinions, and of the dramatic changes that characterize our society. Furthermore, social problems, if examined with intellectual vigor, combine the need for reliable information, intellectual skills, and an examination of values. No other kind of content has the same potential for synthesizing these important dimensions of learning and, at the same time, contributing to the quality of citizen participation.

The second source of content can be found in the conventional topics and disciplines that are usually treated in the secondary social studies curriculum. These include the study of history and the social sciences. While it is our position that social problems could well serve as the organizing vehicle for all of the content employed by the social studies curriculum, we also recognize that the reasoning skills needed for democratic citizenship can be facilitated by the topics conventionally used. However, while such conventional topics as the Roman Empire, the Age of Exploration, the Industrial Revolution, Slavery, and the Populist Movement can serve as a focus, the instructional treatment of these topics must depart dramatically from conventional practice. In order to foster reasoning skills, the issues associated with these conventional topics must not be treated as if a fixed and certain set of facts needs to be learned about them. Rather, thoughtfully conceptualized, the study of these issues can serve to identify a number of thought-provoking questions that can guide the instructional process.

There are five types of questions that can be used in organizing a unit for reflective decision making. The examples given assume that the teacher and students are about to participate in a unit on slavery.

DEFINITIONAL QUESTIONS. The first type of question calls for definition—for example, "What is slavery?" However, definitions provided by textbooks or the dictionary will not suffice, since the point here is to explore the concept of slavery in as much depth as possible. We know that slavery exists when one person is legally owned by another in order to have the advantage of that person's labor. While such a statement may define slavery in a technical way, it does not suggest the wide range of practices—from atrocity to generosity—that characterized the relationship between slaveholders and slaves. Neither does it speak to forms of slavery that are not based in law but exist where individuals have no choice about the treatment they receive or the working conditions to which they are subjected. To probe student thinking teachers can offer a hypothetical case of mine workers who are both poorly paid and forced to tolerate working conditions that are detrimental to their health. Because they lack other occupational skills, these workers do not have the choice of taking other jobs. Are these people also slaves? Why? And if so, how should we define slavery?

EVIDENTIAL QUESTIONS. The next type of question requires that the students produce evidence to support their answers. In a unit on slavery, these might include:

- Why did slavery take root in the United States?
- Where did slavery originate? Why?
- Slavery has existed in many places at many times. How are these conditions similar? Different?
- What were the lives of slaves really like?
- What impact has slavery had on our society?

The manner in which answers to such questions are found is central to the process of countersocialization and to reflective decision making. Simple textbook answers won't do. The challenge is not to memorize a trivial, watered-down answer but to actively search out possible answers, using a wide range of sources that include competing interpretations. Here, the task of the teacher is to involve students actively in a critical search for dependable evidence. As students present their answers, they need to be challenged to defend their claims. Why do you think you are right? On what basis? Do other experts agree? All of these are questions that press students to evaluate evidence.

POLICY QUESTIONS. Another type of questions asks the students to decide and support their own position on an issue. For example, the teacher engaged in the unit on slavery might ask: "If you were Lincoln (or William Lloyd Garrison), what would you have done about slavery? Why?" While this is a hypothetical question, it is also a policy question because it compels the student to take a stand regarding a significant historical issue and, most importantly, to justify that stand. Students need be challenged to present all the reasons and all the evidence they can muster to defend their position. They should be called upon to justify their stance in the face of alternate views presented either by other students or the teacher. Here, students can experience the conflicts and the competing points of view that are part of democratic life. They can experience a wide range of perspectives. In brief, it is here that their minds are being prepared for their role as citizens of a democracy.

VALUE QUESTIONS. While policy questions encourage students to become involved in an issue by taking a personal stand, they do not call for consideration of ethical and moral dimensions. This is the role of the question. For example, the teacher might say to the class, "One result of the Civil War is that slavery was no longer legal. Does the abolition of slavery justify the use of violence? Why?" This challenges the student to weigh the merits of freedom against the tragedy and atrocity of war and to appraise the consequences of maintaining the institution of slavery. Students again need to harness all reason and relevant evidence. This task can trigger thinking about what reasons for violence are justifiable or whether it is ever right to tolerate practices that deny human beings fundamental freedoms.

SPECULATIVE QUESTIONS. The final type of question calls on students to creatively and imaginatively utilize all the information, ideas, and thinking skills they have been accumulating. For example, the teacher might ask, "If slavery had never existed, how might race relations in the United States have been different?"

This speculative question encourages broad thinking about whether slavery set the stage for conflicts between blacks and whites or whether these conflicts would have occurred anyway. Another related question, also speculative, is: Would the absence of slavery have minimized the chances of the Civil War? In addition, the residual impact of slavery on the last hundred years, as well as other factors that have given rise to racial tensions, needs to be considered. Such questions encourage a long-term view of history. What happens in one century can and does affect the next. Most importantly, such questions expand the intellect and engage the learner in a significant exercise that explores causes and effects across time.

If the issues raised by these kinds of questions serve as grist for the study of conventional topics, so that students examine competing accounts of events, evaluate contradictory evidence, and reach their own defensible conclusions, they will be engaging in the kind of intellectual activity required of democratic citizens. At every turn, students should be involved in the process of examining the evidence that lies behind statements that are proffered as truth. Who made a particular statement? Why? What is its basis? Can we accept it as accurate? Why? Any of the conventional topics in the social studies curriculum can be organized in this manner.

We have identified two kinds of content that are appropriate for countersocilization. By calling for content whose basis is found both in social problems as well as in conventional topics and disciplines (but treated in thought-provoking, rigorous, and honest ways), we are emphasizing that the content necessary for countersocialization must approximate the kinds of issues faced by citizens and that the intellect of the student and the substance of the issues considered need to be closely intertwined.

This view of social studies content is a far cry from the dry, descriptive narratives that students are too often required to recall and recite in social studies classrooms. Moreover, this approach to social studies content presents students with knowledge as it is—tentative, perplexed by questions, and subject to continuing reinterpretation.

Method

As students mature intellectually, the role of the teacher changes. During the secondary school years teachers still need to serve as examples of reasoning and thoughtful democratic citizens. However, their audience is increasingly capable of independent thought. Unlike the unquestioning acceptance of young children, this more mature adolescent population is able to question, criticize, and challenge the teacher or the textbook. Moreover, the education of democratic citizens requires that these kinds of student responses be accepted, nourished, and encouraged. Most importantly at these levels, the teacher is no longer socializing by fostering democratic attitudes with children of limited intellectual experience and abilities. Instead at this level, the teacher guides the process of countersocialization by stimulating independent, critical thinking with young adults.

Three approaches deserve serious attention as methods of encouraging countersocialization at the secondary level: questioning, presenting discrepant points of view, and classroom discussion.

QUESTIONING. First of all, since stimulating the student's intellect is the overarching consideration during these years, the teacher's use of probing questions merits further discussion. Probing questions are open-ended. They do not have predetermined answers. Their answers do not lie ready-made in the textbook or the teacher's lecture. Rather, probing questions trigger the reasoning process in students, who are called upon to organize the information at hand in order to arrive at their own defensible answers. These student responses can be expected to be more informed and more complex, and the teacher needs to be more demanding and challenging, than was the case during the elementary years. The following kinds of questions need to be constantly evident:

- What does that mean? (*Definitional Question*)
- Why is that so? (*Evidential Question*)

- What if that hadn't happened? *(Speculative Question)*
- What should be done? *(Policy Question)*
- How do you know that is accurate? *(Evidential Question)*
- What reasons can you give for your belief? *(Evidential Question)*

For classroom purposes some specific examples of probing questions follow:

○ Today we have the technology to minimize most of our problems with air pollution. Since the problem could be largely eliminated, why do you think this hasn't happened?

○ What if there was no system of checks and balances? What do you think would happen to the way our country is governed?

○ Our textbook says that the settlement of the West owed more to the endless toil of frontier women than to Indian fighters, fur traders, and prospectors. What do you think this statement means? Is it true? Does the textbook supply any evidence to support it? How can we find out if it is true?

○ Terry, you just said that you think that everyone should be allowed to own a handgun if they wish. For tomorrow, would all of you think of the best reason you can that explains why you agree or disagree with what Terry has said.

For every topic or issue selected for classroom study, teachers need to identify similar questions to stimulate student thinking, guide classroom discourse, and serve as the basis of student projects.

It needs to be emphasized that these kinds of questions all have a tentative, uncertain nature. That is, answers cannot be proved to be correct beyond a shadow of a doubt. Likewise, citizens can never be totally sure that their views are completely correct, that they always voted for the right person, or that they supported the "right" cause. The recognition that ambiguity and uncertainty accompanies much of what citizens know and do is basic to minimizing the chances that students will develop dogmatic and authoritarian views. The best that any of us can do—teachers, students, and citizens alike—is reach conclusions in a reasonable, thoughtful, and informed way, knowing that all the facts are not in and that, in the last analysis, we might be wrong. Students who appreciate the tentativeness of knowledge and opinions are in a stronger position to participate responsibly and reasonably in negotiating the consensus required in a democracy.

DISCREPANT POINTS OF VIEW. Confronting students with discrepant points of view serves as another strategy teachers can use effectively.

If only one point of view is evident in the classroom, there is no basis for challenge. Further, if competing arguments are not presented, the initial material, whether based on the textbook or the teacher's lecture, will, in all probability, prevail without question. One example of classroom materials that present two discrepant views follows (*Parallel Passages*, 1983). The material concerns Commodore Perry and the "Opening of Japan." The first account is a composite based on several recent U.S. history textbooks. The second account is translated from a history textbook used in Japan.

U.S. VERSION

Commodore Perry's trip to Japan was more successful than he had expected. He sailed into Tokyo Bay with four black warships on July 8, 1853. It was the first time the Japanese had seen steamships which could sail despite the wind and current. Perry, aware that the Japanese might resent outside pressure, negotiated with the Japanese calmly and effectively. After he had given them gifts and asked them to trade with the U.S., he left. He realized that they would need time to think about this request.

Perry returned with seven warships to find out the Japanese reply in February 1854. With Japanese representatives in attendance, there was a feast and an exchange of presents aboard Perry's ships. The Japanese were delighted by the miniature telegraph and toy steam locomotive shown to them.

According to the trip's official reporter, exchanging presents was very successful.

> It was now sunset and the Japanese prepared to depart with quite as much wine in them as they could well bear. The jovial Matsusaki threw his arms about the Commodore's neck crushing . . . a pair of new epaulettes, and repeating, in Japanese . . . these words, as interpreted into English: "Nippon and America, all the same heart."

On March 31, 1854, they signed the treaty which opened Japan to limited trade with the U.S.

JAPANESE VERSION

In June, 1853, the American emissary, Perry appeared at Uraga with four warships. Perry brought a letter of friendship from the American President which sought the opening of Japan.

In January, 1854 Perry came once again, this time with seven warships, and he forcefully sought the acceptance of his demands. The feudal government was overwhelmed by the might of the Black Ships, and in March concluded the *Japan-U.S. Treaty of Friendship* (the Kanagawa Treaty) at Kanagawa. This treaty did not approve the opening of trade relations, but it did agree to the provision of supplies to American ships and assistance to shipwrecked vessels. It also promised to open the two harbors of Shimoda and Hakodate for those purposes. In addition, it gave unilateral most favored nation status to America. Thereafter, the feudal government concluded similar friendship treaties with England, Russia, and Holland.

The U.S. version is deceptively simple. It creates the impression that in less than a year Commodore Perry made two trips to Japan and was able to persuade the Japanese to sign a treaty in which they agreed to trade with the United States. The reader is even left with the impression that the Japanese were quite happy with these circumstances. On the other hand, the Japanese version suggests that Perry gained Japanese compliance by a display of power (seven warships) and the use of force. Furthermore, the passage states that the treaty *did not* approve the opening of trade.

Which account is more accurate? Which impressions are correct? Did Perry use force or didn't he? Were the Japanese pleased with the treaty or not? Did the treaty explicitly approve the opening of trade or didn't it? Why do the textbook accounts of these two nations differ?

These competing passages accompanied by probing questions raise doubt, challenge the intellect, and confront the learner with alternative perspectives. Such questions can serve as the basis of serious classroom study, student assignments, and vigorous classroom discussion.

CLASSROOM DISCUSSION.   Facilitating classroom discussions is the persistent role of teachers who are fostering the process of countersocialization. Probing questions and the presentation of discrepant points of view are grist for discussions where students are challenged to reason independently. To serve the purpose of countersocialization, these discussions should not be merely bull sessions where different opinions are exchanged. Rather, they should take the form of serious dialogue where students are called upon to support their ideas with evidence, where their opinions are subject to challenge by their peers as well as the teacher, and where the teacher's ideas are equally open to criticism. This kind of dialogue calls for the teacher to create a climate in which students feel free to enter any ideas for consideration and know that their ideas and their reasoning will be taken seriously. It is the kind of classroom climate where any idea can be openly and freely examined and where the best idea is the one that is supported by the most powerful evidence available.

SUMMARY

In this chapter, we have highlighted only some of the methods that distinguish countersocialization from more conventional socializing methods such as lecturing and question-answer recitations, the conventional use of textbooks, or the use of dramatic films that sway emotions. While there are ways to adapt such methods to the goal of countersocialization, typically they are used in ways that encourage the learner to accept unquestioningly the interpretation offered in the text-book, the lecture, or the film, where the student's only intellectual challenge is to memorize enough material to pass a test.

Each of the considerations that have been presented in this chapter regarding content and methods appropriate for countersocialization is based on a deep respect for individual students and their capacity to reason independently. Honest respect for each individual further requires that the minds of students not be manipulated in ways that they are not conscious of. In effect, the content and methods employed by the teacher should engage learners in a thoughtful, not mindless, manner. Students have the right to be explicitly aware of the content and methods being used and the reasons for their use. Teachers need to clearly explain why they employ the content and methods that they do. To neglect this matter is to treat students as dependent subjects, rather than as thinking individuals worthy of respect. In the context of democratic education, students are not bundles of stimulus and response connections, nor are they mindless robots. Democracy as a political system is distinguished by the high value it places on each individual. Democratic education must do no less.

4

The Social Sciences
and the Humanities
in Citizenship Education

It is not uncommon for educators to speak of the social sciences and citizenship education as being one and the same. Characteristically, as a kind of afterthought, it may be recognized that citizenship education, in addition to drawing on the social sciences, also takes content from the humanities. Yet almost never is it made clear how very differently the social sciences and the humanities relate to citizenship education and how the two might relate usefully to each other. In the absence of clarity on this point, the humanities are often seen merely as a supplementary source of information (a role that they are not well equipped to perform), or they may be construed to be an alternative approach to citizenship education based on emotional persuasion rather than on the presentation of hard facts.

We see these conceptions of the possible roles of the humanities in citizenship education as inappropriate both to the nature of the humanities and to the needs of democratic citizens. Rather, we see the social sciences and the humanities more as symbiotic partners, the first focused on empirical findings, the second focused on values and individual perspectives, but each providing equally important contributions to the decisions which citizens must learn to make in an intelligent and socially responsible way. The following pages will demonstrate the necessary symbiotic relationship between the social sciences and the humanities in citizenship education.

LIMITATIONS OF THE SOCIAL SCIENCES
IN CITIZENSHIP EDUCATION

Since the goal of social studies is democratic citizenship, social studies is not adequately defined as merely the teaching of the social sciences and history. This definition is inadequate for a number of reasons. To begin with, the experiences and issues encountered by citizens in real life are far broader and more complicated than those represented by one or all of the social sciences. This lack of correspondence between the holistic life experience of the citizen and the specialized perspective of the social sciences is exacerbated when each of the social sciences is studied separately, as they generally are in school.

The social sciences, either separately or collectively, provide a limited perspective on a given topic or issue. While their study may yield significant and interesting findings, they do not and cannot illuminate a specific social issue fully. For instance, an urban geographer may study the uses of land in large metropolitan areas and the results may well increase our understanding of what is possible in developing a complex urban area; but the geographer is ill prepared to deal with conflict over values or human preferences that may be the real issue involved in such questions as desirable zoning regulations or the appropriate location of industry or schools. The burning question may concern what is considered beautiful, and a poet may well have more to say about this than a geographer.

The real life of citizens includes significant learning that is influenced by the home, the workplace, and religion, as well as by exchanges with peers and adults, the media, and the world of entertainment: all contribute to citizens' knowledge and influence their attitudes profoundly. It would be at least possible to conceive of a citizenship education program built wholly around the firsthand experiences of youth. In any case, in an effective program of citizenship education, we ignore this experience at great peril. Lessons learned outside the context of life experience, as with a curriculum based solely on the social sciences, are likely to be sterile and unconvincing.

The exclusive study of social science disciplines provides only a part of the intellectual skills needed by a citizen in real life. Citizens must somehow integrate all of their knowledge and experience into workable solutions to complex social problems. They must develop the broadest possible base of knowledge to guide their decisions and actions, which usually concern problems that cut across disciplinary boundaries, as, for example, the problem of pollution of the earth's environment. Often, because of their very narrow and specialized concerns, different individuals and special interest groups may stand in opposition to each other. Moreover, the problems themselves are viewed differently by experts having different backgrounds. Economists may see the problem of pollution in terms of the trade-off between the cost of pollution abatement and higher prices for commodities or in terms of the effect on job opportunities, while geographers may be more concerned with long-term effects on the earth's biosphere, and sociologists with how a people's way of living is threatened. For citizens to somehow resolve or at least accommodate these conflicts requires an intellectual, disciplined way of thinking, which we will refer to as the discipline of citizenship. This discipline is not only different in kind but broader in scope than the discipline exercised in any one social science. The discipline of the citizen includes making judgments about the kinds of knowledge and data, from whatever source, that are relevant to broad social problems; making judgments about the credibility of conflicting sources of information, including alternative interpretations among the social science disciplines; and, most importantly, identifying and making judgments between the competing values that are at stake in a given situation. The discipline of the citizen also includes making judgments about practical matters such as what possible spin-offs from any course of action may result, how the interests of various groups are affected, and what is politically possible.

Further, citizenship education in a democracy requires not only the development of appropriate intellectual skills that exceed those required of the study of any of the social sciences but it requires as well that citizens learn how to engage in the political process and how to pursue power and influence government. It is difficult to see how these particular intellectual skills and dispositions can be developed exclusively within the separate disciplines of any, or even all, of the social sciences.

Another problem with the total emphasis on the study of the social sciences comes about in the translation of these disciplines into teaching subjects which, though they go by the same name (we say we teach history or economics), are very different both in structure and intent. The goal of a discipline is the discovery and interpretation of new knowledge; the goal of the subject, on the other hand, is the transmission of information, presumably from those who have knowledge to those who do not. The discipline, as a research enterprise, is conducted in a hypothetical mode. It is open to new facts, to new theories, and to new interpretations. In contrast, subjects are usually taught in an expository mode. The goal is possession of the correct answer, the achievement of which tends to close the matter to further investigation. The prevailing interest in a discipline is with raising questions and exploring new avenues of thought. In contrast, the subject is directed to mastering answers and conveying to others facts based on the authority of experts who write textbooks and teach.

Subjects attempt to encapsulate and summarize the accumulated knowledge of a discipline. In doing this, the real and varied insights of the discipline are usually distilled into a single version of affairs, presumably the consensus of scholars in the field and without consideration of how this version of events came to be preferred over others. This preferred version is then represented as true on the authority of scholars, an authority about which reasonable questions can be raised.

Yet the so-called facts are not so easily achieved. The disciplines upon which subjects rest are all hotbeds of controversy. Not only are real scholars not all of one mind, but there are numerous respectable scholarly explanations for almost any human phenomena. Scholarly works are continually being rewritten as new facts or new insights are brought to bear. For example, even the members of the President's Board of Economic Advisors, all presumably conservative, free-enterprise economists, are hard pressed to agree on any set of economic causal relationships.

The conclusions of scholars are open-ended conclusions awaiting the next onslaught of scholarly criticism. In stark contrast to these scholarly principles, the subject based on a discipline is often taught as though the facts were closed to further questioning. The subject is a compendium of answers to be narrated to students, to be accepted by them on the authority of the textbook and the teacher, and usually to be returned as fixed answers on quizzes and examinations. Seldom are the assumptions, qualifiers, and doubts of the real scholar shared with the students. Research has demonstrated time and time again that much that passes for fact in textbooks is not fact at all.[1] Oversimplified and misleading interpretations of human events are easily found in subject presentations and, in some cases, overt propaganda is passed off as fact. Such practice is complete anathema to the very conception of the social sciences.

Too many educators appear to be insensitive to the distinctions being made here. In fact, many scholars in the social sciences ignore these distinctions in their role as teachers, behaving as authority figures when they teach but as scientists when they carry out their research. Genuine teacher-scholars, however, recognize these distinctions. Frederick Paxson, for example, who probably had more right than many other scholars in his time to pose as an authority on the history of the West, freely admitted to his classes that he had many more problems in interpreting Western history than he had certainties. In such a spirit, rare indeed among social studies teachers noted for their insistence on correct answers, teaching and scholarship might become a more congruent enterprise. In a similar vein, the drive to cover "all of the material," also a characteristic of social studies teaching, largely eliminates the possibility for real scholarship, for scholarship is necessarily a deliberate and an open-ended process.

There is still another difference in the intellectual outcome between the scholarly pursuit of a discipline and the teaching of a subject that has not been fully recognized. The genuine study of a social science discipline, as a discipline, has a countersocializing influence on students, whereas the teaching of a subject based on a discipline has a socializing influence. The pursuit of a discipline teaches students how to question conclusions and how to go about validating factual claims. It teaches them to be more open to different points of view. It raises reasonable doubt about what is presumed to be fact. In general, the scientific approach of the disciplines is conducive to greater open-mindedness, which is an important ingredient of democratic citizenship. In contrast, the teaching of subjects, by way of textbooks and lectures, tends to be an influence for socializing students. It teaches students to accept the facts presented as the unmitigated truth, based on the authority of the author. It presents little opportunity to question or doubt. The world is seen as less open to change, as a place more fixed and final than it is in reality. Independent thought is discouraged, and there is little opportunity to learn the skills of inquiry so important in democratic citizenship.

The social sciences are frequently biased accounts of reality (Barnes, 1937; Cohen, 1947; Myrdahl, 1944; Ogburn, 1922). The value judgments and factual assumptions sometimes unknowingly held by scholars color their works. History and the social sciences, as they are taught in schools, are usually oversimple and truncated versions of the disciplines and carry with them an extra burden of unexamined and possibly fallacious factual and value assumptions. These disciplines, when presented in teaching as the unquestioned truth, with qualifiers left out, can be a powerful force for maintaining the status quo, making them, in Myrdahl's (1944) phrase, "do nothing social sciences." Thus in our country, the injustices suffered by blacks, Native Americans, immigrant workers, and women were long covered up in our history under a cloak of ungrounded facts and assumptions until finally unmasked by more persistent scholarship.[2]

It is just these kinds of oversimplified, unexamined versions of human affairs that have characterized the teaching of school subjects based on disciplines. Subjects are almost never examined for their veracity or credibility. Children are manipulated by the textbook and the talk of the teacher into thinking not only that they are getting the unvarnished truth but that the way it happened is the only way it could have happened and, therefore, the right and just way for it to have happened. Nothing could be better calculated to stifle inquiry and to produce acquiescent, passive, accepting citizens or citizens who feel there is little connection between social studies and the real world.

Another basic limitation of the social sciences as the sole source of content of citizenship education is that they leave values and valuing out of the decision-making process. It is never the facts alone, the ordering of which is the long suit of the social sciences, but their associated values that the citizen decision maker, knowingly or unknowingly, brings to an issue and that ultimately rules his or her decision. Citizens may have their facts in some order, but if their values go unrecognized or are in disarray, they are helpless to make an intelligent decision. The social sciences strive to order the facts but they tend to ignore—or to take for granted as unrecognized assumptions—the values that are involved in a social problem. A more dependable source for the orderly study of values lies in philosophy and the arts. While historians and even scholars in the social sciences sometimes take on the role of philosopher, it is seldom explicitly recognized that they are doing so. Further, the standards of scholarship in matters of values are not so likely to be persistently pursued as are the canons of objectivity in matters of fact. It is for such reasons that the education of citizens must be based squarely on the humanities as well as the social sciences. It is for such reasons that we accord the humanities an equal place with the social sciences as the basis for citizenship education.

THE USES OF THE SOCIAL SCIENCES
IN CITIZENSHIP EDUCATION

All of this is not to say that the social sciences are of no use in citizenship education. Quite the contrary. The social sciences, if appropriately used, are of basic importance in citizenship education. The question is, what are these appropriate uses?

Democratic citizens do not make decisions in a factual vacuum. The more information they have at hand and the more reliable that information, the better are the chances for sound decision. However, the social sciences are not the sole source of information needed in democratic decision making. Journalism and the media, literary works, the arts, philosophy, ethics and religion, along with the firsthand and vicarious experience of the individuals and groups actually involved in a decision, are all invaluable to the citizen decision maker. The social sciences are the one source that has been most thoroughly thought out, systematically investigated, organized, summarized, and criticized by able scholars, and they merit very serious consideration in the decision-making process. The dominant ethic of the social sciences, along with the other sciences, is to be concerned above all with facts, a condition that sets the sciences apart from all other sources of information. It is important to enter two caveats on this point, however.

First, a decision maker using a given social science or several social sciences as a source of information should understand that the social sciences are not fixed bodies of information good for all times. Rather, they are continually changing as scholars unearth new evidence. Social science is merely the best possible approximation of what scholars believe to be true at a given time. The fact is that social science will almost certainly be different tomorrow than it is today. Understanding of this important fact about the social sciences is deepened if students have engaged in scholarly criticism and investigation. This experience permits them to appreciate more fully how difficult facts are to come by and how tenuous and temporary is our hold on them. In other words, the social sciences are to be taken seriously, for they are the most systematic body of knowledge we have at hand, but not too seriously, for they are subject to change. Teachers and their students should not be led into the trap of accepting as true a particular version of economic events, for instance, that economists have long since abandoned as untenable.

A second caveat is that facts derived from the social sciences achieve their meaning only as they are used in solving problems or making decisions. Facts learned just to be held in memory are most resistant to being retained and are quickly put out of mind. Learning them for no other reason is next to useless, if not actually harmful, and it is certainly a waste of time.

With these caveats in mind, the citizen can use the social sciences to gain reliable knowledge essential in decision making. Young citizens in particular need to learn to seek out the facts relevant to a given set of questions and decisions. They need to learn to respect facts and to reject ungrounded claims to truth. At the same time, they need to learn to look at all factual claims with a critical eye. It is probably more important for young citizens to master the ways of judging the reliability of so-called facts than it is to remember the facts themselves. To paraphrase Alfred North Whitehead, the first question that a citizen-scholar should ask of any set of facts is: Are they true? The second question is: What use can be made of them?

If one can make the intellectual leap of assuming, as does Jerome Bruner (1965), that one learns best to think systematically by engaging directly in the process, then the social sciences afford a most favorable opportunity to develop this skill. But if this is to happen, instruction in the social sciences must necessarily be organized around the problems of fact and interpretation that confront the scholar in each social science area. It is not enough, or even appropriate, merely to relate to students the conclusions reached by scholars about matters of fact and matters of interpretation. The expository mode in which most social studies instruction is carried on is wholly self-defeating if development of the capacity for critical thinking is our goal. The hypothetical mode, which would necessarily organize instruction around problems of fact and vigorously seek answers to what the facts mean, is a more appropriate form for such instruction. It is difficult to conceive of how the memorization of textbook expositions of the social sciences leads in any useful way to learning the skills of systematic thinking that are so crucial to the citizen in a democracy.

THE USES OF THE HUMANITIES IN CITIZEN EDUCATION

We have suggested earlier that literature, art, music, drama, religion, photography, philosophy, and journalism must be recognized along with the social sciences as valuable resources in citizenship education. The unique role of the humanities is to provide a rich arena for thoughtful exploration of the meaning of human experiences. Scholars in the humanities seek to illuminate the meaning of life. Further, they are not limited by the canons of objectivity that guide the work of social scientists. Rather, they permit their subjectivity and their value judgments to freely influence their thinking. For example, John Steinbeck's novel *The Grapes of Wrath* presents a poignant and wrenching picture of the Great Depression as seen through human lives. From it, one gains a more holistic view of that era than from the unemployment statistics of that period, as garnered by social scientists. Our point here is that both the humanities and social sciences are essential to citizen education. However, heretofore the humanities have not played a significant role in citizenship education, and their potential for providing future citizens with compelling insights into social issues in human terms has not been realized. Considered below are a number of ways that the humanities can be usefully incorporated into citizenship education.

Describing Human Events

A picture may be more telling than a thousand words. A fictional account in the hands of a skilled writer may paint a more vivid and even more accurate picture than many pages of historical writing. Children may gain greater insight into feudalism from speculating about and exploring the meaning of a photograph or a clay model of a feudal castle than in reading about feudalism from a history textbook. Add to the photograph a model of the castle, a picture of a feudal knight in full armor and one of a peasant's cottage, and you have rich material for exploring and understanding a way of life completely foreign to most children. How

did the people who lived in such buildings and who possessed such ac-
coutrements probably make their living? What did they value most in life?
Why did this way of life disappear in modern times? Are there any relics
of this way of life around today? Notice that this line of questioning is not
only problem-oriented (there are no sure and definitive answers), it is also
thought-provoking. Further, making value judgments is an integral part
of this questioning. Still further, the photograph or model can and should
be tested against the facts as obtainable from other sources. Questions such
as the following may be raised: Is this a true or complete picture of feudalism? What may have been left out or distorted in this representation
of feudalism?

In like vein, historical novels such as those written by Victor Hugo,
Toni Morrison, Howard Fast, Alice Walker, or Gore Vidal, even when
they are distorted or biased versions of events, may be used to produce a
lively discussion of what really happened in a period of history and how
that period should be interpreted.

How better to instigate a lively discussion of what really happened in
the French Revolution than by comparing a number of history texts with
Charles Dickens's *A Tale of Two Cities*. Or a journalist's account of a
strike could be checked out against what historians have said about important labor disputes in history. There are thousands of books, journalistic accounts, and paintings that could be used to include a genuine
exploration of almost every important episode in human experience. Students would learn that the search for what is accurate and certain is not
so simple as merely memorizing the facts as laid out in a textbook. It is
also a matter of knowing the meaning of events, of seeing and feeling them
in detail as the writer or painter might express them, of making them a
part of one's own consciousness. In these ways studies drawn from the
humanities can make a rich contribution.

Posing Value Questions

The problems which citizens must deal with in real life always involve value judgments as well as questions of fact. For instance,
it may be determined through factual research that a certain percentage
of the children in the United States suffer from a lack of sufficient food
to sustain a healthy life. It may be determined that this condition bears a
constant relationship to the poverty level of the child's parents. But what
is to be done is still a question of values. Those who value self-reliance
and independence of the individual or who believe in the classical theory
of economic welfare as a law of nature, may say to do nothing. Under-
nourished children are simply the losers in the struggle for existence. They

should be allowed, if need be, to sicken and die in order to maintain the classical economic system which is thought to be best for all in the long run. In contrast to these values, those who believe in the democratic principle that everyone, including every child, deserves an equal chance at the good life or those who believe that we should help the poor and downtrodden may argue that society should subsidize the poor with food at the expense of those who have grown rich.

At the point that the two contrasting positions clash new facts may be brought into play. For instance, humanitarians may argue that children of the very poor frequently do, in spite of poverty, grow up to make great contributions to society as scientists, writers, artists, musicians, and the like, while children of the rich frequently grow up slothful and mean. In contrast, the classicist may cite facts to prove that these cases are exceptions and that recipients of welfare grow up to be dependent on handouts and unable to escape their dependency. So the argument may go. This is the stuff of the real world, where the best possible decision must be made and where citizens must deal not only with the facts as best they can be known but also with their own values as best these can be applied to the problem. Serious works of literature, art, and music afford the clearest expression of values. Citizens may explore these values in light of the facts they must confront in their own lives. Without the inclusion of the humanities in citizenship education, young citizens are denied the opportunity to look at social problems whole, to consider the entire range of evidence, including, importantly, values as well as facts. Without the humanities they are denied the opportunity to master the process by which problems in real life may be intelligently resolved. This process involves not only learning to identify the values that relate to a problem but also learning to sort out and arrange values in hierarchical order from the most important to the least. The process involves learning to validate values against facts and to decide between conflicting values, including values of lesser and greater good.

To take some examples, Myra MacPherson's *Long Time Passing,* when compared to an historical account, could focus attention on the important question of whether the Viet Nam War was morally justified. In like vein, Erich Remarque's *All Quiet on the Western Front,* a book banned in post-World War I Germany, could engender a lively rethinking about the moral justification for war. Or Frederick Douglass's *Narrative of the Life of Frederick Douglass,* despite inaccuracies, could be used to reopen the moral issues surrounding slavery and the Civil War. So conceived, the humanities may provide the case studies whereby the social sciences may become operational in the real life of students. It is in some such rich interplay of the factual and the judgmental that young citizens learn how they can deal with the real problems in life. There is no end of possibilities for this kind of factual-judgmental interplay once we have accepted the humanities as a full partner in civic education.[3]

THE SOCIAL SCIENCES AND THE HUMANITIES IN THE SOCIALIZATION AND COUNTERSOCIALIZATION OF YOUTH

Is it possible for the social sciences to be taught in such a way as to contribute to the countersocialization of youth so essential if democracy is to survive and flourish? Most assuredly, and without too much strain, for we would need only to teach the social sciences as they really are, as inquiry-oriented disciplines. We would need to abandon straight expository, textbook-based teaching as it is now so widely practiced. To the extent that textbook subjects are used at all for the purpose of gaining a grasp of affairs, we would need to make a special effort to help students understand what a textbook really is—a single, simplified version of affairs—and what its shortcomings are. We should deliberately help students to experience different versions of a human event and to look for and question the assumptions that underlie a particular version. In short, textbook expositions should be questioned and criticized and students should be helped to develop the skills of criticism. Students should not be punished, as with failing grades, for quarreling with the text.

In a broader sense, the social sciences should be treated as they really are, warts and all. The problems of fact and interpretation confronting scholars should be honestly shared with students. Any study of a social science might well start with the problems and uncertainties which face the scholars in the field. Thus economics, the social science that makes the strongest claims to being a "hard" science, would be revealed as a cacophony of economic problems and issues and theories, rather than a unified set of theories that can provide the final answer to all of the economic and social problems of mankind. From such an experience, students should learn to be observant inquirers better able to cope with the kind of changing, open world in which democracy can flourish.

Some may object that we have veered too far toward countersocializing over socializing experiences. What is the glue that will hold democracy together? We rest our case in this respect on the belief that the strongest attachment to democracy is that which is based on reasonableness and fairness. Once the mature and the maturing citizen sees democracy in this light, its very openness to contrasting and changing views becomes the tie that binds its people together. It is out of character with democracy to expect its citizens to be blindly loyal. It is out of character with democracy to expect its imposition by force or even by persuasion.

The social sciences do provide a wealth of reasonably dependable information which, if understood as we have indicated above, is vastly superior to guessing about the facts or consulting a soothsayer. Interestingly, this body of information actually gains in usefulness if taken, as we have suggested, with a proper grain of salt. The humanities taken as a whole are a mixture of the bizarre as well as the substantial. In the face of this array, the student who has learned to be intellectually honest and humble in the search for truth and who is not thrown into intellectual paralysis by the absence of absolute answers has learned the very essence of democratic citizenship. Such students are not likely to become easy prey to ideologues. Their commitment to democracy will be persistent because it is a reasoned commitment, a product of their own intelligence. Citizenship education in this vein will be both socializing and countersocializing at one and the same time.

5

Reflective Decision Making in a Democracy

Democracy envisions an open and dynamic society in the governance of which individual citizens are privileged to play the deciding role. In contrast to an autocracy where all important decisions are made at the top and where most citizens are expected merely to be compliant, the citizens of a democracy are ultimately responsible for the policies and actions implemented by their government.

Citizens in a democracy make a host of decisions that affect their own welfare as well as the welfare of others. Two levels of decision making are involved.

At one level citizens must decide on the dependability of the information that they use as evidence to support their positions on complex social problems. Among competing claims to truth they must decide what to believe and what not to believe. They must learn to distinguish claims to truth that have validity from those that do not.

At a second and higher level citizens must decide how to deal with complex social problems: how to define the problem, what values should be pursued, what public policies should be supported, what candidates should be elected to office, what actions should be taken with respect to social concerns. These tasks are critical to the effective functioning of citizens. The knowledge and skills needed to deal with such problems usually exceeds that included in any one discipline or field of knowledge or expertise.

The quality of decision making at the first level contributes to the quality of decision making at the second. Social problems cannot be soberly dealt with out of ignorance or naïveté.

Improvement in the quality of decision making at each of these levels is best gained by seriously engaging in it. The huge amounts of information that we impress on children in school, with scant opportunity for them to question or examine its validity and with little or no opportunity to apply the information as evidence in support of one action or another, may well do more to hinder than to develop decision-making skills in citizens. Education that emphasizes isolated facts is not only useless, it is above all things, harmful. "There is only one subject matter of education, and that is life in all its manifestations. Instead of this single unity, we offer children, geometry from which nothing follows; science from which nothing follows; history from which nothing follows" (Whitehead, 1967).

If education is to go anywhere, if more skilled decision making is to result from education, then as Whitehead suggests, we must engage students in decision making, not at some distant time, but here and now. If content is to be useful and relevant, then the first question students should be encouraged to ask of any content is, "Is it true?" The second question is, "What is it useful for?" We must ask ourselves, What light does it throw on some value that I am about to embrace or some policy that I am about to support, some action I am about to take or some social problem about which I am concerned?

With only a little imagination we can refocus the study of any of the social sciences or any other content that lays claim to accurate information. By involving students in a reexamination and validation of key truth claims, we can create for the students an authentic decision-making situation. Furthermore, this is not an artificial exercise. The reexamination of truth claims is precisely what social scientists continually do in real life. Key truth claims are held with great tentativeness by social scientists and are frequently controversial. Frequently social scientists have already disproved or qualified the truth claims found in textbooks before other educators get around to publishing and teaching them. By teaching these already invalid versions as truth, without the opportunity to question them, we not only rob young citizens of their right to develop decision-making skills, but we also destroy our own credibility as scholars by fostering inaccurate knowledge as if it were the whole truth.

With only a little more imagination we can focus the study of any piece of social science content (or any other discipline) on the resolution of some important and complex social problem involving such questions as what values should be pursued, what public policies should be supported, or what actions should be taken. Or we may study such problems directly, guided by any one social science discipline. By doing this we substitute for the passive learning of inert ideas the opportunity to apply knowledge in an immediately useful way. Students are given the opportunity to develop the whole gamut of decision-making skills which are so important in democratic citizenship. It is reasonable to conclude that any piece of social studies content, for which no connection to real life, here and now, can be made or in which no decision-making opportunities can be provided, should be dropped from the curriculum.

DECISION MAKING IN THE TESTING OF TRUTH CLAIMS

Something more needs to be said about the distinction between the two levels of decision making cited above. Decision making in the validation of truth claims closely parallels the scientific method. Scientists observe, collect, and evaluate data, and draw conclusions. In this process concern for evidence and reason are paramount: scientists strive to be objective and to reduce or eliminate the effect of their own personal feelings or emotions. In describing human behavior, social scientists experience some difficulty in adhering to a strict scientific order for, in contrast to physical scientists, their subjects are human beings who may change their behavior from time to time on the basis of new experience and among whom emotions may run high. These factors may work to produce ambiguity or to invalidate their findings. Because of the complexity of human beings and the constantly changing nature of human society, as compared, for example, to that of Japanese beetles, knowledge about humans is often incomplete and the real meaning of human behavior may be obscure. Nonetheless, social scientists do their best to be scientific with, of course, a considerable margin of error, which it is important for the student citizen to understand.

In the study of truth claims, how do we get students into a decision-making posture? Jerome Bruner (1965) has most usefully pointed out that we do this by treating key truth claims as hypotheses whose validity should be tested by the students. Students are helped to devise intellectual strategies for testing these truth claims against the evidence. Or, continuing with Bruner's thought, we may encourage students to develop their own truth claims from raw data. Treating truth claims as hypotheses to be tested stands in contrast to the frequent practice in teaching that treats truth claims as facts merely to be remembered. As Bruner points out, to treat a truth claim as a hypothesis rather than as a fact amounts to placing the student rather than the teacher in the decision-making position. To quote Bruner (1965), "Emphasis on discovery . . . has precisely the effect on the learner of leading him to be a constructionist, to organize what he is encountering in a manner not only designed to discover regularities and relatedness, but also to avoid the kind of information drift that fails to keep account of the uses to which information might have to be put." Treating truth claims as hypotheses is particularly appropriate in the study of the social sciences, for social scientists are much less certain of their truths than are their counterparts among the physical scientists. Appropriately, social scientists are more modest and tentative in their claims to truth.

DECISION MAKING IN THE RESOLUTION
OF SOCIAL PROBLEMS

Decision making at the higher level of solving social problems takes on a somewhat different form than does decision making which is limited to validation of truth claims. How can we make intelligent and socially responsible decisions in such matters as what problems deserve attention, what values to pursue, what public policies to support, what actions to take in matters of social concern, and the like?

Certainly the facts play an important and necessary role in the intelligent solution of social problems. The facts of the case must be pursued at every stage of the process with the same relentlessness and objectivity that scientific study demonstrates. But the resolution of a social problem can seldom be postponed until the facts are all in—indeed, some kind of action may be necessary before the crucial facts can even be known. Nor would having all the facts, even if that were possible, resolve the problem, since all alternative solutions are freighted with conflicting values. Value conflicts, which are not strictly amenable to factual validation, must be resolved. Furthermore, human beings are involved in the resolution of social problems. Each may perceive the problem somewhat differently and may bring different needs and perspectives to the problem. The long years of conflict between the United States government and Native Americans arose not so much because of a dearth of facts but because two very different perceptions of the good life were in conflict. Values can, of course, be subjected to some probing questions: Is the value involved consistent with other highly regarded values? What consequences will result from holding this value? However, ultimate values may still come into conflict even within the same person, as will be demonstrated later in this chapter.

What then is to be done with complex social problems? How may they be studied rationally?

John Dewey (1933) was the most influential proponent of the notion that social problems could be solved using the methods of science. He sought a relationship between rationality, which is such an important characteristic of the citizen of a democracy, and the ordered objectivity of sciences. Although Dewey's belief in the scientific method was probably too generous, his analysis of the complete act of thought that follows scientific methodology is useful today in the initial ordering of the study of a social problem. A somewhat modified version of Dewey's steps is: (1) recognizing a predicament, (2) defining or stating the problem, (3) gathering and evaluating relevant data, (4) hypothesizing as to what might remedy the situation, (5) checking out each hypothesis for its plausibility, (6) deciding, and (7) acting.

Dewey's prescription of how thought could be organized for solving social problems is basically sound, but it makes the actual solution sound simpler than it really is. The rub is in making the decision and acting. Decisions must be made, even though the facts are never all in, and action must be taken now and cannot be indefinitely delayed. In fact, some action may be necessary before the problem can actually be probed more deeply and a better resolution reached. Most importantly of all, people bring different values, different perspectives, and different needs to the problem, all of which must be considered. Not only must a solution be worked out that will be the most effective for the society as a whole but it must be one that will accommodate the special needs and desires of the greatest number of people.

Such a solution transcends strictly scientific procedures. It is best reached through a process that we shall call "talking it out," in which individuals make a serious effort to understand and to accommodate to how others feel about the predicament. Facts, values, individual perceptions, and needs should all come under serious review in an unhurried dialogue that seeks to reach some accommodation among the individuals involved. In a classroom situation, role playing of unrepresented or underrepresented points of view might serve as one useful means to promote the dialogue. Thus an accommodation is reached which represents the maximum utilization of all facts, values, and individual needs involved in the problem. Accommodation reached in this way may well be the highest expression of democratic decision making.

DEMOCRATIC VALUES AND DECISION MAKING

Since our emphasis centers on the ability of citizens to make reflective and democratic decisions, we need to explore how the democratic ideal impacts on the process of decision making. Democracy involves attention to values. Democratic values include respect for the individual, respect for the welfare of others, the right to dissent, the right to participate in decision making, and equality of opportunity for each individual. Such values are frequently learned by children at an early age without giving the matter much thought. Stories and simple histories told to young children frequently applaud such values. However, when translated into practical affairs, these values are sometimes in opposition. For example, the struggle to expand civil rights has often created a tension between the value of freedom and the value of equality. The owners of businesses may want the freedom to hire whomever they prefer, while members of minority groups claim the right to equal opportunity. Such examples illustrate the complexity of the problem of applying democratic values.

Using self-interest as a guide to decision making comes naturally to most human beings. All of us want to fulfill our own interests and goals. Participation in a democracy poses a challenge to this natural predisposition. This challenge is embedded in such questions as: Regardless of personal gains, how do my decisions affect others? Does my exercise of self-interest interfere with the welfare of my neighbors, my friends, my co-workers, or my community? Does my chosen course of action decrease the extent to which this society can realize its democratic ideals? Such questions encourage individuals to look beyond self-interest and to consider whether in the long run, their interest is better served by paying attention to those conditions that benefit the larger community and foster democratic values.

The need to nurture democratic conditions and examine the effects of our decisions on others requires that social studies programs lead students to examine questions related to the greater good. If citizens make decisions and take actions solely on the basis of immediate self-interest, democratic values would soon erode and become meaningless. While citizens need to be explicitly conscious of their own goals and interests, they also need to be concerned with the welfare of others and with the preservation of democratic values. Otherwise, the system itself, as well as the opportunity to participate in it, will deteriorate.

The temptation is to indoctrinate children with the "right" democratic values. Children may be told that they should value such things as justice, equality, responsibility, rule of law, freedom, diversity, privacy, and the like. Such values may be presented in simple histories or children's stories as facts to be taken for granted. Indoctrination of values in this way ignores the fact that values are themselves problematic when the effort is made to apply them to specific cases. We say we believe in justice, but what is just in a particular case is seldom easily determined. And if the value of equality also is involved in the case (only the poor go to jail, the rich get a high-priced lawyer), then the problem of what to value or what to value most may become very difficult to decide. We believe in freedom of speech and of the press. Does this mean that newspaper reporters have the right to reveal secret war plans that they were told about in confidence? We believe in the right of the people to information. Does this mean that all governmental affairs must be conducted in full view of the public?

Indoctrination of values is the mode of authoritarianism. Values are proclaimed, even some values that are inconsistent with one another, and no questions are allowed. In contrast, democracy does not rest so much on fixed values as on the process of analyzing values and on their continual reappraisal. We believe that this condition leads to a stronger commitment to values on the part of the citizen and to a growing consistency in reflective decisions based on values.

Alan Griffin (1942) has succinctly summarized the special place of value analysis in a democracy: "The democratic refusal to espouse a hierarchy of preferred values [is] a positive insistence that values originate out of human experience, that standards arise through the common experiences of people living and working and thinking together, and that authoritarianism is simply the arresting of the process through which values and standards are generated" (p. 92).

INTELLECTUAL DIMENSIONS OF REFLECTIVE AND DEMOCRATIC DECISION MAKING

The compelling task faced by social studies programs and social studies teachers is to involve student citizens in reflective decision making around social problems. This task embraces the two levels of decision making described earlier: first, that students need to learn to appraise the validity of truth claims; and second, that they need to learn how to make intelligent and responsible decisions related to public actions and public policy.

In the discussion that follows we identify the major components of each of these intellectual tasks. While each of these components is described separately, we wish to emphasize that they are intertwined and do not follow neatly in linear fashion.

Making Decisions About the Validity of Truth Claims

Testing the credibility of claims made by politicians, journalists, government officials, and other citizens is a constant activity of concerned citizenship, since the ability to test truth claims is fundamental to independent and responsible decision making. The process of testing truth claims includes the following.

AROUSING CURIOSITY.   A textbook passage might state: "Abraham Lincoln came to be known as the Great Emancipator. He freed the slaves." Or a student might say: "Anyone who works hard in this country can make a decent living. We shouldn't have to pay taxes to give money to the poor." Each of these statements contains truth claims that can be challenged and examined.

In order to stimulate curiosity about the merits of a particular claim, it is useful to introduce information or counterclaims that contradict the initial claim. Regarding Lincoln's stand on slavery, a teacher can respond by stating that there are other sources that claim that Lincoln was reluctant to free the slaves and that he did so only because he felt it was necessary to save the Union. Both of these claims cannot be true. By introducing a counterclaim, the teacher has introduced doubt and heightened curiosity.

In effect, the truth claim that is taken from a textbook, a student, or a newspaper functions as a hypothesis to guide further study. The counterclaims (and there may be more than one) serve as alternative hypotheses.

Since stimulating curiosity about truth claims is critical to involving students in the process of testing them, it is important to underscore a condition well known to experienced teachers—namely, that not all students will find the question interesting or be naturally curious about knowing whether Lincoln deserved to be called the Great Emancipator. Making the question relevant to the learner is basic to learning. Relating the question to the learner calls for considerable creativity on the part of the teacher.

Using the Lincoln example, the following two possibilities may be useful.

First, the teacher can create intellectual tension by dramatizing the issue. To achieve this, a teacher can probe students in the following manner; "What we are exploring here is the reputation of an important President. Was Lincoln really the Great Emancipator he is claimed to be? Or, was he more concerned with saving the Union at a difficult time? What were his actual motives? Was he *both* the President who saved the Union and the Great Emancipator? Was he neither? Is this question about Lincoln's reputation an important one? Why, in a democracy, is it important to examine his motives with respect to the abolition of the slaves?"

In this example the teacher has created a tension-filled context for exploring the question. Furthermore, students have been challenged to supply their perspectives about the significance of the question. If the teacher has approached these students with vigor and enthusiasm, they are likely to respond in kind. In the ensuing discussion, they can well develop some identification with the question that will spark their curiosity.

Second, the teacher can personalize the issue. To relate the issue in a personal way to students, the teacher might proceed as follows: "This question asks us to examine Lincoln's reputation. Is it appropriate to think of him as the Great Emancipator? All of us have reputations and we often think of other people in terms of their reputations. However, these reputations are not always accurate. I can recall a person who lived in my neighborhood who was always called the 'Old Crank.' This man kept to himself and barely grunted when someone said hello to him. Most of us were really afraid of him. Yet, I'll never forget the day when my brother was racing down the street on his bicycle and fell to the ground, breaking his arm. No one was home and our neighbor, the 'old crank,' drove him to a doctor to have his arm set. It didn't take us long to realize he didn't deserve the opinion we had of him. Are there people you have known who have reputations they don't deserve? Can you share some examples with us?"

After several such examples have been identified, the teacher can bring the discussion back to Lincoln: "Is the reputation ascribed to Lincoln an accurate one? Was he really the Great Emancipator? How can we find out?"

Here, the teacher has cast the issue in terms of personal experiences and has asked students to share theirs. The matter of reputation is likely to be of interest to adolescents and the preceding discussion can serve to relate that interest to the question about Lincoln.

These two examples do not exhaust the ways that student awareness in a problem can be heightened. Each issue and each group of students will have to be met on their own terms.

SUPPORTING TRUTH CLAIMS. Assuming Lincoln deserves to be called the Great Emancipator, what evidence would we need to find to support this position? If Lincoln freed the slaves reluctantly, what evidence would we need to find to support this counterclaim? Letters Lincoln wrote, speeches he gave, newspaper accounts, and historical scholarship are all important sources of needed evidence. The nature of the evidence will vary from question to question. However, in each case students need to identify the sources of evidence that might be useful.

COLLECTING EVIDENCE. Evidence can be found in many settings. Libraries, experts, films, art, music are only a few. Realistically, students will be limited in the kinds of evidence available to them. They will not be able to read Lincoln's letters or the newspapers of Lincoln's time. But they can probably gain access to selected historical works, to someone in the community who is a Lincoln buff, or to a historian whose specialty is the Civil War. They can also, with guidance from the teacher, explore the relative worth of these different sources of information. Which would be the best source of evidence: a letter, a newspaper, or an historical account? Why? It will not be possible for them to exhaust all the information that is related to the topic, yet this condition is exactly that faced by citizens who are also unable to examine all the related evidence. Nonetheless, if students are to learn how to function as democratic citizens, they need to be actively involved in identifying the available sources of information that can be most useful to them.

EVALUATING EVIDENCE. Evaluating evidence is one of the more intellectually challenging aspects of testing a truth claim. For example, it might be possible for students to find several secondary school history textbooks, in addition to their own, that also claim that Lincoln deserves to be called the Great Emancipator. However, students need to be aware that corroboration from textbooks does not represent a strong base for concluding that the claim is valid. Textbooks are, at best, tertiary sources—that is, they are at least three times removed from the original evidence. Textbook authors often use secondary sources (historical works) developed by scholars who in turn may have relied on primary sources (personal letters, government documents, contemporary newspapers, and the like). Consequently, textbook information is remote from original sources and is simplified for use by secondary school students. Furthermore, the textbook is likely to represent the bias of the publisher and the author. Critical appraisal of all the evidence gathered, including textbooks, is necessary if student citizens are to learn to reach thoughtful conclusions.

The following questions can guide students as they evaluate the evidence:

- Who wrote the account?
- What were the author's credentials? (Was the author a firsthand observer, a scholar, a journalist?)
- If a close friend of Lincoln's wrote the account, is it more believable than one written by a historian many years later?
- Is the account biased?
- What evidence does the account use to support the claim?
- Is the account supported by other sources?

Learning to detect bias is an especially important part of evaluating evidence. All authors bring a set of attitudes and opinions to the topics they write about. In some cases, the opinions of the author may be very clear, as in the case of an ardent abolitionist who writes about Lincoln. In other cases, the opinions or bias of the author may need to be inferred. The use of emotional language, the emphasis given to some facts or the omission of others provide clues to the author's perspective. The credibility of evidence is directly influenced by the bias of the author. Citizens need to gain experience in detecting bias and in making judicious decisions about its effect on the credibility of the evidence presented.

For instance, if a textbook passage states, "Abraham Lincoln is often called the Great Emancipator. He freed the slaves," the claim has little credibility. The passage is merely making a claim without providing any supporting evidence. Students, like all citizens, need to be able to identify these unsupported claims and recognize their serious limitations. They need to explore the basis on which any claim rests. Does the author use original sources? If the author cites support from another source, is that source credible? As students learn to analyze the evidence critically, they can develop an understanding of how to build a strong case for the arguments or claims that they themselves advance.

In addition, seldom does any one source provide a definitive answer. If two or three soundly researched historical works present support for the idea that Lincoln reluctantly freed the slaves, such evidence is stronger than if a secondary school history text states that this is the case. Similarly, if Lincoln's personal papers support this conclusion, this evidence will be stronger than the opinions of people devoted to preserving a positive image of Lincoln. In evaluating evidence students need to be encouraged to find several sources that corroborate the claim. One source, however strong it may be, is not sufficient to justify a given claim—even though it may serve as an important beginning. It still needs further substantiation.

Evaluating evidence is at the heart of the search for truth. In this context students need to recognize that their answers can never be definitive but that at the same time, like all citizens, they need to reach the best conclusion possible on the basis of the evidence available to them.

DRAWING CONCLUSIONS.   Is there enough evidence to support the truth claim? Or the counterclaim? Does one or the other need to be modified? How? At this point, students need to pull together the evidence that they have gathered and evaluated and decide what conclusion might be justified on the basis of what they have found. Students need to be challenged to present their conclusions with the strongest justification possible, knowing full well that they will be probed by both their peers and their teacher. Classroom dialogue needs to be focused and rigorous. Both students and teacher need to challenge the presenter with the same kinds of questions that guided the process of testing the truth claim. How do you know that is true? Who wrote that? Why is that author believable? Did you find supporting evidence for that in other sources? Such questions should characterize the interactions in a classroom where students are engaged in serious reflective thinking.

Making Decisions Related to Public Actions and Public Policy

Learning to make decisions that are intelligent and responsible is the essence of democratic citizenship. Without decision-making abilities, citizens become more susceptible to external manipulation. To that extent, democracies can deteriorate and even perish. Consequently, student citizens must have concentrated and intensive experience in wrestling with decisions about social problems in all of their complexity. Making such decisions includes the following dimensions.

Before the process of decision making can be set in motion, individuals must sense that a problem exists. Creating the need to resolve a sense of doubt or confusion is essential (Festinger, 1957). What problems individuals perceive and whether they perceive them or not is related to their interests, goals, and values. The problem of what is to be done with industrial waste may be a vital question for a student whose parents belong to the Sierra Club, while others may have no interest in the matter at all. Moreover, individuals may identify a problem only in terms of their immediate context. For example, automobile workers might view the importation of foreign cars as threatening their employment. On the other hand, a foreign car dealer might find it financially lucrative, since these cars are selling well, and soybean farmers might recognize that increased foreign imports would enhance the capability of the exporting nations to buy soybeans from them.

The challenge for reflective decision making is to perceive the problem in its broadest possible context so that its many-faceted implications are apparent. From this broad perspective, students need to make decisions that consider the welfare of all parties and that are not solely limited to satisfying the immediate needs of any single interest group.

The problems selected for classroom discussion must be directly connected to the interests of students. Otherwise, student involvement will not be fostered or maintained. Due to their limited experiences, student interests can be narrow and sometimes trivial. However, their interests are an important starting point and can be linked to the larger questions present in the community, the society, and the world. For example, such immediate student concerns as drug and alcohol use can be linked to public issues such as what constitutes the appropriate treatment of drunk drivers and what should be the legal drinking age. Student concerns about fairness, even at the elementary level, can be tied to minority concerns and equality issues. Problems of local unemployment and rising costs can be broadened to include national and international economic issues. To start the decision-making process with student interests does not limit the scope of decision making to those interests. Rather, the challenge for social studies teachers is to expand the vision that students have of those issues so that they can be examined in a context that requires consideration of the fullest range of consequences possible.

To summarize, problem awareness is influenced by the goals, interests, and values of students. Every effort needs to be made to relate classroom issues to these interests and goals. Finally, the problems selected need to be related to a broader context in order to broaden student perspectives.

IDENTIFYING AND DEFINING THE PROBLEM. Determining what problem is being addressed is a key consideration for any decision-making group (including the classroom group). Whatever the issue under discussion, the class needs to reach agreement on what the problem is. How the problem is defined will influence the proposed solution. Students, like adults, may perceive the nature of the problem differently, and considerable discussion may be needed before agreement can be reached about what will be examined. Regardless of the difficulty involved, identifying a problem is part of the reflective process and broadly based student interaction on this question should be encouraged.

Once the problem is identified, the task of defining key terms in the problem statement is likely to follow. If the identified problem statement is, "What should be done to keep people from littering?" the meaning of "littering" must be defined. Does littering refer to depositing waste and leftovers on public property? On private property? Or on both? Before decision making can proceed productively, the class needs to reach agreement on such key terms.

An important caution in the context of identifying the problem and defining terms is that students should be involved in reaching their own conclusions, albeit with the teacher acting as facilitator. If the teacher preempts the class by providing them with a succinctly stated problem accompanied by a clear definition of terms, students lose the opportunity to develop significant reflective thinking skills.

IDENTIFYING VALUE ASSUMPTIONS.   Identifying the values that an individual or a group wishes to maximize in the context of making a decision is essential to reflective decision making. These values serve as criteria for assessing both alternatives and consequences. Being explicitly conscious of these values guides all the thinking that is done relative to a particular decision. Of course, value assumptions will differ from individual to individual, and it will probably be neither possible nor desirable to reach consensus on the value assumptions held by the group as a whole.

However, identifying value assumptions is not limited to any one phase of the decision-making process. If a class is exploring the problem, "Should our community restore its old library?" some students may feel that preserving historic buildings is a valuable thing to do. As the discussion unfolds, they may come to recognize that the costs of preserving the library would be very high. They will then be faced with tension between at least two values—that of preserving the past and that of higher community costs. This tension becomes the foundation for learning. Which is more important? Why? To what extent would they be willing to trade off the initial value for lower costs? Like this one, most issues will cause ambivalence between short-term self-interest (lower cost, lower taxes) and long-term goals that might have more impact on others (beautification of the community for the future).

Since students will hold different values, any effort to force classroom consensus is likely to be counterproductive. Students could easily feel pressured to comply with their peer group or the teacher, and as a result the level of their participation and autonomy will be minimized.

IDENTIFYING ALTERNATIVES.   Values, previous knowledge, and experience are all involved in identifying alternatives. People are likely to generate alternatives that are consistent with their own predispositions. Furthermore, the more knowledge they have about the issue, the more likely they are to generate thoughtful alternatives. Before students are asked to generate alternatives, they need information about the problem so that their ideas are based on as broad an understanding of the problem seen in as great a context as possible. Contrasting proposals and viewpoints need to be included.

Another consideration regarding the identification of alternatives is that listing them does not imply commitment to them. More specifically, judgment of the merits of all alternatives should be suspended to the fullest extent possible until more information is available and consequences have been seriously considered. Premature evaluation of alternatives can either minimize consideration of other alternatives or can preempt consideration of an attractive alternative.

Finally, the sum total of alternatives needs to be as balanced as possible. If a class of students is of like mind on a question, only alternatives that represent that point of view may be identified. Reflective decision making requires that students experience the tension generated by alternatives from all points of view. Guided by the teacher, students need to be presented with conflicting views.

PREDICTING CONSEQUENCES. Once the consequences of each alternative are explored, these predictions serve as a basis for evaluating the worth of the alternatives being considered.

Two questions are pertinent in predicting consequences. First, what effects will follow from each alternative and what effect will each have on all parties concerned? Secondly, will the alternative enhance or limit the realization of certain values, especially democratic values? This process involves higher-level thinking skills with special attention to analysis, synthesis, and creative thinking.

In order to predict consequences additional information is usually needed. For example, if the city council doesn't restore the library, what will happen? If the building is torn down or left empty, will the neighborhood surrounding the library deteriorate? What secondary effects will this have? In this case students need to know what has happened in similar cases. Some selected student readings or a conversation with a city planning expert may be in order. This process involves gathering of evidence and is crucial to reaching sound decisions.

Examining consequences also involves a logical analysis of whether specific alternatives will enhance values, particularly democratic values. If the government limits welfare funding, will democratic values, such as the dignity of the individual, be eroded? This matter is complex. Some would argue that helping individuals meet their basic needs would enhance human dignity. Others may claim that welfare contributes to slothfulness and therefore contributes to poverty—a condition that violates the dignity of the individual. In short, no clear-cut answer emerges. Regardless of the complexity of this task, student citizens need to relate consequences to democratic values in order to reach thoughtful decisions.

REACHING DECISIONS. After identifying as many alternatives as possible and determining their likely consequences, students need to rank and prioritize the possibilities in terms of the values they are trying to realize. This aspect of the process can be filled with tension, since there is often no clear answer that fulfills all a student's hopes and goals. A question that often needs to be raised at this point is whether the decision should serve the individual's self-interest or whether it should contribute to the common good? It is here that sensitivity about the welfare of others can be addressed.

JUSTIFYING DECISIONS.   While learning to make decisions is critical, citizens must also be able to defend their decisions with reasons and evidence if these decisions are to represent grounded and reasoned choices. These reasons may involve the use of specific evidence as well as of values in justifying the outcome. The social studies classroom provides a setting where students can justify their decisions in either oral or written form, exchange and challenge one another's ideas, and revise their decisions if their arguments are found wanting.

TENTATIVENESS OF DECISION MAKING.   Even when large amounts of information are available for decision-making purposes, total knowledge is seldom available. Yet emergence of additional information can alter the nature of the decision-making process as well as the decision itself. In part, this is why there are no perfect decisions. Rather, citizens can only try to make the best decisions in light of the information they have and the values they hold. At the same time, they need to recognize that complete knowledge will never be available. An attitude that is open to new and conflicting ideas and information has great importance in making reflective and democratic decisions. Rigid views and fixed opinions contribute to an authoritarian posture that reduces the chances for further intellectual growth and the free exchange of ideas. The right to change one's mind or to revise one's decision needs to be emphasized to all students as they develop the intellectual strength necessary to function as citizens in a democracy.

6

The Learning Process
in a Democracy

In this chapter we will examine the relationship between democratic citizenship and the body of scholarship related to the learning process. Our purpose is to derive implications that can guide the implementation of a decision-making curriculum.

In particular, we have searched for scholarly perspectives that contribute to fostering the learning process in a democratic context, and we will describe the perspectives we have selected in some detail. We have accepted only those views that demonstrate respect for the individual, that develop intellectual abilities, and that support the growth of autonomy in individual decision making—qualities which are so vitally needed by fully functioning citizens in a democracy. Other views that are inconsistent with or contradictory to democratic principles, we have rejected.

Reflective decision making entails making decisions by using the broadest possible base of knowledge about the problem being examined. It involves skill in explaining and theorizing about the issue involved. In addition, it includes the ability to ask pertinent questions, weigh alternatives and consequences, synthesize data, and analyze the values at stake.

THE RELATIONSHIP BETWEEN THE ENVIRONMENT
AND THE LEARNER

Learning is influenced by the individual's perception of the environment. At any given point in time, the individual selects from the environment those factors that are of interest. An individual's perception of the environment is influenced by past experiences as well as by his or her view of the present and future. The family, the peer group, religious institutions, and the media combine to shape the framework each individual brings to learning and to decision making.

It is important to note that the forces shaping the perception of the individual have both rational and nonrational qualities. Families, for example, can exercise a very powerful influence over a person's attitudes. If an individual's family experience has nurtured open exploration of issues, he or she will more likely bring that perspective to further learning. Such an individual is more likely to examine diverse points of view freely and rationally. By contrast, other individuals who have been influenced by rigid, inflexible family views may hold their views arbitrarily, even in the face of competing evidence.

Self-knowledge—in particular, explicit awareness of one's values, beliefs, and emotions—can liberate the decision-making process. Individuals who are explicitly conscious of conditions that have influenced their personal views are better able to mediate the extent to which these influences control the decisions they make. For example, if individuals are aware that they hold a negative view of a particular religious group, the recognition and admission of this attitude make it somewhat more likely that they will be able to examine the basis for such an attitude reflectively.

The work of Kurt Lewin (1936), a Gestalt psychologist, speaks to the relationship between the environment and the individual in a compelling way. One of Lewin's key contributions is found in his principle that the behavior of individuals, at any given time, depends on how these individuals conceptualize what Lewin called their "life space." The concept of life space embraces both the individual and the individual's environment, including all those factors that influence the individual's behavior, whether the individual is conscious of them or not and even whether they are real or not. For example, if a person thinks there is a burglar on the porch, his or her behavior is likely to be consistent with that belief, whether there really is a burglar there or not.

According to Lewin, an individual's life space is shaped by four factors: (1) the goals an individual is trying to achieve; (2) the barriers the individual is trying to avoid; (3) the things the person wants to approach (those having positive valence); and (4) the things the person wants to avoid (those with negative valence).

It should be clear at this point that Lewin's concept of life space is not concerned with physical or geographic space but with the total environment as perceived by the individual. Life space refers not to objective reality but to the subjective reality that the individual has constructed with respect to the environment. Learning, in Lewinian terms, involves a change in an individual's perception of life space. This relationship between the learner and the environment carries several implications for fostering the learning process in a democracy.

First, it is especially important that teachers recognize that students will have a distinctive perspective, that is, a unique view of their social world. That perspective may or may not be compatible with the goals of a reflective curriculum. Nonetheless, the connection between students' previous experiences and their individual perceptions needs full recognition by teachers. From the student's perspective, the views he or she holds are legitimate and useful. These views can also be reasonably explained in terms of the previous experiences a particular student has had. An old teaching maxim is underscored here. Teachers must accept and understand students on their own terms, regardless of how different their values may be from the values the teacher holds. At the same time, the student's vision or life space needs to be expanded to entertain competing knowledge and diverse alternatives. To foster such growth, the teacher's full awareness of the student's experience is critical.

Second, both rational and nonrational factors are involved as young people (and for that matter even adults) make decisions. Emotion, impulse, and intuition are an inherent part of the human condition. They enter into our conclusions about the correctness of factual information as well as into our private and public decisions. Whether students are trying to prove that George Washington was an honest man or whether they are trying to decide whether this country needs a ban on immigration, their feelings, impulses, and previous experiences will influence their decisions. It is the teacher's role not only to recognize these nonrational factors but to make them evident to students so that their influence is not so overwhelming that reason and evidence are rejected. At the same time, it needs to be recognized that nonrational influences cannot be eliminated.

Third, Lewin's work emphasizes that learners must see a clear connection between subject matter and their lives. This emphasis suggests that the topics and issues studied need to be defined in terms of the interests and concerns of the students. If the students do not perceive the classroom situation as meaningful, their engagement with the topic is likely to be minimal and ritualistic. Teachers, then, must come to know their students, and to know them well. Their hopes, their fears, their backgrounds represent essential knowledge for teachers who seek to foster reflective decision making. Only then, can teachers effectively relate their instruction to the experiences and interests of students.

For example, students—especially adolescents—might find more meaning in the American Revolution or the French Revolution if these events were portrayed as illustrating the struggle between, on the one

hand, *individuals* seeking to realize their own goals and establish autonomy and, on the other, of the state seeking citizen conformity. To begin
with, students can be asked to provide examples of situations where they
have had to follow the rules whether they liked it or not. School authorities, law enforcement agencies, parents, and other adults regularly impose themselves on students to preserve order and foster conformity.
Having explored this matter as it relates to their own lives, students are
likely to be in a better position to view the American Revolution in a
somewhat similar framework. In this way, the teacher promotes more
meaningful learning by tying instruction more directly to the experiences
and interests (the life space) of students.

In Lewin's theory, life space is personally defined by the individual—
hence the compelling importance of connecting what is taught to the interests of the learner. This conception of the learner is compatible with
the principles of democracy. It honors the individual, respects individual
differences, and implies that the teacher must engage the minds of learners on their own terms.

In addition to Lewin and his concept of life space, the work of other
Gestalt theorists is helpful in understanding learning in a democratic context. Gestalt theorists view learning as the process by which individuals
restructure perceived patterns or configurations in their environment.
They emphasize that thinking involves the perception of meaningful
wholes, called *gestalten,* and that these wholes are more than the sum of
their parts. Further, whole patterns perceived by the individual cannot
necessarily be inferred from the sum of the parts, nor does understanding the separate parts, by themselves, necessarily lead to understanding
the whole.

Wertheimer, a key proponent of Gestalt psychology, provides numerous examples of this principle (discussed in W. F. Hill, 1953). In one case
he refers to the lights on a flashing billboard that are perceived as moving
from one place to another. In fact, all that is happening is that one light
is turned off, while the light next to it is turned on. What the observer
perceives is an impression of movement and not the separate lights, which
are the components of this impression. Importantly, the configuration that
is perceived is more than the sum of the individual light bulbs, and
meaningful understanding of the whole requires more than an understanding of each separate light bulb. It is important to note that Gestalt
psychologists do not deny the importance of understanding the component parts and the relationships between them; rather, they insist only that
an integrated whole cannot be inferred or understood from an analysis of
the individual parts.

In addition, Gestalt theory enlightens and supports the reflective process which involves learners in perceiving problems, giving meaning to phenomena in their environment, and making reasoned decisions. Such activities involve individual perceptions and, more importantly, require some understanding of unified wholes, whether those come in the form of problems or academic topics. To address a problem, an individual must first perceive it; the form of that perception should be holistic, so that the problem is seen as more than a collection of separate elements. Therefore, if students are to learn to make decisions about social problems, educators need to fully recognize that the quality of student decision making will be related to the perceptions they hold of the nature of the problem being considered. In terms of Gestalt theory, asking students to memorize a set of discrete facts about a particular topic—people, places, battles, dates—does not constitute meaningful learning or understanding. Indeed, it is likely to prevent students from seeing "the forest" because they are caught up in the task of identifying a selected number of "trees." Further, reflective thinking calls for judgments made from the broadest possible base of considerations. The more differentiations that individuals perceive in their environment, the more sophisticated their thinking will be. For example, a particular issue can be examined from a narrow or broad perspective. One can examine the impact of anti-pollution regulations on smoke-stack industries from the narrow vantage point of the increasing costs that these industries will have to assume and of how these costs will affect prices, production, and employment levels in a given community. Conversely, the issue can also be examined from the standpoint of the future health of the community and the long-term economic and social costs involved. The latter is a broader view that requires a more comprehensive examination of the issue. Consequently, it is necessary to broaden and deepen student perceptions of a given situation and to facilitate more complete configurations of it. Students can then draw on these broadened configurations and make their decisions based on a wider and more informed orientation.

Fundamentally, Gestalt theory is useful because it provides educators with a view of learning that emphasizes that thinking is based on holistic impressions which need to be developed and nurtured and that these impressions will vary with each individual. Without such efforts to recognize the diverse and holistic nature of individual impressions, teaching and learning can easily revert to the trivial, to the arbitrary memorization of facts or principles, instead of expanding the images students have of social conditions and issues.

Today's world finds citizens struggling in their efforts to make meaning of broad and complex human issues that are both domestic and global in nature. To be able to grasp the breadth and complexity, as well as the interconnectedness, of these issues, future citizens will need to envision the broadest possible context. Gestalt theory provides a view of learning that is compatible with fostering the capacity to think widely and holistically in a manner consistent with the skills needed by democratic citizens.

By accepting the holistic perspectives associated with the work of Lewin and the Gestaltists, we have deliberately rejected reductionist theories that are not consistent with developing the independence and thinking skills essential to democratic citizenship. One such theory is behaviorism, whose applications take the form of controlling the individual. Theoretically, behaviorists see prediction and control as defining characteristics of their science (Zuriff, 1985). Specifically, they focus on the narrow concept of *behavior,* which does not necessarily account for the power and energy that generates from human thought and feeling. They further reduce behavior to its component parts and assume that if they can control the part, they can control the behavior, and in turn, can control the individual. Inadvertently or not, applications of behaviorist psychology encourage conformity to authority and afford little dignity to the vitality that individuals can bring to their own set of circumstances. This denial of the individual's autonomy, combined with the overarching weight that behaviorists assign to the power of the environment as a controller of human activity, is impossible to reconcile with democratic principles. To use controlling mechanisms to manipulate human beings, often without their knowledge, fosters mindless and thoughtless actions. These characteristics flagrantly deny a central democratic principle: the inherent worth and dignity of the individual.

INTELLECTUAL ABILITIES

Reflective decision making is a complex process that requires that a broad range of intellectual abilities be brought to bear on specific issues. Although scholarship related to these processes will increase our understanding of them, our present knowledge is not sufficiently complete to permit us to present detailed descriptions of how these intellectual activities develop, prescriptions of how to nurture them, or the exact procedures that teachers need to employ.

The work of Jean Piaget makes an important contribution to our understanding of intellectual development (Ault, 1977). His observations of children and youth led to an identification of major stages of intellectual development. These stages are based on the principle that the capacity to handle abstract ideas develops sequentially in young people. Consequently, sixteen-year-olds can grasp abstract ideas and relationships more easily than can eight- or nine-year-olds, who are intellectually dependent on concrete referents. Piaget identified three stages of intellectual development: preoperational, concrete operational, and formal operational. While his observations led him to approximate these stages to specific age groups, these estimates should not be viewed rigidly. Intellectual development proceeds at different rates for different individuals and may be influenced by experience. In the following discussion, we focus on Piaget's concrete and formal operational states since these are particularly applicable to young people of school age.

Concrete Operational Period

Intellectual abilities show dramatic growth during this period (7–11 years of age, approximately). While children are completely dependent on real objects and events and cannot reason hypothetically, they are far less egocentric than ever before and even begin to demonstrate the ability to understand another person's point of view. This capacity expands their functioning as social beings. They are more likely to listen to others and to understand how others feel. They can participate in role playing and act out problems depicting simple social situations. Anyone observing children playing "house" or "school" can confirm that during these years children are capable of assuming the perspective of others, although they are limited to the range of their own experiences. In addition, they can engage in sharing and in small group activities if these activities are carefully planned. Sharing work space, sharing art paper to make a drawing, and eventually working in small groups where each child is responsible for a different aspect of a simple project are all possible and desirable activities.

In the concrete operational stage children are able to classify. They are no longer limited to classifying objects in only one way, but can focus on two or more dimensions and can even comprehend and construct hierarchies of concepts. Along these lines, Barry Beyer (1984) has proposed that a sequential thinking curriculum be developed. Such a program would emphasize, at the early elementary grades, simplified versions of such skills as recall, comprehension, and comparing and contrasting. Children can engage in such intellectual operations in limited ways. In turn, teachers need to provide opportunities for classroom tasks that will strengthen their intellectual functioning.

An important limitation during this period is that physical, concrete props are needed as a basis for intellectual functioning. Relying exclusively on language, whether oral or written, is not likely to be helpful unless it is tied closely to the children's immediate or recent experiences. During this stage children also begin to give explanations for what they observe and do. These abilities—classification, explanation, and role taking—make the concrete operational period one that is rich in its potential for building a foundation for the reflective process.

For example, young children can participate in the following kinds of experiences. Given selected pictures of different landscapes—rural, urban, mountain, lake, desert, and grassland—elementary school children can group these pictures together on the basis of similar qualities as they perceive them. They can also give reasons for their groupings. Furthermore, young children can engage in simple role playing, based on problem situations, such as the following:

> On her way home from school, Cindy saw an older woman up ahead of her drop her purse. The woman picked it up and walked on. Cindy followed and saw a five dollar bill on the sidewalk.

Young students can then roleplay the parts of Cindy and the woman and act out what Cindy should do. Gaining experience with these relatively simple intellectual tasks sets the stage for more complex thinking in later grades. The stage of concrete operations should be viewed as a significant time when the reflective process gains an important foothold.

Piaget's conclusions regarding young children suggest that these children can participate in some of the intellectual tasks involved in the reflective process. While they need concrete referents and cannot handle abstract ideas well, they can classify objects and events, offer explanations, and to some extent understand the perspectives of others. Providing young children with experiences that tap these abilities is critical to the development of reflective thinking.

CLASSIFYING. Many learning tasks can be structured so that children have an opportunity to sort objects and events according to observable criteria. Probably no one has addressed this intellectual operation more effectively than Hilda Taba (1967). The Concept Development task that she designed involves children in listing items out of their own experiences or observations, grouping these items, giving reasons for their groupings, and giving labels to the items they assemble. Further, children also consider alternative ways of grouping. In the process of creating collections of similar items, children discern differences and similarities and make comparisons. When they label groups that describe a particular set of items, they are, in effect, forming their own concepts. Teachers of young children would serve the cause of reflective decision making well if they employed Taba's Concept Development task with regularity.

EXPLAINING. The inclination of young children to give explanations provides a basis for involving them in hypothetical thinking, an intellectual activity critical to reflection. Teachers should ask such questions as:

- Why do *you* think our city is located here?
- Why do *you* think people who live in warm countries wear light-colored clothes?
- Why do *you* think we have had so many fights on the playground this week?

Each of these questions allows children to draw on their own experiences and to develop their own explanations. But children can also learn that their explanations are only guesses whose accuracy can be tested. Rather than simply giving children explanations or relying on those provided by a textbook, teachers would be well advised to pose hypothetical questions about appropriate issues or topics. An important guideline to bear in mind is that every time teachers tell students what the "right" answer is, they are preempting those children from exercising their own intellectual abilities. Furthermore, they are increasing the child's dependence on authority. The key point here is that young children can engage in hypothetical thinking even though such thinking must take place in reference to concrete objects or events found in their experience.

ROLE TAKING. The capacity to engage in perspective taking assumes a developmental dimension. As described by Selman (1980), between the ages of 5 and 9 children come to understand that their perspectives will differ from those of others. Between the ages of 7 through 12, the child develops a capacity for self-reflection. Children can place themselves in the shoes of another person and also recognize that others can do the same. In short, the child has developed the capacity for reciprocity and mutual awareness.

The capacity to perceive a situation from the standpoint of another, to be aware of another person's point of view, is an intellectual operation that is developing during the elementary school years. It is worth noting that role taking has an emotional dimension, which involves feelings of empathy, as well as a cognitive dimension, which requires awareness of the characteristics of other people. Since reflective decision making requires role-taking abilities, teachers of elementary children can foster these abilities through carefully planned classroom activities. Dramatic play, for example, allows children to represent the life of early pioneers or the story line in a children's book. In dramatic play, children portray previously defined roles. For example, once they have learned about pioneers, they can base their dramatization on what they have learned. A more dynamic approach is found in role playing, where students address an issue within their own experience. The issue, which must be relevant to their experience, could be of the following order: "As a class, what should we do about fighting on the playground?" Small groups of students can then assume the roles of the teacher, of students who are in fights, and of other students who are not involved in fighting. In these kinds of role-playing experiences, children define their roles and bring their own experiences to them. As they put themselves in the shoes of another, they can suggest ways of dealing with the problem from that perspective. In this way, they learn about the implications of other points of view. By fostering understanding of several perspectives, role playing supports reflective decision making.

Dramatic play is especially useful for children in the primary grades. While it involves taking the role of another, it is not tied to decision making. Rather, it emphasizes reenactment. Role playing, however, is more appropriate for the intermediate grades when children have a broader base of experience from which to define their roles and can better weigh alternatives and make decisions.

Role-taking experiences during the elementary years can provide strong support for the development of reflective thinking not only by emphasizing the importance of understanding other points of view but also by allowing children to recognize that the points of view of others need to be considered in making decisions. Role taking fosters individuality as well as concern for others, both of which are important dimensions of democratic citizenship. Further, role taking calls for active, not passive learners. This capacity needs to be strengthened in every elementary classroom.

Period of Formal Operation

During this stage (11+ years approximately), learners are no longer dependent on concrete referents. They can use verbal statements rather than concrete props as the content for their thinking and can grasp relationships as well as abstract ideas. In addition, these learners can classify hypothetical objects outside of their experience and can draw conclusions about hypothetical statements and situations. Further, classification comes easily during this stage along with the recognition that objects, events, or ideas can be classified in many ways.

In the formal operations stage, learners are more completely decentered. They come to understand that their own point of view is only one point of view. Further, they develop the capacity to argue an opposing point of view, even if they do not agree with it.

However, it is important to bear in mind that adolescents face certain conditions that can limit their intellectual functioning. One such condition is found in their self-consciousness regarding their own physical and social changes. Still another is their inclination to view the world in idealistic terms—a condition that may cause them to be limited in their openness to alternative points of view.

During this stage young people exhibit an intellectual readiness to participate in the reflective process. Their abilities to engage in multiple classification, to identify and understand relationships, to draw conclusions, and to recognize points of view other than their own provide a sound basis for engaging them in more advanced intellectual skills. At this stage young people can be profitably engaged in the investigation of social issues and in exploring topics that are related to these issues critically. Continuous opportunities should be provided for students to frame hypotheses, collect and evaluate data, draw conclusions, and make decisions. Further, teachers can engage students in vigorous discussions that explore value and policy issues. Early adolescence represents the right time to develop the intellectual abilities of learners to their utmost and thereby foster effective democratic citizenship. Challenging questions and probing classroom dialogue between students and teachers and among students themselves are the major strategies that can trigger the development of advanced thinking abilities. Jerome Bruner (1972) supported this claim when he stated: "One of the most crucial ways in which a culture provides intellectual growth is through a dialogue with the more experienced and the less experienced, [thus] providing a means for the internalization of dialogue in thought" (p. 53).

The work of Leon Festinger (1964) also is applicable to reflective thinking. His theory of cognitive dissonance is based on the idea that individuals strive to establish internal harmony among and between their various opinions, attitudes, knowledge, and values. In brief, a condition of dissonance exists when two elements do not fit together. For example, if a woman supports equal rights for women but allows herself to be subservient in her relationships with men, a dissonant condition exists. Festinger's theory implies that when individuals experience such dissonance, they will strive to reduce it. Dissonance can be triggered by various conditions. One way is to be confronted with the logical inconsistency of one's beliefs. To present students with information or opinions discrepant from their own can stimulate the reexamination of knowledge and values.

The following implications are drawn from the work of Piaget and Festinger.

HYPOTHETICAL REASONING. Since adolescents are no longer dependent on concrete referents, they can examine ideas that are not present in their immediate environment. They can also begin to understand more abstract concepts, such as freedom, cooperation, equality, democracy, and the like. They can reason hypothetically and can examine ideas with which they have had no direct experience. Speculative questions such as the following can stimulate hypothetical reasoning:

- What would have happened if the American Revolution had not been won by the colonists?
- What would happen if we did not have rules in school?
- What do you think our community will be like twenty years from now?

Carefully exploring questions such as these permits students to cultivate more advanced intellectual operations needed by citizens in a democracy.

STIMULATING COGNITIVE DISSONANCE. The following classroom example illustrates one way of stimulating dissonance. In the context of discussing the problem of unemployment, a student concludes: "I think we ought to stop buying cars from Japan—that would get rid of our unemployment problem." To stimulate thinking, the teacher responds: "But you need to consider that if the Japanese sell fewer cars, they will be less able to buy farm products from us. That would be a disadvantage for U.S. farmers." In this case the teacher has confronted the student with a competing claim. At this point the teacher can seize the moment to encourage further investigation of each of these statements. Teachers of adolescents need to recognize these factors but at the same time make every effort to expand student thinking beyond these constraints. First of all, students need to become conscious of these factors. Secondly, at every opportunity they need to be confronted with the need for reasons and evidence in grounding their decisions. The more citizens are self-conscious regarding the nonrational forces that influence them and at the same time are able to explore ideas and values critically, the better able they will be to exercise their individuality and to contribute to the dynamics of democratic citizenship.

Irving Sigel (1984) has further underscored the critical place of inquiry in the classroom. His constructivist view of learning draws upon both Piaget's developmental stages and Werner's orthogenetic principles.[1] Sigel proposes that teachers use what he called "distancing strategies" to foster intellectual functioning. These strategies require the child to deal with experiences (objects, events, actions) that are not part of the immediate present. To ask a child to discover the relationship between two events is, for example, more distancing than asking a child to label an object. Figure 6.1 shows how Sigel refines his concept of distancing strategies.

Sigel encourages teachers to:

1. Place cognitive demands on the child.
2. Draw the child's attention to discrepancy and contradiction.
3. Involve the child in mental activities that require going beyond obvious, concrete events.

He also observes that in typical classrooms teachers interact with students on a one-on-one basis. Seldom do students interact with each other. He suggests that teachers need to deliberately encourage student-to-student interaction where students will place cognitive demands on each other.

Figure 6.1 Types of Distancing Strategies

High-level Distancing	Medium-level Distancing	Low-level Distancing
Evaluate consequences	Sequence	Label
Evaluate competence	Reproduce	Produce information
Evaluate effect	Describe similarities and differences	Describe: define
Evaluate effort and/or performance	Infer similarities and differences	Describe: interpret
Evaluate necessary and/or sufficent	Sense differences	Demonstrate
Inferencing, for example, causal relations and their effects	Classify symmetrically	Observe
Generalize	Classify asymmetrically	
Plan	Enumerate	
Confirm a plan	Synthesize classification	
Conclude		
Propose alternatives		
Resolve conflicts		

Source: Sigel, 1984, p. 20.

Sigel's constructivist view of learning, his distancing strategies, and his research findings strengthen the basis for a curriculum that demands vigorous intellectual activity in order to prepare citizens for democratic life.

SUMMARY

In this chapter we have selected scholarship relevant to learning in the reflective decision-making tradition. We have derived implications for fostering this process with students. We have emphasized that reflective decision making is a form of complex learning that is not fully understood. To the best of our ability we have suggested conditions of learning that can support reflective decision making. Moreover, we wish to emphasize that the scholarship was selected on the basis of two criteria:

1. The scholarship had to embrace assumptions compatible with the goals of reflective decision making.
2. The principles embedded in the scholarship had to be consistent with a fundamental democratic principle: the dignity and worth of each individual.

The latter criterion led to the exclusion of behaviorist (stimulus-response) theories, which pay minimal attention to human thoughts, feelings, and emotions and view learning only as a change in external behavior. In our view, these theories have no place in the context of democratic education.

What is centrally important to fostering reflective decision making is the view of the learner held by those who work with students. If educators see learners as people who should be obedient, compliant, and passive, they will behave in ways that encourage such behavior by exposing students to static information and by offering praise, recognition, and rewards for deference to authority. In the short run they may be successful in nurturing compliance. However, the result is not likely to be individuals who can either think for themselves or function effectively as citizens in a democracy. Rather, those who wish to promote reflective decision making need to view the learner as independent, active, self-directing, and socially responsible. In this chapter, we have tried to shed some light on learning conditions that can contribute to this goal.

7

The Present Status
of the Social Studies:
What Is Needed?

In Chapter 2, "The Citizen We Need in a Democracy," we distinguished the citizen of a democracy from the citizen of an autocratic society by noting that the democratic citizen needed not merely habits of good behavior but also, along with broad knowledge of the society and skill in critical thinking, a commitment to the democratic process. In a democracy we are not preparing citizen drones but active participants in the governance of the communities of which they are a part.

This chapter will examine practice in the social studies in light of the criteria for the democratic citizen, by undertaking the following:

1. Examining the sources of confusion over the definition of the social studies.
2. Describing the deficiencies among the various configurations of the social studies.
3. Describing present practice in the social studies.
4. Suggesting the broad lines which reform in the social studies must take if the criteria suggested in Chapter 2 are to be met.

CONFUSION OVER THE DEFINITION
OF THE SOCIAL STUDIES

The social studies may be defined narrowly as the study of the social sciences and history—which usually means the mere exposition of facts and generalizations about which social scientists, at a given point in time, are in reasonable agreement. However, the social studies may be defined more broadly as the *critical* study of the social sciences and history—which usually means engaging directly in the intellectual process by which social scientists and historians verify truth. Finally, the social studies may be defined even more broadly as the process of solving social problems, a process in which the social sciences and history become instrumental in the learning process rather than the ends of education. From these three basic definitions at least seven distinguishable configurations of the social studies can be identified, each with a different conception of purpose and different projected outcomes, which in some cases may run counter to one another. Nor do all configurations promise to serve equally well, if at all, the unique needs of democratic citizenship.

In the following pages each of these configurations of the social studies will be described and the potential of each for citizenship education in a democracy will be delineated.

The Social Studies As the Social Sciences Simplified for Pedagogical Purposes

A definition of the social studies given currency years ago by Edgar B. Wesley (1937) and still widely accepted in the field is that "the social studies are the social sciences adapted and simplified for pedagogical purposes." Whatever meaning Wesley may have had for this definition, in practice it has meant the mere exposition of a relatively small number of facts and generalizations selected from history and the social sciences and presented to students as truth to be committed to memory. Seldom is the opportunity to examine the validity of these claims to truth given to students. Rather it is often expected that they be accepted as true on the authority of the textbook and the teacher. Frequently, there is no opportunity for students to know or to question the scholarly assumptions upon which the validity of these truth claims rests. There is also little opportunity to question how the narrative might have been different if facts that were left out had instead been included. Finally, there is seldom an opportunity to consult and compare other versions of the same events.

Three configurations of the social studies emerging from the simplistic use of Wesley's definition are described below.

THE SOCIAL STUDIES AS THE EXPOSITION OF THE SEPARATE SOCIAL SCIENCES. The most common configuration of the social studies is the exposition of the facts and generalizations that scholars in the various social sciences at a given point in time claim to be true. Historians tell us what happened and why. Economists tell us how economic phenomena are invariably related. And so forth. These truth claims are filtered through, selected out, and arranged by textbook writers. The result is that teams of professional textbook writers, who are seldom themselves scholars, produce a more or less complete but vastly simplified story of events. These events are explicated to students by means of teacher lectures or by reading the textbook and being quizzed on its content. Students are expected to remember and presumably to understand these selected facts and relationships. The bottom line is that the student must be able to recall the facts and generalizations covered. Under this configuration students are not encouraged to question the factual claims made or to argue with the authority. Teachers, scholars, and textbook writers are assumed to be authorities and to know the facts. Nor are students encouraged to utilize the facts in thinking about some problem, either their own or someone else's. Knowledge of the facts and retention of them in memory are the end in view.

A number of problems exist with this configuration of the social studies. In the first place, it overlooks the fact that the social science fields which it seeks to explicate are within themselves hotbeds of dispute. The scholars who write the textbooks are in continual and sometimes sharp disagreement over what the facts are and what they mean. On the basis of new research findings, scholars are continually revising their conception of what is true. The real field of economics, for instance, as contrasted with textbook versions of economics, is currently in almost total disarray.[1] The very best scholars in the field are hard pressed to explain, with any degree of certainty, the economic circumstances in which the peoples of the world find themselves today. There are dozens of equally respectable theories which purport to explain the current economic situation. Because many of the so-called facts of the field of economics are so undependable, it is useless as well as dishonest to teach them to students as if they represent the whole truth.

It is also somewhat of a misrepresentation to hold out the promise that the social sciences can be successfully simplified for purposes of pedagogy. To simplify involves leaving out part of the story, for example, the Indians' side of the Colonial-Indian wars or the American Revolution as seen from the perspective of the Loyalists. This simplifying process actually works to distort the social sciences, making them say something that they did not actually say. The social sciences are not sciences if facts are withheld for whatever purpose. They are not sciences if other, possibly unpopular versions, are suppressed. They are surely not sciences if the assumptions and qualifiers upon which the claims to truth are based are not laid bare. Simplified social science is only one short step removed from propaganda, however sincere the simplifiers are. It defeats the possibility that students will get a balanced, even if less certain, view of society.

A related problem with a social studies configuration based on the exposition of the facts of the social sciences is that it teaches students, inadvertently, to be accepting and unquestioning of authority, as befits autocracy, rather than to be the inquirers and skeptics that democracy requires. The weight of such teaching fosters conformity, in contrast to the questioning attitude of democratic citizens. It is healthy skepticism that keeps the democratic engine running.

Still another problem with the expository configuration is that teaching in this mode is unbearably dull and unexciting. Such teaching trivializes the study of the social sciences. It burdens the mind with what Alfred North Whitehead (1929) called "inert ideas" that go nowhere. It is dull and unexciting because it puts off indefinitely, usually forever, the opportunity to ask really important questions, which are characterized by uncertainty and controversy and seldom have definite and final answers. Only in the open-ended exploration of such questions does excitement enter learning. The focus of the exposition and memorizing of facts and generalizations which this configuration entails denies students the opportunity to explore really exciting questions.

THE SOCIAL STUDIES AS INDOCTRINATION.   A variation of the expository teaching of social science facts and generalizations—and one that rivals it in frequency of school practice—is the use of the social studies for purposes of propaganda, There are those who believe that it is the role of the social studies to indoctrinate students with certain understandings and points of view that are thought to be better than others or to be necessary to unify the people and preserve a particular way of life. Some individuals and groups within the country fear for its future unless their particular ideas of what is good and right are imposed upon all. They would skew the facts to be taught in history or economics in such a way as to advance what they see as the common interest. For instance, only the good about capitalism would be presented, with no mention made about its problems. Similarly, the violence committed against people and property by the patriots in the American Revolution might be soft-pedaled, lest it suggest that disobedience to unpopular government action, as with anti-nuke protests, is a tolerable practice. Or the Viet Nam War, which historians for the most part agree was a disastrous defeat for the United States, could be described as a tactical retreat or even a victory because young people are not to be told that America can ever be wrong or not invincible. There are those, including many teachers, who seemingly believe that tender minds should be told not the facts but the facts as someone would like them to be. It is but one short, easily taken step from teaching unquestioned truth, as in the exposition of facts and generalizations taken solely on the authority of the textbook, to teaching the truth dressed up a bit or skewed to serve what someone sees as a patriotic responsibility or even self-interest. Such a fragile and deceitful treatment of truth is contradictory to the tenets of a democracy.

Textbook publishers, driven by the necessity to sell books and afraid of self-appointed censors, contribute to indoctrination by either omitting or watering down the coverage of any topic that occasions controversy. For instance, a recent study of ten social studies textbooks series for the elementary level found them uniformly superficial in their treatment of important topics, arbitrary in their selection of topics, and neglectful of topics deemed controversial (Elliott et al., 1985). They found coverage of such topics as civil rights stylistic rather than substantive and the treatment of women and minorities unrealistic. There is also the distinct possibility that the truth may be distorted unwittingly by teachers and others who may lack scholarly acumen and intellectual persistence.

Scholars contribute to this skewing of the facts when they write, out of ignorance or from ill-founded assumptions. For instance, it is now clear that historians, many of whom were also textbook writers, wrote in the post-Civil War period with an anti-women, anti-black, anti-Native American and anti-labor union bias, a bias which only later historians have tried to correct. What were purported to have been the facts about Reconstruction turned out to be not the facts at all. Historians wrote mistakenly about blacks because they really did not know blacks. Seeing them only as slaves, they misinterpreted the potential of blacks in circumstances other than slavery. Unwittingly or not, they wrote history with a decidedly white bias, which for years was taken as the truth. Teaching history in straight expository fashion, without questioning, contributes to fixing such bias in students. Such teaching is really a subtle form of propaganda.

Still other problems exist with a configuration of the social studies that intends to indoctrinate. While small children who have not reached the age of full rationality are inevitably subject to indoctrination by parents, teachers, and even their own peers, the appropriateness of such indoctrination disappears once children have reached the age of rationality, surely by the time they are in middle school. In a democracy citizens are expected to learn to think for themselves and to make up their own minds. To allow anyone, either self-appointed or legally authorized, to decide what is safe for others to know or to think is a complete negation of democracy—which is nothing if it is not the right to know and the right to make one's own decisions based on the facts, wherever the facts may lead. Denial of the right to know is a significant step toward dictatorship and tyranny. Democracy prospers only in the full light of day. We do not advance democracy by imitating the educational methods of dictators.

There is still another problem with indoctrination. It robs the student of the opportunity to learn the skills of questioning and criticism so necessary in the development of the democractic citizen. Indoctrination dare not be conducted in any mode but the expositive. As with the straight transmission of facts described above, indoctrination is intolerant of questioning or hypothesizing. Students must be believers.

In a very real sense the exposition of a lie is not too different than the exposition of the facts, for any single truth is never the whole truth. Truths must be questioned and continually refined to achieve a greater truth. This process is the hallmark of scholarship. Both a lie and a half-truth may be exposed by further questioning. The intellectual process in either case is the same. Thus, whether we insist on a configuration of the social studies that transmits mere facts or that transmits lies posing as the truth, students are denied the right and the opportunity to hone their critical thinking skills.

Despite their widespread use, it is difficult to see how either of these approaches contributes usefully to the development of democractic citizens. Each denies to young citizens the right to know all of the facts as is their right in a democracy. Each denies to young citizens the right to develop the critical intellectual skills so central to democracy. Instead children learn to be accepting of whatever they are told by their elders. One can hardly conceive of citizen characteristics that serve democracy less well than these.

THE SOCIAL STUDIES AS THE STUDY OF TOPICS.   The topical configuration of the social studies is simply a variation of the exposition of facts and generalizations or of lies being passed off as facts. It is different only in that the subject matter being transmitted is broader in scope and cuts across the boundaries of disciplines or, as in the elementary grades, the subject matter is too simplistic and general to be treated reasonably in separate social science disciplines.

As Barth and Shermis (1979) have clearly pointed out, we frequently confuse the study of a topic with the study of a social problem. For instance, the problems suggested for study in the 12th grade by the Committee on the Social Studies in 1916 were, in fact, topics, and that is the way they were generally treated in the schools of the United States for many years to come. The purpose was not to involve students in problem solving but to inform them about what were then called social problems. It was believed that the social sciences could resolve all social problems as soon as the facts were known. Students were taught the solutions to social problems, just as social scientists, in all of their scientific wisdom, then saw them being solved. Today, social scientists are far less certain about the power of science to solve social problems. Social problems are seen as far more complex entities, involving moral, ethical, and political questions as well as cultural differences that, presently at least, cannot be solved by science alone. Nonetheless, we persist in schools with what is really a topical rather than a problems approach to the study of social problems.

From this perspective, the difference between a topic and a problem is in large part a matter of the mode in which we approach study. Is our purpose merely to inform students about the problem, even its supposed solution, or to engage them in the more knotty effort to work out real solutions? The first is conducted in the expository mode, the second in the more difficult and intellectually agonizing hypothetical mode. The outcome of the first is information about the problem that can be held in memory. The outcome of the second is a much less definitive sense of the whole problem, where efforts at resolution are always only approximations of a final and definite solution. In this approach solutions are always temporary, until the emergence of a new set of circumstances, and they always entail compromises between contending forces and opinions. This is the real stuff of problem solving, a condition from which a topical approach recoils.

Everyone seems to agree on the propriety, if not the necessity, of a topical approach with very young children, who are deemed too immature intellectually and socially for the introduction of uncertainty that hypothesizing entails. Disagreement occurs over how long to continue in this vein. Judging by current practice, most teachers would never wean students from dependence on lectures and the textbook to hear the facts and commit them to memory. Others, less numerous, believe that children at an early age, possibly as early as the third grade, should be introduced to the necessity of deciding for themselves between alternative versions of truth. In any case, the burden on teachers of small children to teach the truth as best they know it is indeed an onerous responsibility.

In addition to the topical study of problems, the topical approach has been utilized by a number of curriculum reformers, who insist that a study of social science disciplines needlessly divides the field and makes a proper understanding of the broad sweep of human events impossible to transmit. Social scientists bring a general background of understanding to their disciplines, which students in elementary and secondary school have no means of achieving. Notable among these reformers was Harold Rugg of Columbia University, who attempted a general discourse on human events in the United States that encompassed all of the disciplines (Rugg, 1921).

Another was Paul Hanna and his students at Stanford, who identified generalizations cutting across disciplines, which became the basis for the none-too-successful California Social Studies Framework (California State Department of Education, 1921). Still another reformer was Lawrence Senesh at Purdue, who wrote textbooks for the lower grades attempting to orchestrate all of the social sciences, ostensibly around an understanding of economics (Senesh, 1966).

The overriding goal of these efforts was to unify the social sciences and make them more comprehensible to students. All were attempts to explicate the facts to students as the authors saw it, which left little room for questioning. All fall in the expository mode, not unlike the expository approach to teaching the disciplines described above. In addition, not only did the disciplines prove to be difficult, if not impossible to orchestrate, but each discipline presented a different, rather than a harmonious way of looking at society. Students were left burdened with unassimilated information which they had memorized but had not learned to utilize. In any case, none of these efforts justified the enthusiasm of their authors.

Another, wider use of the topical approach comes about when someone decides that a particular area of concern is of such far-reaching importance that it deserves special treatment not accorded it in a curriculum devoted to the exposition of disciplines. There exists a more or less continuous flow of pamphlet materials, either privately engineered or published under the auspices of the National Council of the Social Studies or some other professional organization, which provide information on a broad range of such topics. A recent publication of the National Council for the Social Studies, *Perspectives on Japan: A Guide for Teachers,* may be taken as fairly typical of such publications (Cogan and Schneider, 1983). The extent to which such materials are used and just how they are integrated with regular social studies programs is not definitely known. One observation is pertinent, however. For the most part such materials are strictly topical, rather than problem oriented, being by and large narrative treatments of the topic. That they may be used by resourceful teachers to exercise the intellectual skills of problem solving is of course a possibility, but they are seldom designed to achieve this end. Taken at face value, they are subject to all of the problems that beset expository teaching with its overload of poorly utilized information.

The Social Studies as the Critical Study of the Social Sciences

Attempts to reform the teaching of the social studies have frequently taken the form of the critical study of the social sciences, in contrast to their exposition. Fundamentally, such reform involves a switch from the expository mode of teaching to the hypothetical. The truth claims made by social scientists are treated as hypotheses for further study and validation, exactly as they are treated among social scientists themselves. Students are expected to take on the active role of fledgling social scientists. The purpose is to help students to become critical consumers of social science scholarship as well as critical thinkers in their own right.

Such reform is consistent with the nature of the social sciences, since truth claims among social scientists are always taken to be tentative and open to further study. Factual claims are taken to be only approximations of truth, always subject to revision as new light is shed on them by further research. History is always being reinterpreted, sometimes dramatically so, as new facts come to light. Economists are always at each other's scholarly throats, as there are always other respectable versions of claims to truth.

Further, the reformers are more concerned that students learn to think and to be open to new evidence than merely memorize unrelated and sometimes invalid factual trivia. To the reformers, the exposition and memorization of information is not a sufficient end for the social studies. They believe that it is more important to advance knowledge based on reason and develop the skills of critical thinking upon which more dependable knowledge rests. They see these ends better accomplished by putting students through their scholarly paces rather than by telling them merely what the scholar has learned. Two different configurations have emerged from this orientation toward social studies.

THE SOCIAL STUDIES AS THE CRITICAL ANALYSIS OF THE SOCIAL SCIENCES. This configuration takes its inspiration from such scholars as Gunnar Myrdahl, who years ago warned in his book, *The Great American Dilemma*, of the misinformation and misconceptions of society that accrue to a simplistic and uncritical exposition of history, without knowledge of the assumptions and qualifiers known to the historian and without the consideration of other possible versions of the same events (Myrdahl, 1944). In addition, Alfred North Whitehead in *The Aims of Education* warned about not only the uselessness but the harmfulness of education which fills the mind with "inert ideas"—that is, with ideas that are merely received into the mind without being utilized, tested, or thrown into fresh combinations. Whitehead said that the first thing to do to any idea was to prove its truth, and that the second was to prove its worth or usefulness. In the social studies field the most illustrious proponent of this point of view was Alan Griffin (1942) of Ohio State, who focused the teaching of American history on the validation of the beliefs of students about both matters of fact and matters of value (Engle, 1982). Griffin's student, Lawrence Metcalf of the University of Illinois, extended this idea to cover the validation of beliefs of students in "closed areas" of society, that is, in questions so controversial that they are not freely discussed (Hunt and Metcalf, 1955).

The Indiana Experiments conducted at Indiana University in the 1960s under the guidance of Shirley Engle demonstrated that the use of the Whitehead formula—"Is it true and what can it be used for?"—in studying textbook courses in world history, United States history, and government not only was enthusiastically received by students but led to a sounder grasp of the subject matter and a greater development of critical thinking skills. It also proved to be very exacting on teachers and, as a possible result, was never widely emulated in schools (Massialas, 1963).

A somewhat simpler version of the "critical analysis of texts" configuration would consistently introduce an alternative version into the study of a textbook version of events, as was suggested even for third graders by the eminent scholar at Columbia University, Henry Johnson (1940). Such a practice rests on the knowledge that facts, at best, are hard to come by, even when sought after by careful scholars. It recognizes that scholars are continually revising their beliefs about what the facts are and how they should be interpreted; that there is usually more than one reasoned interpretation of any social phenomenon; and that social science scholarship is an open-ended process, resulting usually in tentative conclusions rather than in unquestioned truth. Such an approach further recognizes that it is far more useful in dealing with human affairs to have the whole picture in all of its variations than to have one limited and possibly erroneous view. This approach is therefore consistent with the nature of scholarship, in that it continually considers alternative versions of affairs. Recent scholarly reinterpretations of important events can be an excellent source of alternative versions to compare to textbook accounts. New perspectives that may have a far-reaching impact on how we view the world and society can be discovered in news reports of research and in current scholarly publications. For example, new research on Christopher Columbus, conducted by noted biographer Frederick J. Pohl (1986), gives a very different account of the life and times of Columbus than that which appears in most United States history textbooks.

One problem with the critical analysis approach is the greater time required to carry out the study. In place of the superficial coverage of large amounts of material, which the expository configurations make possible, is substituted the patient and more leisurely treatment in great depth of a relatively small number of topics. One must ask, however, whether the expository ground-covering which characterizes so much of the social studies really achieves what it is intended to achieve— that is, an understanding of our social heritage—and whether it provides students with the kind of intellectual experience needed in a democracy? Would not the more leisurely and critical study of a smaller number of topics in depth serve us better?

A related problem is that many teachers are not well enough prepared to lead the study of important content in the depth required by this configuration. Additionally, a rich collection of resources other than textbooks is needed to buttress the investigations that this configuration requires. It is of course possible that over a period of time a teacher, a social studies department, or a school could collect files of materials which present alternative views of events not commonly presented in textbooks.

In any case, the advantages of using a configuration of social studies that focuses on the critical analysis of the textbook are persuasive. The critical analysis configuration presents the social sciences as they really are, as scholarly, open-ended ways of studying social phenomena, not merely compendiums of sometimes badly skewed and outdated information. The social sciences represent live and viable tools for understanding the human condition, and an overwhelming advantage of critical analysis over exposition is that it cultivates these tools of questioning and making critical judgments, both so necessary for citizens of a democracy.

THE SOCIAL STUDIES AS THE REPLICATION OF SOCIAL SCIENCE SCHOLAR-SHIP.   The configuration of the social studies just described places the emphasis on students learning to be critical consumers of the social sciences. A kindred version places the emphasis on doing social science as nearly as possible as the social scientist does. Jerome Bruner, who popularized the idea of "discovery" teaching and who taught the social sciences in the "hypothetical" as contrasted with the "expository" mode, is the best known exponent of this approach to teaching (Bruner, 1962). Bruner sees the student learning by actually doing social science and at the same time mastering its structure. This could conceivably be accomplished in one or both of two ways: by replicating selected work of social scientists from raw data, or by engaging the student in heretofore unresearched studies of selected human phenomena.

In the first instance students would be given raw data and then helped to replicate the work of scholars in organizing and interpreting the data. Students would be encouraged to hypothesize concerning the meaning of the data, to set up strategies for testing their hypotheses and correcting them for error, and eventually to draw conclusions from their data, much as social scientists draw conclusions from their own research. Students could, of course, compare their findings to those of social scientists.

A variation of this configuration would have the students engage in real, and as yet unresearched, areas of social investigation. For instance, students could write their own history of the community in which they lived or conduct sociological or economic surveys of their community.

Bruner's claim for such strategies is that they would transform students from passive receivers of information into active constructionists, better able to use information to solve a variety of problems. Seeing information as useful, students would be motivated by a love for learning rather than by grades and the approval of parents and teachers. Information learned as it is used would be much easier to remember, and, most importantly, students would learn problem solving, a skill which Bruner sees as best learned by actually solving problems (Bruner, 1962).

Although these heady claims to excellence have never been conclusively established, they were nonetheless compelling enough to have furnished the impetus for what became the most extensive reform movement ever undertaken in the social studies. The "New Social Studies" movement of the late 1960s and early 1970s enlisted the support and effort of thousands of social scientists, educators, and teachers, most of whom were thoroughly disenchanted with the more traditional exposition of textbook versions of events. Hundreds of curriculum projects were undertaken, more or less embracing Brunerian ideas, and some excellent work, such as *Man: A Course of Study* (1969) and *The High School Geography Project* (Association of American Geographers, 1969) was completed. But despite generous support by the federal government to develop the materials and to train teachers in their use, the acceptance of these projects by teachers was limited. Teachers were unprepared to deal with materials that led to no correct and final answers, and they felt insecure and out of control when faced with students who were thinking and asking questions. Furthermore, the traditional achievement tests based on the recall of factual trivia no longer could be used to measure progress in learning. Parents and conservative patrons were upset because children were excited, sometimes upset, by the controversy that had been introduced. The change from memorizing facts to using them in thought upset traditionalists. In any case, hardly a trace of the New Social Studies remains today. Despite this, many in the field of the social studies still believe the new social studies movement was on the right track and its revival is still a distinct possibility.

There is no question that the implementation of a configuration of the social studies which would have students doing the social studies would require resources and teaching personnel far greater than any alternative suggested thus far. For instance, textbooks would need to be replaced by a far richer variety of materials of many kinds. Teachers would require a far more thorough breadth and depth of training than most teachers have. Evaluation would have to be drastically revised to accommodate a far more comprehensive set of outcomes including process outcomes that are difficult to measure.

But it is argued by those who see open-ended intellectual development as the best, if not the only, road to democractic competence that the result would be worth the price.

The Social Studies as the Examination of Social Problems

Still a third group of reformers would organize the social studies around the study of social problems. Social problems as conceived by these people are not to be confused with the study of topics referred to above as a configuration under the expository approach to teaching. Nor are they to be confused with the involvement of students in the study of social science disciplines as proposed by Bruner. While each of these may have its place, the first stops short of real social problem solving and settles for merely providing students with information; the second stops short of social problem solving by limiting study to the academic problems of particular social sciences. In fact, social scientists as social scientists seldom concern themselves with social problems as citizens meet them in real life. The President's Board of Economic Advisors, the best example we have of social scientists advising on social policy, is of limited usefulness and is frequently ignored by policy makers because its members understand only the economic factors in a social situation and are blind to other, possibly more compelling factors that may be operating. Social scientists are of only limited usefulness in resolving social problems and in fact are seldom called on to advise in such matters.

Those who see the social studies as usefully organized around compelling social problems believe that a significant part, if not all, of the social studies should be devoted to a direct attempt to resolve significant social problems in all of their ramifications. Only in this way, they would argue, can the citizen learn to deal intelligently and responsibly with such problems. They would criticize education on two counts: for devoting itself almost exclusively to providing background information, without teaching students to apply what they have presumably learned in school to real-life situations, and for avoiding the controversy and uncertainty which inevitably surround the study of real issues in real life. Two possible configurations of social studies arise from this thinking, and it is important to note that in both of them the social sciences and history become instrumental to the learning rather than ends to be mastered. This condition may actually work to enhance, rather than diminish, their influence in the learning process.

THE SOCIAL STUDIES AS THE STUDY OF PERSISTENT SOCIAL ISSUES. An outstanding example of this configuration is the Public Issues Series/Harvard Social Studies Project produced by Donald W. Oliver and Fred M. Newmann (1967). In this series, topics in U.S. history such as the American Revolution, the railroad era, religious freedom, the rise of organized labor, the New Deal, and the like are each taught around central issues of great concern, both then and now.

For instance, the American Revolution is taught around questions that retain an importance and relevance in today's world, questions such as: What is patriotism? Were Samuel Adams, Patrick Henry, Benjamin Franklin, and Thomas Paine patriots or traitors, and would the same standards apply to modern heroes such as Martin Luther King? Under what circumstances, if ever, should people refuse to obey their legally constituted government? Is violence ever justified in the pursuit of political goals? Who had the most reason to refuse to obey their government, the Committeemen at Lexington or the blacks at Pettus Bridge?

Cases are provided in which actual people, past and present (the Committeemen at Lexington and Concord, the blacks at Pettus Bridge), have been faced with deciding these issues. Facts from history are used rather than memorized to help students decide the issues. Students are guided to reach conclusions to the best of their ability in light of the facts.

Scattered throughout the country are teachers who use such an approach, particularly in the study of United States history and to a lesser degree in the study of economics, but to our knowledge, there is no systematic use of this configuration, as we envision it, in any school in the nation. Resourceful teachers who are bored with and discouraged by the results of expository textbook teaching are the most likely to use this configuration. They usually do this without the material support needed for its optimum success. However, the Harvard Public Issues Series was the best seller among the materials growing out of the New Social Studies movement.

THE SOCIAL STUDIES AS THE DIRECT STUDY OF SIGNIFICANT SOCIAL PROBLEMS. It would seem obvious that the direct study of social problems should serve not only as the central focus but as the capstone experience of the social studies. Actually, among the configurations identified, it is the least practiced in schools. In a recent study, social studies teachers reported their overwhelming belief that significant social problems, such as nuclear disarmament and pollution of the world's environment, should be studied in school but they just as overwhelmingly reported that such issues were not being studied (Molnar, 1983). It is as if the social studies have a persistent failure of heart that leads to pulling back at the brink from really coming to grips with what the field is all about: the education of citizens who have the ability to participate intelligently and responsibly in resolving our persistent social problems.

In the name of objectivity, social scientists, have always stood aloof from the maelstrom of social problems. This they leave to politicians and just plain citizens. In a similar vein, social studies is hard pressed to prove that it has any real impact on the behavior of citizens. There is ample evidence around us that speaks to the impotence of citizens who have attended our classes to deal with the problems of our society. It may be overly simplistic to conclude that our ineffectiveness as citizen educators lies in the fact that we are so preoccupied with teaching facts that we have no time to deal with problems or to teach young people to think critically. Or perhaps it is that we know that dealing with problems is a difficult, imprecise, uncomfortable, controversial matter into which we fear to enter. Whatever the reasons, it is not illogical to suggest that without the study of significant social problems the whole social studies enterprise loses its reason for existing. If effective democractic citizenship is our goal, the persistent study of social problems is the very heart of the social studies endeavor.

An approach to the study of social problems, based on Deweyan ideas as refined by, among others, Broudy, Smith, and Burnett in their book *Democracy and Excellence in American Secondary Education* (1964) is spelled out in Chapter 8 of this book. In our view the implementation of the direct in-depth study of our persistent social problems is the greatest imperative facing social studies today.

AN ASSESSMENT OF SOCIAL STUDIES PRACTICE

The social studies as practiced in schools today fall almost totally under the framework of the "Social Studies as the Social Sciences Simplified." The other configurations are found infrequently and spottily, if at all. Further, as pointed out above, the social studies have dealt inadequately, if at all, with values and value problems and have been ambiguous in their relationship to the humanities, usually using them inappropriately. Nor has all of this changed very much in the nearly three quarters of a century since the term social studies began to have currency. Yet over the same period of time there has been a persistent demand for reform in the field. Numerous educational leaders have called for a social studies more in line with the unique needs of democracy and one utilizing more intellectually sophisticated ways of learning that involve inquiry and reason over the rote memorization of facts. Most have recognized the central role of values analysis and learning to resolve value problems in social education.

These reformers included, prominently: John Dewey and others at Columbia University; Bode and Hullfish and their student Alan Griffin, along with his students Hunt, Metcalf, and Martorella, at Ohio State University; B. O. Smith and William Stanley and their students at the University of Illinois; Donald Oliver and his associates at Harvard; and most recently the devotees of the federally funded New Social Studies Movement of the 1960s and 1970s, revolving around the work of Jerome Bruner. Others who have urged reform include such illustrious scholars as Gunnar Myrdahl, James Harvey Robinson, Alfred North Whitehead, Margaret Mead, Robert Redfield, Henry Steele Commager, and Paul Starr.

In one way or another, all these reformers urged that education in general and the social studies in particular should be a hands-on, open, questioning, active enterprise, consistent with human intelligence and consistent with a democracy that presumably prizes the rational and the intellectual. The important concern to all of them was the quest and skill of asking questions and pursuing one's own answers. The mere possession of facts and explanations, from the disciplines or from anywhere else, was thought of as the means rather than the ends of education. Education was seen as the mastery of a process as much as the mastery of a content. The primary function of education for democracy was to develop the capacity for social criticism and the political skills needed to be an influence in the society. These are principles which the social studies, as they are constituted today in most classrooms (including the introductory social science courses in college that make up the bulk of the training social studies teachers receive), strictly violate.

Despite the vigor of this reform movement and its intellectual appeal, there is hardly a trace of it in the social studies as actually taught in the nation's schools today. Instead, school people have followed the lead of Edgar B. Wesley (1937), who defined the social studies as the social sciences simplified for purposes of pedagogy. Or perhaps *he* followed *them*, in that he merely described what educators were already doing and continue to do to this day. They do this, without too much thought, because it is the natural and traditional way to teach, predating democracy; its presumption is that elders (and this has been extended to include textbook writers) always possess superior knowledge of facts and values which it is their duty to pass along to youth. No matter that the world is faced with unprecedented change and social turmoil and that ancient values were everywhere coming unglued.

Wesley's way was the simple, easy way. It was easily accommodated by straightforward exposition and textbooks. It seldom occasioned controversy. Most teachers were comfortable with it, for they were left in complete control.

Even the National Council for the Social Studies, for the most part, fell in line. Its annual meetings and its publications were dominated, over the years, by so-called practical, "What do I do tomorrow?" matters and by gimmickry, by which children could be induced to learn unpalatable and frequently useless lessons. The curriculum influence of the Council was indicated in its publications, which, in close alliance with textbook companies and textbook writers, were largely additive in nature; there was a cacophony of new topics to be covered in an expanding world—career education, consumer education, economic education, global education, multicultural education, moral education, law-related education, and much more—with not enough serious thought as to how all of this was to be orchestrated or how all of this could be brought to help young people gain some comprehensive understanding of and power over their world, as befits citizens in a democracy.

What Is the Practice?

Despite the potential of the reform movement for providing citizenship education more in line with the needs of democracy, actual practice in the classroom has changed little over the years. The persistent practice is the exposition, via textbook and lecture, of a simplified version of facts and generalizations from history and the separate social sciences.

A spate of studies concerning current practice, clustered around 1980, attest to the current practice and register almost complete agreement as to its characteristics (Stake and Easley, 1978; Shaver et al., 1979; Goodlad, 1983; Superka et al., 1980). The textbook is the standard fare of social studies in the schools. The goal is to reduce the text to memory. Students are regularly examined by oral questioning and written examination, usually of the short-answer type to see to what extent they recall text material. Materials other than textbooks, including those produced by the federally funded New Social Studies projects of the 1960s and 1970s are not extensively used in social studies classrooms (Shaver et al., 1979).

An exhaustive study of American history textbooks completed in 1979 by Frances Fitzgerald has demonstrated both the scholarly unreliability and the inappropriateness of the textbook as the sole arbiter of the content and the method of social studies teaching. Textbooks normally present one uncomplicated and overly simple version of events, with no mention of the qualifiers and assumptions being made by the author, with no mention of the existence of other scholarly and respectable versions of the same events, and with no mention of facts that run counter to the conclusions drawn. Rather than being objective accounts, textbooks are easily observed to sway hither and fro to suit the passions of the day. And because they are produced to be sold in a market full of politically powerful, self-appointed censors, they customarily soft-pedal, or omit entirely, social problems or controversial issues. Textbooks have largely been written from the point of view of the powerful. Textbook writers have been reluctant to give equitable and balanced treatment to blacks, Native Americans, women, the labor movement, environmentalists, and the like. The result is a history, like a fairy tale, devoid of the conflict and problem resolution so typically democratic. At best, such history is sterile and unexciting; at worst, it is a fraud (Fitzgerald, 1979).

The studies cited above report that social studies, among all subjects taught in school, is clearly the one least liked by students. Students generally find social studies content uninteresting. It is also the subject most resistant to learning, students report. This is probably not so much because of the intellectual rigor with which the subject is taught, but because of the incredible amount of trivia which students are required to remember, at least temporarily. The author of the comic strip "Shoe" demonstrates rare insight into the extent to which the social studies is the memorization of trivia when he has Skyler's little friend inquiring, "What is the name of the game when you try to answer a bunch of questions for points?" To which Skyler answers, "Oh yeah, we play that in school. We call it American History." Social studies is also reported to be the subject about which there is the most ambivalence among both students and their teachers as to the purpose for which it is studied.

Because of the preoccupation with mastering textbooks, there is little time in the social studies classroom to study social problems, although most teachers say that social problems should be treated. Most will also admit that these problems are not being treated in social studies classrooms (Molnar, 1983). Controversial issues are usually avoided, and if they are mentioned at all, it is likely that they will be treated superficially as merely the reporting of current events or the pooling of ignorance, rather than with the depth of consideration that the serious study of social problems requires.

The mode of instruction common to the social studies is to read the text and be quizzed on its content. This may be supplemented by other largely teacher-controlled modes of instruction, such as lectures or filling in blanks in workbooks. There is little genuine discussion of topics and little opportunity for either the teacher or the student to raise important questions for which there are not set answers and which require systematic reasoning and inquiry. The teacher, usually lecturing or quizzing students for recall of facts, dominates such discussions as do occur. Genuine discussion, which involves an extended exchange of ideas among students and between students and the teacher on some important topic, seldom occurs and is not encouraged by the kinds of questions asked.

Evaluation of social studies instruction is based, for the most part, on students' demonstrating that they can recall and reproduce the information given in the text, frequently in the very language of the text (Shaver et al., 1979). More persuasive evaluation, which would require students to apply what they have learned to new situations or which would inquire into the actual behavior of students as citizens, is almost nonexistent.

What Are the Results?

It is germane to ask, What are the real outcomes of social studies teaching as pictured above? We do not know, because the profession has never systematically and persistently investigated the basic questions about the effects of schooling on the real-life behavior of citizens. Nor have public agencies, which are responsible for schools, done so. Some of these basic questions would be: What kind of citizens do our graduates actually become? What are their actual reading habits after leaving school? What do they read and how much? Do they keep themselves well informed? Do our graduates vote and take an active part in civic affairs? Do they demonstrate in their daily lives an understanding and appreciation of the freedoms and responsibilities of citizens in a democracy? Such questions are seldom investigated, nor are they easily answered. Yet they are the only kinds of questions that will tell us how we are actually doing.

In the meantime, it is important to recognize that such spotty evidence as we have is none too reassuring. There is good reason to believe that large numbers of our graduates have generally poor reading habits, do not keep themselves informed on important issues, participate very little, if at all, in public affairs, and generally underestimate or misinterpret the importance of the most basic democratic principles. Such a conclusion is suggested to almost anyone who looks around at the behavior of citizens in the day-to-day affairs of our nation.

However, some more concrete evidence on these questions, while by no means definitive, can be cited. Discerning students of citizenship education have no doubt observed, possibly with dismay, how ill-informed is the U.S. citizen about the most pressing problems of the day, as revealed over and over again by such indices of public opinion as the Harris and the Gallup polls. The level of ignorance about crucial public issues revealed in public opinion surveys, interviews, and inquiries borders on the ludicrous. The citizen frequently appears to be a buffoon and a dupe, rather than a serious student of public affairs. One possible indicator of the intellectual level of our citizens is the trend in magazine publications. Nearly all of the serious journals of public opinion, once held in high esteem, are in trouble for lack of subscribers. At the same time, trash publications, the slicks which deal superficially and even frivolously with civic affairs, are sold in ever-increasing numbers. Such public evidence has led such a serious observer of our democracy as Walter Cronkite to conclude that the majority of our people are not adequately informed to intelligently exercise their franchise (Cronkite, 1983).

Cronkite places much of the blame on television and the newspapers, which report the news superficially without the analysis and interpretation necessary for understanding—one is tempted to add, much as we teach the social studies. Television and the newspapers these days must be brief and entertaining if they are to hold the public interest. Newspapers, in particular, in order to compete with television, have abandoned their time-honored role to report the news in depth.[2]

It is possible that the fault lies not so much with the media, as Cronkite suggests, but with citizens who accept and even demand the fare they are getting.[3] In turn, from our point of view, a good share of the blame may be placed on schools in general and on the social studies in particular, which turn out citizens who are intellectually shallow and superficial.

For a number of years, H. H. Remmers of Purdue University tested large numbers of graduating high school seniors on their knowledge and attitudes with respect to the most basic beliefs that undergird democracy. The preponderance of these seniors were confused and ill-informed about our most basic rights (Remmers, 1957). This finding is confirmed to some extent by the National Assessment of Education Progress reported in 1976 (Forbes, 1976).

Citizens who graduate from our schools seem to have a low estimate of their own ability to affect public policy or exert control over government. The failure of large numbers of citizens, frequently a majority, to vote in elections borders on the disgraceful and compares unfavorably to the voting records in most other democracies. For instance, just 53.3% of our citizens bothered to vote in the 1984 Presidential election.[4]

Recent studies point to the lack of interest in civic affairs among college students, the cream of the crop, who have graduated from our high schools. According to one writer, David Matthews, who has reviewed several of these studies, college students are not interested in government or in public questions (Matthews, 1985). Few are interested in public service. Instead, they are interested in themselves and how to get ahead in the marketplace. Matthews cites one study by Alexander Astin who found that among college students only about 40% are interested in public affairs and only 20% are likely to become involved in community activity, while 80% cite affluence as their top priority. Such data speaks poorly for the influence of the social studies on the civic education of our most promising citizens.

The low intellectual level at which political campaigns are waged in this country also testifies to the lack of political sophistication on the part of large numbers of our citizens. Politicians find it to their advantage to conduct their campaigns in the most simplistic terms, which frequently distort or even misrepresent the real issues. Citizens seem to have a low tolerance for the politician who is scholarly, who talks about issues as intellectual problems, who does not propose a quick fix. The susceptibility of many citizens to the propaganda blitz and to "Madison Avenue Slick" is attested to by the increasingly large sums of money that candidates need to raise and spend on their election. For instance, reported expenditures of the two major Presidential candidates in 1984 exceeded 95 million dollars. It is no longer unusual for a senatorial election to cost the candidate in excess of 25 million dollars.[5] The impression that the candidates make or that is created for them by the media seems to speak louder to the voter than does the substance of their campaign. We are perilously close to the time when candidates can simply buy their way into power, when the control of government passes from the people to the money powers. At the same time citizens seem to display very meager intellectual defenses against such an eventuality.

One cannot help but ponder the possibility that the force-feeding of unexamined truths and the emphasis on the right answer, which characterize so much of citizenship education today, may have contributed to the quiescence of so many of our citizens, or at least to have rendered them helpless to resist the propaganda onslaught we are observing in this country today.

PROBLEMS IN THE SOCIAL STUDIES

When looked at in terms of its generally accepted goal to prepare citizens for a democracy, social studies as it exists in schools today, is confronted with a number of vexing problems.

To Socialize or Countersocialize Youth?

Social studies is strong on socializing youngsters, leading them to accept and acquiesce to the teachings of adults. It is woefully weak on countersocializing youth, teaching them to question, to inquire, to make judgments, and to participate actively in the improvement of society.

In an autocracy, all citizenship education is appropriately devoted to socializing youth to accept without question the present ways of the society and the authority of whoever is in power. Citizens are not expected to have a voice in managing or changing the society. The role of the citizen is unquestioning obedience and blind loyalty.

In this respect, democracy is starkly different. Change, progress, and improvement are endemic to democracy and citizens are expected to participate freely in charting the direction of the society. If they are to do this, they must be able and inclined to think independently. It is not the blind loyalist but the person of independent mind who represents the goal of democratic citizenship.

While all citizenship education in an autocracy can be socialization, in a democracy only part, a minor part at that, can be. The basic principles of democratic behavior can and should be learned at an early age through example and more formally by reading or being told simple stories and histories that exemplify these principles. Even then, in a democracy, we are obliged to help children, as soon as possible, to have reasons for accepting principles they earlier accepted from elders on faith.

But in later years—as mental maturity develops, in the upper elementary school and certainly by the middle school—the emphasis can and must change toward countersocialization. Children should be helped to question and to develop the capacity to pose their own questions more effectively. They should be helped to build the capacity to conduct their own investigations and should be encouraged to engage in independent thinking and in the development of new forms of democratic expression. They should achieve what Paul Starr refers to as the art of criticism (Starr, 1971).

Socialization is easy, simple, and straightforward. It leaves the teacher in complete control, eliminates controversy, and is easily accommodated by textbooks. The results are easier to measure, and the real goals need not be made explicit. But despite all these managerial advantages, countersocialization is by far the more important for democracy. Countersocialization is fraught with difficulty: it is more intellectually demanding of both teachers and students; it introduces elements of uncertainty and controversy into the school and the classrooms; the results are more difficult to measure; suitable materials are more difficult to come by; and the defense of academic freedom becomes more challenging. Despite all these difficulties, countersocialization is the real goal of citizenship education in a democracy and we should hasten to embrace it before it is too late. One certain result will be more exciting, more stimulating, and more challenging classrooms.

Confusion Between the Exposition of Subjects and Teaching Critical Thinking

In a somewhat related vein, the social studies as currently taught in schools today mistakenly confuse the mere exposition of social science disciplines by way of lectures or textbooks, however simplified for purposes of pedagogy, with citizenship education. This process, so common today, is not only an insufficient basis for citizenship education, being far too narrow and fragmented, but in some ways it is a counterproductive process, negating rather than supporting democratic citizen behavior.

The social sciences—taught as though there were one agreed-upon version of truth—become, if taken seriously by students at all, a powerful socializing force, a force for maintaining the status quo (Myrdhal, 1944; Johnson, 1940). Students are moved to conclude that what is reported to have happened is the only thing that could have happened and is therefore the right thing to have happened. We all know of the tremendous errors of fact and of precept that have been engraved in the minds of students through this process, on such important matters as slavery and Reconstruction, treatment of Native Americans, economic conflict, and, more recently, the Great Depression (Miller and Rose, 1983).

In stark contrast to the homogenization, oversimplification, and even distortion of affairs that go on in our classrooms under the label of teaching the social sciences, scholars in the social sciences, behaving as scholars, are often at each other's throats. Unfortunately, they frequently do not carry this contentious scholarly behavior over into their lectures in History 101. History is continually being rewritten as new evidence and new insight, frequently borrowed from the other social sciences, comes to light or as we ask more penetrating questions of it. There are a thousand economic theories, no one of which explains all economic activity and no one of which survives for long the barrage of criticism leveled by other economists. Consider, for example, the President's Board of Economic Advisors: All of them are considered conservative economists, but they are unable to agree on anything. Or consider the recent Nobel prize winner in economics who was awarded the prize because he proved mathematically that the law of supply and demand really works. He admits that his findings apply only in the theoretical realm of mathematical modeling and that his equations leave out of consideration labor unions and wage contracts, tariffs, subsidies, differential taxation, cartels, monopolies, regulatory boards, advertising, unequal access to information and to education, and plain human compassion. In the light of this unsettlement in economic thought, it is difficult to understand how, with a straight face and a clear conscience, we can teach some version of the free enterprise system as invariant truth. As Frederick Paxson, the scholar generally recognized as the leading authority on the history of the West once said, "There are many more problems of understanding and interpretation in the history of the West than there are certainties" (Paxson, 1936).

If honestly taught, the social sciences and history could be a constructive force for countersocialization. But if this is to be, the social sciences must be taught, warts and all. Students must be helped to share in the same problems that concern scholars. The mode of instruction must shift from the expository to the hypothetical, as Bruner advocated and as many of the "new" social studies attempted. There is the opportunity, if we will grasp it, for students to learn from the study of disciplines how to deal with uncertainty, how to marshal and weigh evidence, and how to think about social problems. It is only in such terms that the disciplines are justified as a part of citizenship education in a democracy.

But even if taught with integrity, the social sciences taken alone are an insufficient basis for democratic citizenship education. Taught as separate disciplines, they do not teach the citizen how to deal intelligently with broad social problems involving multiple dimensions of knowledge. The resolution of such problems involves mental operations that go far beyond and are different in kind than those of any single discipline. These include making judgments about the kinds of knowledge and data, from whatever source, that are relevant to the problem; making judgments about the credibility of conflicting sources of information; and, most importantly, making judgments between the conflicting values that are at stake. It includes, also, making judgments about practical matters such as the possible spin-offs of any proposed solution, how various groups see their interest being affected, and what is politically possible. In short, broad areas of social concern with which citizens in a democracy are expected to deal require a special intellectual discipline, a discipline which some have referred to as the "Discipline of Practical Judgment in a Democracy." Such a discipline entails combining and integrating a number of elements and processes only partially served by the study of one or all of the individual social sciences.

Furthermore, useful citizenship participation in a democracy requires not only that citizens develop appropriate intellectual skills but that they learn how to engage in the pursuit of power and how to influence government. Without these political skills, the rest is an exercise in futility.

It is difficult to see how all of these can be developed in the limited confines of a few social sciences that were never conceived in the first place for such a purpose. It is difficult to see how these comprehensive skills of the citizen can be developed short of the direct study of broad social problems in all of their facets.

Lack of Relevance to Current Social Problems

As the social studies exist today in most schools, we somehow manage never to get to the present or, at best, we treat the present superficially. Important contemporary and future problems—such as nuclear disarmament, pollution of the earth's environment, division of our nation and the world into areas of wealth and poverty, alternatives to existing and faltering forms of economic organization, and the like—are passed over in most schools, and young people graduate from high school not only knowing less than nothing about them but having no clear idea as to how to think about such problems. It is no wonder that young people and their parents show little enthusiasm for the social studies and are hard pressed, as are many teachers as well, to suggest their usefulness in real life.

If pushed to give reasons, we say lamely, you must learn this because you will need it someday. Yet we should know that materials learned for no discernible use or for use later in some undefined connection are very resistant to being learned at all, and, if learned, are learned superficially and quickly forgotten. Alfred North Whitehead defines education as the "art of the utilization of knowledge." He warned against an education overburdened with "inert ideas," that is to say, ideas merely received into the mind without being utilized, tested, or thrown into fresh combinations. As Whitehead put it, such an education clutters up the mind with a "horrible burden of inert ideas" which are "not only useless but above all things harmful" (Whitehead, 1929). This is precisely what we do when we teach for later use.

A second argument that will not hold water is that students are too immature to deal with difficult and complex social problems. The answer to this is: If not now, when and where will students have the opportunity to learn to deal sensibly with the conditions that face and threaten their world? What agency is better situated than the school to provide a balanced and unpressured environment in which students can try their own wings at dealing with reality?

There is no way out of our present state of irrelevancy except to make social problems the continuing focus of the social studies and to weave them into the very fabric of the curriculum throughout the years of schooling.

How is this to be done? There are at least two possible approaches to this problem. Neither excludes the other; in fact with planning, each could be made to complement and strengthen the other.

The first is reform in the way we teach the social sciences and history, along the lines suggested earlier in this chapter and somewhat along the lines initiated, but regretfully rejected by most teachers, in some of the "new" social studies projects of the 1960s. Social studies instruction would need to abandon the expository mode and the single version textbook as its stock in trade in favor of a variety of materials and versions to be treated in the hypothetical mode as Bruner suggested. The disciplines would need to be presented humbly and honestly, as they really are, with all their problems of fact and interpretation laid bare for students to see, just as these problems are confronted by scholars. Questioning and criticism would need to be encouraged over ready answers. The whole process should be directed to opening minds to new possibilities rather than closing them.

Further, with careful planning the social sciences can be used in limited fields to throw light on important social problems. Their study need not be totally ephemeral and unrelated to realities. For instance, the study of geography, without great strain, could be continually focused on worldwide environmental problems, and it should be assigned that responsibility. Economics, rather than being a narrow and unreal economic orthodoxy, could afford students the opportunity to ponder worldwide and national economic problems and consider alternatives to faltering economic systems. The very title, "The Advantages of the American Free Enterprise System," should be anathema. Episodes in history could be made both exciting and useful by focus on current problems similar to, and possibly having their roots in, those described in previous events.

In this vein, it might have been said to the university history professor—who complained in an address on the social studies that because of bad study habits fostered by progressive education, students resist learning the battles of the Civil War and, worse, that they resist in their geography classes learning the names of the rivers in the South, without a knowledge of which it was difficult to learn the battles—that he try asking how the battles of the Civil War would have been different if either or both sides had possessed the atomic bomb. That might have brought a dead class to life, although the conclusion seems inescapable that under the circumstances the war might never have been fought, there certainly would not have been so many heroes on both sides, and the names of the rivers would, in all probability, not have mattered. High interest could be brought to a unit on the American Revolution which, using the Harvard Social Studies Public Issues Series materials, is organized around such questions as:

- Under what conditions should individuals disobey legally constituted authority?
- Is violence ever the right course? What about the Boston Tea Party, the March at Pettus Bridge, picketing atomic energy installations, and so forth?

Such excursions of the social sciences into problem areas, not leaving them to incidental treatment or to chance encounters, can contribute significantly toward resolving the problem of irrelevance. But taken alone, even this is not enough.

The most powerful statement for relevance that could be made to our students would lie in the direct and regular study of a few persistent and important areas of social concern, such as those mentioned earlier, and employ all of the intellectual and political skills that have been touched upon above. The very best that could be done for a somnambulistic social studies today would be to devote a significant period of time at least once each year, during which all of the resources of the social studies department in a school at all grade levels from at least the middle school up would be brought to bear on the study of a broad area of social concern in all the breadth and depth that can be mustered. Even better, a whole school in all of its departments might be brought into such an undertaking. Not only do other departments have much to contribute but their own programs would be helped by such a venture.

Children could not help but conclude that citizenship is important, after all. They would see their teachers in a new light, as being real and committed citizens. Students would be likely to take a new interest in other subjects toward which they are now indifferent. Attacks on academic freedom, which will surely follow if teachers begin to talk about anything worthwhile, would be easier to deal with, for there is power in numbers. The really effective teacher could no longer be singled out and silenced as is frequently the case at present.

The Neglect of Values and Value Problems in the Social Studies

A serious shortcoming in most of the configurations of the social studies enumerated above is their ambivalence or outright neglect of the key role of values in understanding and resolving social problems. The three expository categories described above either behave as though values do not exist or they teach values that are tucked away covertly in the text as unrecognized assumptions never to be questioned or as fixed beliefs to be taken on authority or faith. It is seldom recognized that the values we hold, recognized or not, are the key to the facts we collect and the key to how these facts are interpreted and utilized in problem solving. Even more importantly, it is seldom recognized that social problems arise not so much because the facts are unknown but because the parties to the conflict bring differing values to the situation. In large measure social problems are value problems. Nonetheless, the key role of values in resolving social problems is largely ignored by the expository approaches to the social studies. These approaches are seldom concerned with problems of any kind. The easy assumption is made that the facts are known beyond doubt and that all we need to resolve a social problem is to have the facts in mind.

The categories based on the critical study of the social science disciplines described above, while immensely more respectable as intellectual exercises, are the victims of their own narrow orientation to the scientific process. They are dominated by the idea of scientific probability: only that is true which can be proven by marshalling the evidence and by knowing all the facts beyond doubt. It follows that all we need to resolve a social problem is to have the facts in mind.

It is true that facts may play a role in selecting among values. For instance, values may be tested factually against various courses of action to see if a particular course does indeed lead to the value desired. Conversely, holding to a particular value may be tested factually to see if it leads to a desired course of action. However, this kind of factuality is seldom associated with the scientific pursuit of the facts within a discipline that is usually—and erroneously—assumed to be value free. Thus the critical study of disciplines does little to clarify the nature of valuing or to teach how to go about resolving social problems.

Even the categories that focus on social problems can shortchange values and valuing by treating social problems as entirely amenable to the application of facts. We may teach about toxic waste, for instance, by presenting all the known facts but without mentioning the real problem: the conflict between the belief in economic freedom and free enterprise and the belief in the rights of all of the people to be protected in their homes from dangerous substances in water, air, and land. Which is the greater value? To which should we accede, or is some compromise possible?

The proponents of the study of persistent or current social issues usually present the cleanest front, among all alternatives, in recognizing the central role of values in solving social problems. The Harvard Group of Oliver, Shaver, and Newmann, who were prominently associated with this conception of the social studies, developed widely recognized materials that clearly placed conflicts over values in the very forefront of their conception of how the social studies should be taught (Oliver and Shaver, 1966; Oliver and Newmann, 1967). Ironically, those who advocate direct study of significant social problems are frequently less explicit regarding the roles of values in social problem solving. They are more likely to fall into the trap of treating social problems purely as factual problems.

In stark contrast to the neglect of values in most of the conceptions of the social studies, the real world of social affairs and politics is dominated by value considerations. A few examples will demonstrate this fact. One of our leading economists, Lester Thurow, writing in the November 1985 *Washington Monthly*, suggested that the reason Americans are so resistant to sharing the burden of balancing the budget and making the sacrifices needed to make American industry competitive again is that they perceive that the necessary sacrifices are not being shared *equitably*, a value word. The perception is that the poor are being asked to sacrifice while the rich grow richer as a result of that sacrifice. Economic imbalance in favor of the rich, rather than fueling the economy with new investments (as some have argued it would do) is casting instead a wet blanket over the whole economy. Thurow argues that a greater dose of *economic justice*, value words again, would fuel a rapid recovery of the economy (Thurow, 1985).

Whether Thurow is right or not is beside the point. Other economists would no doubt disagree with his analysis. But they too would bring equally potent value orientations into the picture. Thus the real field of economics, a supposedly hard science devoid of values, is seen in the end to be centrally a matter of values.

Another example will be instructive. In his numerous appeals for tax reform President Reagan has forcefully cited *justice* and *fairness*, value words, as reasons for reform.[6] This is clearly a value position not immediately referable to factual determination. Interestingly, in the ensuing debates in Congess over tax reform, differences over what is a *just* and *fair* tax have been the sticking point that has delayed a decision. It is said that Congress has never before in its history collected so much factual information bearing on any decision and yet differences over tax reform have proven obdurate.

Still another example concerns *freedom*, clearly one of the highest values in our democracy. In his speech to the nation on the occasion of his departure for the Geneva Summit, the President referred to a love of freedom on at least eight occasions.[7] But freedom refers to a value which is open to many different interpretations. For instance, freedom is cited as a reason for removing bothersome government regulations from businesses, leaving them free to save money by dumping toxic waste indiscriminately; but freedom for citizens who are forced to live in a polluted environment is also cited as the reason for regulating those industries. Frequently, the pursuit of freedom may run counter to other values as, for instance, security, which is a value of equal or even greater status. The right to be secure in one's life, home, and livelihood is indeed a potent value that excesses of freedom may endanger. For instance, we place great stock in a democracy built on access to information and the right to be informed. Particularly dear to us is freedom of speech, of the press, and of academic freedom. Yet in the face of presumed threats from the Soviets, we are seeing the withholding of information by our government on a scale exceeding that of any period of peace in our history. A government operating in secret is seen as necessary to our security but is also a serious threat to our democracy.

It should be clear from the above examples that value problems are not so neatly resolved as are factual problems. It is much easier and more straightforward to ask what are the facts than to ask what value or values should we subscribe to in a given instance. Despite the difficulty, a social studies program that neglects to deal with value problems stops far short of teaching students how to think intelligently about the real world. We must dissuade ourselves of the belief that facts alone can solve social problems, which are themselves basically value problems. Facts are useful only as they are marshalled as evidence in the conflict between contending values.

It should also be obvious that values are never fixed entities which can be handed down intact from adults to children. How a value such as freedom is to be taken clearly depends on the circumstances. It must be reinterpreted case by case and generation by generation. Its application is very much the same kind of problem for intelligent and well-informed adults as for children. The exact circumstances of its application in one case are never repeated in another. We must abandon the idea that values can be taught, in the abstract, as fixed entities without substance. Such an effort results only in the mouthing of empty words rather than real commitment. Even if one is really committed to a value, it is intelligently and morally respectable to have some doubt about that value.

Nor can the teaching of values be treated as incidental to otherwise purely factual social studies. Value examination, value commitment, and value use in resolving social problems cannot be carried out without facts, any more than facts can be made meaningful without recourse to values. Values command and order facts. Facts explain and substantiate value choices. This exchange operates even among unlettered people who may be unaware of this process. The facts utilized in a problem situation may be little more than myths based on the shoddiest evidence. The values held may be a mishmash of poorly articulated and poorly supported opinions, including opinions in conflict with one another. The persistent goal of the social studies should be to raise the process of valuing in a conscious effort to be rational, logical, and consistent in the ordering of values.

Value examination and value utilization has an emergent methodology and is quite as much an intellectual discipline as is the scientific search for facts that occupies the social sciences and history. It behooves the professional who is really concerned with citizenship education to be quite as familiar with this discipline as with the others. We are sadly remiss as social studies professionals if we are unaware of the rich body of literature in values and valuing. Sadly, social studies professionals, if we may judge by what and how they teach, do indeed show little awareness of this literature. In fact, the configurations that demonstrate the greatest degree of naïveté regarding values are the ones most practiced in schools.

Included in the literature that should be familiar to the social studies professional are basic works on facts and valuations by John Dewey, particularly his *How We Think* (1933), and by Gunnar Myrdahl, particularly the first three appendices of Volume 2 of *An American Dilemma* (1944). Based on such works and others, for instance, *The Structure of Science* (Nagel, 1961) and *Reliable Knowledge* (Larrabee, 1945), a number of social studies professionals have made useful contributions to the literature on values and valuing in teaching the social studies. Possibly the most comprehensive is the work of the Harvard group, particularly Oliver and Shaver, *Teaching Public Issues in the High School* (1966), which was followed by the development of materials by Oliver and Newmann, *The Public Issues Series* (1967), demonstrating the use of this approach. Concurrent work by Alan Griffin's students, Maurice P. Hunt and Lawrence E. Metcalf, *Teaching High School Social Studies* (1955), illustrated a somewhat different approach toward the same general objectives. These works, and to some extent all work in the field along these lines, are heavily dependent on the basic thinking of the Columbia Associates, Benne, Axtelle, Smith, and Raup, who produced *The Improvement of Practical Intelligence* (Benne, Axtelle, Smith, & Raup, 1943).

The most heavily used configurations described above, the Social Studies as the Social Sciences Simplified and the Social Studies as the Critical Study of the Social Sciences, demonstrate scant evidence of familiarity with any of this literature, a fact we view as fraught with grave consequences for citizenship education in a democracy. It is significant in this respect that the "New Social Studies," the most vigorous reform movement to take place in the social studies field in the last three decades, was for the most part directed to teaching the structure of the social science disciplines, while values and value problems were dealt with inadequately, if at all. The "New Social Studies" died apparently because it was too intellectually demanding of students and teachers. This was hardly a fault. However, the New Social Studies was even more remiss for its failure to deal with problems of the real world, which are basically problems of conflicting values and of valuing.

Ambiguity as to the Role of the Humanities in the Social Studies

Because there is neglect in the social studies of values and valuing, there is no clarity about the role of the humanities in citizen education. While it is said that the social studies are based on the social sciences and in some respects on the humanities, it is seldom clear what distinguishes the contributions of each. In the absence of clarity on this point, the humanities are usually treated as a supplementary source of information, a role for which they are not especially well suited. Or the humanities are thrown in to stifle boredom or to create excitement, a role which the social sciences, if properly taught, should be able to shoulder for themselves.

Almost never is it made clear how very differently the social sciences and the humanities relate to citizenship education and how the two might relate usefully to each other in a way better described as a symbiotic relationship than an additive one.

In contrast to the social sciences, which seek to detail, divide, and classify the facts of life, the unique role of scholars in the humanities—novelists, painters, editorialists, philosophers, religious moralists, and even some historians—is to provide a rich arena for thoughtful exploration of the real meaning of large segments of human experience. Scholars in the humanities usually paint with a broad brush. They express a subjective view of events based on their own synthesis and imagination and unashamedly engage in valuations of events in their entirety. They frequently discover truths to which social scientists have no access. In doing so, they provide a scale against which the social sciences can be measured; they powerfully focus attention on values and valuing, which is the touchstone of citizenship education.

Looked at this way, the humanities become not merely something to be added on by way of strengthening the social sciences but as an equal partner in the enterprise called social studies or citizenship education. In this view, the social studies should abandon their overly strong dependence on the social sciences and should embrace the humanities as another useful way to look at the social problems with which citizens, and citizens in preparation, must learn to deal.

SUMMARY

The future of the social studies lies in either of two directions. The profession may choose to risk its future, in keeping with the potential of democracy to chart new courses, with the development of the citizen critic. This goal will certainly demand of us scholarly honesty and willingness to be relevant to the present scene.

Or we can play it safe. We can continue to deal out, via lecture and textbook, "dead education," as Oscar Handlin (1961) referred to it, to passive, acquiescent, and obedient students, as befits affairs in a dictatorship. In this case there is no need for scholarly honesty and relevance. We must only avoid controversy. In terms of the seven configurations of the social studies identified and described in this chapter we need to conceive of the social studies not so much as the exposition of the simplified social sciences as the critical study of the social sciences and social problems. We need to move away from configurations related to Social Studies as Simplified Social Sciences to a greater use of the configurations related to the Critical Study of the Social Sciences and Social Problems, which affords the means for a more intellectually rigorous and democratically oriented social studies. In doing so we need to embrace values and value problems, as well as the humanities, as the center around which all social studies instruction is organized. This amounts to embracing social problems and the hypothetical mode as the modus operandi of social studies. In some reasonable combination of the last four configurations noted above, with their focus on value problems, lies hope for the social studies.

Part II

**A CURRICULUM FOR DEMOCRATIC
CITIZENSHIP EDUCATION**

8

The Framework for the Curriculum

The curriculum that we envision for the citizens of democracy moves away from the conventional implementations of the social studies described above (Chapter 7) toward more open-ended and problem-centered treatments of the social studies. In short, we would move away from the unqualified exposition to students of facts taken as truths, whether embodied in the social sciences or elsewhere, toward the confrontation of young citizens with the problems contained in the disciplines and in the unfolding of society—past, present, and future.

We see the problems of democracy as they have developed historically and the problems of democratic societies today and tomorrow as the appropriate locus for the truly disciplined study of democracy. We see participation in problem solving as the appropriate instructional mode for nurturing citizens who will respect democracy and who will be able to make the decisions needed for its continued development. We do not see democracy as a way of life that can be transmitted unthinkingly to students. Democracy is learned instead as it is questioned, thought about, criticized, and practiced, and as improvements in its workings are achieved.

The key to a curriculum that purports to prepare citizens of a democracy is its capacity to encourage young citizens to think and to make considered decisions. Its content is never merely remembered without being thought about and utilized. This suggests that the curriculum being proposed must provide a more probing treatment of problems, ideas, values, and materials, covering fewer topics than usual, but going deeper into each, and ultimately leading to some worthwhile and reasoned conclusions.

In the light of this general purpose, believing as we do, that improvement in the ability of young citizens to make intelligent and socially responsible decisions is the ultimate goal of the social studies, and also believing, with Dewey (1929) and Bruner (1965), that the only way to learn to resolve problems is to engage in problem solving, we suggest the following guidelines for social studies curriculum development.

1. The curriculum should be highly selective of a relatively small number of topics or episodes, each of which will be studied in great depth. The effort to cover superficially a large number of topics would be abandoned.[1]

2. The topics of episodes to be selected should be those with the greatest potential for encouraging thinking, or even controversy, about matters of fact, or about matters of historical interpretation of events in the past, or about alternative resolutions to social problems in the present. Topics or episodes that cannot be conceived as problematical would be omitted from the curriculum.

3. Students should continually be asked to make judgments about such matters as what really are the facts, how facts should be interpreted, what should be done about a problem or, if the problem is historical, what should have been done differently. Students should continually be asked to make value judgments as to whether the decisions made or about to be made, past or present, are good or bad. The study of such problems needs to be open-ended, in the hypothetical mode (Engle, 1986; Longstreet, 1977), and without pressure for closure for a correct answer.[2]

4. Geography, history, and the other social science disciplines will be treated not as an end product or summary of supposed knowledge to be accepted as true and then memorized but rather as alternative sources of information to be utilized in resolving questions such as those suggested above.

5. Since questions of what is good and what is bad are involved in most or all of these kinds of questions and since models for thinking about questions of good and bad are more likely to be found in the humanities than in the social sciences, selections from literature, art, music, religion, philosophy, and journalism would be utilized alongside and on a par with selections from the social sciences and history in the thoughtful study of any topic, episode, or problem. For instance, historians have much that is important to say about the institution of slavery but so do authors like Harriet Beecher Stowe, William Lloyd Garrison, and Stephen Crane.

6. The curriculum should utilize relatively large quantities of data (much more than could possibly be held in memory) from a variety of sources (more than could possibly be encompassed in a single textbook) to study in depth a relatively small number of topics.

7. The firsthand experience of students and teachers would be respected as one of the important sources of information bearing on any question or problem.

From these guidelines, a number of implications flow. The organization of the curriculum into units around a smaller number of highly selected topics with a focus on problems suggests the virtual abandonment or considerable modification of survey courses, such as those dealing with United States history, that students encounter two and possibly three times in the course of their school years and that usually cover superficially the same ground. It suggests considerable modification of survey courses in geography and the other social sciences, which frequently require memorization of the abstract ideas which frame a discipline, without sharing with students the problems within the discipline or the relationship of the discipline to the problems of society. If survey courses are to exist at all, they need to include major social problems pursued in depth, which means that the current time allocation for survey courses would have to be extended. Furthermore, the often repetitious coverage of survey courses would need to be avoided.

In addition, the study of the social sciences needs to be approached with an attitude of tentativeness. Even economists, notwithstanding their air of certainty, have difficulty agreeing on the meaning of economic events. Problems that students experience in their own studies and investigations are also worthy sources for curriculum development. The attitude of tentativeness is equally valid for their real-world problems. Of course, the study of students' problems is likely to require the breaching of strict disciplinary lines, as relevant data is pursued wherever it may lead.

The focus on problems should make possible the introduction of greater flexibility into the selection and sequencing of study. To accommodate the study of newly developing problems or the fading of problems no longer significant, there will be an ongoing need to revise the curricular selection of social problems. Chronology and the abstract framework of disciplines, the usual bases for sequencing social studies curricula, are not necessarily the best way to handle the problem of sequence, and certainly should not be the only way. An equally important approach might be called that of currency or perceived immediate utility. To search in history for the background of recognized social problems may in some cases be a more effective way to open up the study and utilization of history than to move through history from beginning to end with no other reason than to follow a time sequence.

For instance, must we wait to study the problem of terrorism, which is on everybody's mind at the time this is being written, until we reach its temporal place in history, when it will be treated superficially (if ever) in a survey of U.S. or world history? Terrorism, which is being considered today in a state of great emotionalism and with many half-truths, does in fact have a long history. It has taken many different forms. It has served many different purposes. It has been used by many different peoples including, at times, some of our own. It has been used for what were perceived to be honorable purposes as well as for dishonorable ones. It has been utilized in history by the oppressed to escape their oppressors and by the oppressors to keep the oppressed in check, as well as by religious fanatics to destroy those they saw as their enemies. Would not the study of this problem in a balanced way be better dealt with now, when it is on everybody's mind, than to wait until its time comes, if ever, in the survey of U.S. or world history? The topical approach focused on problems affords greater opportunity for teachers and students to take charge of the curriculum and to make reasonable modifications, from time to time, that would render the curriculum more relevant to the real world.

Another implication of the guidelines suggested above, is the inappropriateness of basing the assessment of achievement on the measurement of isolated bits of information that can be recalled on short-answer tests. More appropriate assessment of achievement would attempt to deal with the degree to which problems are understood, the ability to gather and interpret evidence, and mastery of the intellectual processes needed in the resolution of problems.

These are not altogether new ideas. They were embodied in most reform movements in the social studies for at least the last fifty years, from the time of John Dewey to the present. John Dewey (1929) brought to the forefront of our thinking the idea that, in a democracy, learning is not a passive receiving of knowledge or truth but is instead the active involvement of the student in problem solving. Alan Griffin (1942), one of our yet unrecognized great thinkers in the social studies, saw the teaching of history not as a matter of requiring students to store up the facts of history but as the opportunity to lead students to test their beliefs, both about what the facts are and about what the facts mean. What to believe and why were the persistent problems with which Griffin, not unlike Socrates, continually confronted students (Engle, 1982).

The reform movement of the late 1950s, to the 1970s, culminating in the "New Social Studies," included the work of Hunt and Metcalf (1955), both of whom were Griffin's students, as well as Fenton (1967), Oliver and Shaver (1966), and the numerous projects spawned from the ideas of Jerome Bruner (1962). All of these were efforts to turn the social studies from the mindless exposition and memorization of facts to the more thoughtful study of problems, including problems of what are the facts and what can be concluded from them within the study of the disciplines and problems of what should be done as public policy.

In all of these reform efforts, the hypothetical mode of thought was substituted for the expository mode of teaching. All of the reform efforts afforded students the opportunity to become thinkers and decision makers and all of the reform efforts afforded teachers the opportunity to demonstrate that they really understood their subject and that they could really relate their subject to the problems of society. The error within the profession was that it so quickly deemed the projects unworkable rather than putting forth the effort to refine and improve them (Engle, 1986).

This book is written in the belief that the reformers in the field who followed Dewey's educational philosophy were on the right track. It is a modest effort to push once again at the frontier of transforming the social studies into something more meaningful and useful in preparing citizens to become the participants and intelligent decision makers they must become if democracy is to survive and prosper.

In some respects, the curriculum we envision is a modest change from the traditional curriculum. For instance, heavy reliance will continue to be placed on United States history, world history, and geography, but they will be taught in a very special way. The subjects will be less concerned with memorization. Instead, they will focus on problems, past and present, which students will be encouraged to think about and reach decisions on. Furthermore, the usual content of these subjects will be broadened and, in some cases, combined with content from other disciplines and fields of study to accomplish the broad purpose of being fully relevant to society and its problems. But with all this, we believe this curriculum will still be recognized as good geography and good history or, possibly, as better geography and better history.

In this chapter we will take the educational needs of the citizen of a democracy, identified in Chapter 2, as determining the content of the social studies curriculum, and consistent with these guidelines we will develop the following suggested curriculum strands:[3]

Environmental Studies
Institutional Studies
Cultural Studies
Social Problems
Problems in Decision Making
Internship in Citizenship
Electives
A Democratic School Environment

ENVIRONMENTAL STUDIES

Environmental Studies is the study of problems that surround human use of the environment. The study should be focused on a problem that arises out of this relationship. This strand should be organized around a listing of important environmental problems, which should be revised from time to time to bring it into correspondence with current realities and concerns. For example, at this writing, the problem of what to do about nuclear waste and nuclear fallout from testing of nuclear weapons may well be our most pressing environmental problem in the local community, in the nation, and in the world. But there are other problems of almost equal weight, such as the problems of what to do with industrial toxic waste, what to do with the rapidly growing shortage of potable water all over the world, what to do about the destruction of the rain forest and swamplands so essential to ultimate survival on the earth, what to do about the growing shortage of viable agricultural soils and the related shortages of food which confront many of the world's people,[4] what to do about the extinction of many plant and animal forms and the loss of genetic materials useful to science in the further development of the earth's resources, or, to cite a more exotic problem, one that might be of immediate interest to third-graders, what to do about the whales.

This list could be extended many times over. The questions will change from time to time as science discovers new truths about the earth, its organic composition, its ecology, its climate, its relation to the universe; as technology invents new ways to utilize the earth; and as people develop new ways to relate to one another. But in any case, it is to such a list of problems that environmental studies should continually relate. The goal is that young citizens will not only come to understand the various ramifications of environmental problems but that they will come to appreciate the seriousness of the problem and enlist themselves in doing something sensible about it.

Obviously geography can play an important role in furnishing the materials for thinking about such problems as those listed above. However, we envision not the study of geography for its own sake but geographic information brought immediately to use in thinking about a significant problem. Remembering the products of the nations of the world is of little use and is quickly forgotten unless one puts this information to use in thinking about problems such as the increasingly unfavorable balance of trade faced by the United States. Furthermore, such a list will probably be out of date by the time it is memorized.

Sequencing content from grade to grade may be based on selecting problems for higher grade levels that are more difficult or more comprehensive than problems studied at lower grade levels. For example, what to do about whales is not really a simple problem. The issue could theoretically be expanded to encompass the ecological crisis of the whole universe, but even then it would not be as complex as the problem of how to reconcile the need of advancing nations for technological development and the tendency of those same nations to produce unmanageable quantities of toxic waste that are spread over the lands and waters of the world.

In the process of assigning problems to be studied to particular grade levels, we should studiously avoid the fiction that children cannot deal with problems at any acceptable level until they have a vast background of memoriter knowledge of geography. Such memoriter knowledge, superficially learned because it is not used immediately, is quickly forgotten, and students are not any more ready to deal with problems than they were in the first place. We have only wasted time and the intellectual resources which even young children have in great abundance.

To the extent that the discipline of geography is to be the primary source of information for studying environmental problems it must be expanded to include elements of geology, astronomy, and possibly paleontology, as well as some aspects of biology, ecology, physical anthropology, and climatology. The point is that information that will throw light on our environmental problems should be readily sought wherever it may reside.

Much of the most readily available, interestingly written, and up to date information on the environment is to be found in magazines and in the daily press. *National Geographic* immediately comes to mind, but tremendously informative articles on some aspect of the environmental problem have appeared in such magazines as *Time* and the *Progressive*, which have devoted special issues to such appropriate topics as, "Buried in Waste," "Garbage," and "Not in My Backyard." A library of such materials could be quickly collected from popular magazines and newspapers.

Not to be overlooked are popular books by such writers as Hans Zinsser, Barbara Ward, Lewis Thomas, David Attenborough, Lester Brown, Kenneth Boulding, Carl Sagan, Rachel Carson, Garrett Hardin, John Hersey, John Naisbett, Adam Suddacy, and John Berger. By no means to be neglected are articles by scholars in the field which appear regularly in scholarly publications. Especially noteworthy is the annual publication of the Worldwatch Institute entitled, *State of the World*. In short, prerequisite to the serious study of the environment is a well-stocked library.

INSTITUTIONAL STUDIES

Institutional studies is the study of the origins and the present circumstances of the broad range of social institutions of the United States, including the study of the problems that these institutions faced as they developed and the problems that they face in their further development. This study is an attempt to move beyond the superficial understanding of our democracy exhibited by so many citizens and to achieve instead a more fundamental understanding of our most important institutions and the problems that confront them. It is intended to involve the young citizen in a meaningful defense and improvement of democratic institutions, somewhat along the lines suggested some years ago by Harry Elmer Barnes (1942):

> The real friends of the American way of life are those who recognize and fearlessly reveal the obvious danger signals that are evident on every side, and who seek to eliminate the threat to our social order while there is time and opportunity. . . . The real menace to our civilization is to be found in those who insist on living in a "fool's paradise" of smug conceit and compliancy, conducting a sort of "sit down strike" against intelligence and insisting that nothing is wrong in the best of all possible worlds. (p. viii)

The study of the social institutions of the United States might be divided as follows: 1) institutions that express and protect the fundamental freedoms of the United States, the rights and beliefs which underlie all institutional arrangements, 2) economic institutions, 3) political institutions, 4) institutions that define our relationship to other peoples of the world, and 5) institutions that exist primarily in the private sector, as the family, religious groups, and social groups of all kinds. In all cases, public or private, attention needs to be given to equity issues that directly affect less powerful individuals and groups.

The study of institutions would focus at all times on the hard questions that confront institutional development in the United States today, always of course in the light of institutional history and the nation's democratic aspirations. By hard questions we mean questions that are in fact problems because there is no certain and immediately obvious answer and because decisions must be made, even if tentatively, about them. They may in fact be open issues in the society at the time they are being studied.

For instance, in the case of fundamental rights and beliefs, to the study of which the history of the Revolutionary Period and the Constitution would contribute much useful information, such questions as the following might be used to give focus to the study.

What does it mean to be free? What does it mean to have freedom of one's person or freedom of one's home? What does it mean to have freedom of the press, or freedom of speech, or freedom of religion? Which of these freedoms are the most basic or important? Are there limits to the exercise of any of these freedoms? Who has the right to limit one's freedom? For which of these freedoms, if any, would you lay down your life? Should one's ideas of what it means to be free ever change?

Do you think all citizens of the United States are equally free? Are the poor as free as the rich? Are minority groups as free as the majority? Are the uneducated as free as the educated? How can we know when our freedoms are being violated? What do we really mean when we say we are the "land of the free"? What do we mean when we say that we will defend the freedom for which many fought and died?

How do you think conflict between rival conceptions of freedom, such as those that follow, should be resolved? The conflict between religious freedom and compulsory school prayer, the conflict between freedom of the press and censorship to protect national security,[5] the conflict between the idea that citizens may do what they want with their property and the right of the citizens to be protected from toxic wastes, and the conflict over whether it is constitutional to establish quotas to insure that the hiring and firing practices of employers do not discriminate against the members of any minority group or women.

In the case of economic institutions, to the study of which the history of the post-Revolutionary War period would make important contributions, such questions as the following might be the focus of study. What are the most basic economic institutions in the United States? Which of the following has had most to do with the development of these institutions: the hard work of individuals wanting to improve their economic lot; and open land of rich natural resources; the help of the government in building major industries such as railroads, waterways, air transport, irrigation, dams, and canals; provision by the government of the infrastructure for the nation's industries, such as highways and the postal service; foreign investors; immigration; a seemingly insatiable market in Europe for exports; governmental regulation of business practices and trade; wars and/or avoidance of international entanglements; or free public education? If all of these factors contribute, in what order of importance? What are the relationships between them? To what extent is it a misreading of our history to reduce the role of the government in the economy?

Does economic conflict have a positive or negative influence in the following cases: the struggle between organized labor and the employer for the control of industry; the struggle between those who believe in un-

limited free enterprise and those who believe the government should reg-
ulate industry to protect the consumer and labor rights; the conflict
between different sections of the country for economic advantage; and the
struggle of minority groups for economic opportunity?

How are we to meet the economic problems that beset our country
today? For instance, unprecedented levels of unemployment and poverty
exist at the same time that many are better off than ever before; a growing unfavorable balance of trade, increasing both public and private in-
debtedness; agricultural bankruptcy; the declining efficiency of basic
industries such as steel, electronics, and automobiles in the face of stiff
foreign competition; the problem of how to control, if at all, the activities
of multinational corporations; a circular economy that alternates between
boom and bust; neglect of the public parks; welfare; pollution.

In similar vein, the problems that face other institutions would need
to be identified and used as the guide for study. For instance, one important question that could guide the study of political institutions would
be: What should we do, if anything, in light of our history as a democracy, to change a governing system in which it costs a single con-
gressperson or senator millions of dollars, paid by those who expect fa-
vors from the government in exchange for their support, to run for office
(see *The Washington Spectator* for February 15, 1986, and *Harper's* July
1982)? What should we do, to change a legislative system in which highly
paid lobbyists, who outnumber congressmen in Washington by nearly 20
to 1, play such a decisive role in determining legislation (See *Time*, March
3, 1986)? Equally compelling questions could also be used to identify the
study of other domestic institutions.

It is obvious that United States history would serve as the primary
source of information for the study of such questions as are posed above.
This is true despite the importance of current periodical material. Some
will say that this is nothing really new, that institutional studies is just a
new name for the study of United States history. But this observation
misses the critical point that the study of the American Revolution, or any
historical period, takes on an entirely different meaning when it is focused on the resolution of significant issues such as the one emphasized
in the Oliver and Newmann Public Issues Series unit on the American
Revolution (Oliver & Newmann, 1967) when they asked, "Who had the
best grounds for refusing to obey their legally constituted government, the
Minutemen at Concord or the blacks at Pettus Bridge?" This question,
which closely parallels events today, requires a far more serious and
meaningful study of history than is ordinarily the case in survey courses
in United States history. Furthermore, the intellectual skills called into
play are those of thinking, not just remembering.

But if United States history is to be used to explore questions such as those posed above rather than to be merely remembered, it will need to be a very different kind of history. Such history would need to go both wide and deep. It would need to expose the problems of interpretation and the problems of verification that confront the historian honestly. It would need to afford the opportunity to examine alternative versions of history. In short, it would need to provide young citizens with the opportunity to think about the history of our democracy and to think about its problems in the light of that history. Its continuing purpose would be to enlist young citizens, here and now and not at some future time, to work to preserve and improve the democratic institutions they have inherited from their elders and to do this with the fullest possible understanding of the origins and problems of those institutions.

Obviously, this kind of historical treatment could not be of the ordinary textbook variety. It would need to include both broader and deeper versions of events than those ordinarily provided by textbook writers. Textbook versions of events are ordinarily, and with very few exceptions, too narrow in scope, too shallow in their treatment of events, too parsimonious in providing detail, and too preoccupied with merely chronicling a highly select set of events that are supposed to be remembered. It is not this kind of mastery of events that the active democratic citizen needs but a much deeper and more involved grasp of the meaning of democratic institutions useful to the challenges of citizenship.

If textbooks are to be used at all, generous references should be made to content written by historians writing as historians rather than as textbook writers. Historians who range widely over events, as do George Bancroft and William McNeill, would need to be consulted, as well as historians whose best-known works go deeply into the investigation of particular events, as William Prescott, Francis Parkman, Samuel Eliot Morrison, Bruce Catton, Barbara Tuchman, and David Potter. Frequently such work is found in scholarly journals or even in such serious and respected periodicals or newspapers as *Atlantic, Harper's,* the *New York Times* or the *Washington Post.* Not to be overlooked are biographical and autobiographical accounts, diaries, and copies of original documents.

The purpose of this study is much more to make factual and moral judgments about events than merely to remember them. As Henry Steele Commager has so brilliantly argued in his essay "Should Historians Make Moral Judgments?" (Commager, 1966), history is not so much to be remembered as to be judged. Quite aside from the argument that has raged among historians since history was first written by Herodotus, Thucydides, Livy, and Plutarch as to whether historians pass judgment on the events they record, the usefulness of historical writing to the citizen comes from its efforts to pass moral judgment on the events in history. Great historians such as Edward Gibbon, David Hume, Voltaire, Thomas Carlyle, Theodore Parker, Henry Adams, Charles A. Beard, John Latrope Motely, and Vernon Parrington, to mention just a few, were quite as much moral philosophers as historians, quite as much concerned with passing moral judgment on history as with recording it. Still other great historians, such as Leopold Van Ranke, Mandell Creighton, Arnold Toynbee, E. H. Carr, and Allan Nevins, tried to record events with complete impartiality. In either case, students of social institutions are best instructed by historical writings when they place themselves in the position of passing moral judgment on the events of history. As Carl Becker once argued, "every man must be his own historian" (Becker, 1936), or as Commager put it, "The assumption behind the expectation that the historian should make our moral judgment for us is that the reader has no mind of his own, no moral standard, no capacity to exercise judgment. . . . Are those mature enough to read serious history really so obtuse that they cannot draw conclusions from the facts that are submitted to them?" (Commager, 1966).

Since the making of moral judgment is the most basic of all functions of democratic citizens, we would continually cast students in the role of making judgments about events rather than merely remembering them. Therefore such questions as the following are appropriate: Was the violence and terror perpetrated on Loyalists during the Revolution justified in the cause of freedom? Was the forced ejection of Native Americans from lands they had occupied for centuries right or wrong? Was there a better way to deal with conflict between the Indians and the settlers? Were John Brown and his followers at Harper's Ferry justified in killing people in their effort to free the slaves? Were the oppressive measures taken to keep workers from organizing and striking at Haymarket Square right or wrong? How might the conflict between workers and their employers have been more fairly settled? Were people who were out of work during the Great Depression deserving of help from the government? Why? What is the basis of your judgment?

Not to be ignored in the study of social institutions is the contribution of great works of literature, art, music, and journalism. Great literary and artistic works are more likely than historians to capture the broad meaning of events and to emphasize the moral issues that are embodied in them. Historians are often too engrossed in establishing the facts objectively to speculate about their broad meaning. The authors of great literary or artistic works are concerned about the facts, to be sure, but they are more concerned with interpreting and evaluating human events. Through subjective reasoning they are able to discover truths that elude the historian using a more scientific approach. Through creative imagination they confront their audience with fresh points of view. Great breakthroughs in thought occur in this way—for instance, the writings of Thomas Paine and James Otis on democracy. Many of our social problems today require such imagination for their solution.

Such significant works are likely to have a moral focus. The author and the artist are likely to take sides, to cast judgments about what in history is most valuable, on what is good and what is bad, and to make statements about what needs to be changed in human society. These great works afford models for the citizen of how great thinkers make the moral judgments that are really at the heart of every social problem. These models are indeed an important resource for citizenship education. In a social studies curriculum dedicated to fostering the intellectual skills of problem solving, the great literary and artistic works should be taken as an integral part of the content. They are not merely frills added to embroider social studies instruction.

For instance, how more succinctly could one begin the study of the institution of human slavery than to read Harriet Beecher Stowe's *Uncle Tom's Cabin* or Stephen Crane's *The Red Badge of Courage*? Or, if a somewhat more scholarly version of history is preferred, Bruce Catton's *A Stillness at Appomattox*? How better could one be introduced to the crises in American economic and political institutions and to the issues of the Great Depression than by reading John Steinbeck's *The Grapes of Wrath*?

American literature, art, music and journalism are rich sources of moral commentary on the progress of our social institutions. From the likes of Washington Irving, James Fenimore Cooper, and Thomas Paine in colonial times to modern writers such as Gore Vidal, Alice Walker, Saul Bellow, and James Michener, people of letters have had much to say about the moral quality of American institutions. This body of commentary should be continually utilized both for the stimulation of thought and dialogue about the state of American institutions.

It is obvious that a well-stocked school library is an inestimably valuable resource for an in-depth study of American social institutions. If such a library does not exist in the school, it would be a first order of business to begin the building of one. Serious study of American institutions requires it.

CULTURAL STUDIES

Cultural studies involve the study of differing cultures: of why people of different regions, historical backgrounds, nationalities, and ethnic groups grow up differently; of how we can live usefully in a world of differing cultures; of how, despite cultural differences, people of varying cultures share profound human similarities; and of how we turn cultural differences into assets for betterment of the living conditions of people within our own country and the world.

Questions upon which cultural studies may focus include:

- Why do peoples of different cultures, religions, and historical backgrounds grow up differently, behaving and believing in different ways? Can you accept the reasonableness of these differences?
- Do you know of any people whose beliefs and ways of behaving are so different from your own that you cannot accept the reasonableness of their difference? In what respects?
- Can you identify similarities between these people and yourself?
- What is universal about cultures? What is unique?
- Why have some cultures survived and flourished while others have declined or disappeared?
- Of the different cultural groups in the world, which ones do you have most difficulty accepting? With which do you have least difficulty?
- Suppose a cultural group exhibits behavior that flies in the face of your most cherished beliefs. How should you behave toward them? Suppose they are fellow citizens of the United States. How should you behave toward them?
- What do you think are the most pressing problems which face the world's people today?
- How would you rank the following problems in importance: fear of nuclear war, religious differences, pollution of the world's environment, world hunger, restrictions on the free exchange of goods throughout the world?
- Taking cultural differences into account, where is the point at which the resolutions of these problems might best begin?

It is fairly obvious that world history will be a major source of information for answering such questions. But it should be equally obvious that the study of world history from a textbook for the sole purpose of remembering the chronology of events in the history of nations will not be adequate. The history utilized must present a much more sweeping view of the world, more as it has been treated by such historians as Arnold Toynbee, Will and Ariel Durant, H. G. Wells, and William McNeill. Students would need to be helped and encouraged to read history not to memorize it but rather to use it to throw light on important questions— or even to enjoy it. History should be read as suggested by the noted

English historian, Christopher Hill, who said, "Any serious history deals with questions. . . . The narrative can be rearranged but the true originality of the historian lies in identifying questions that seem new to us. . . . This would help to explain why history has to be rewritten in every generation" (Hill, 1983).

Obvious, too, is the usefulness of materials from anthropology and sociology to buttress the understanding of cultural differences that may be gleaned from history. Optimally, historical study of cultural differences could pause at some point to study in depth, as the anthropologist would study them, a few selected cultures for a clearer idea of how cultures develop.

To support study of the kind described a good library collection would be a necessity. Such a library would include scholarly books and articles on particular cultures, but should include as well serious popular periodicals and even newspaper articles where information may be found that relates to cultural groups and the problems of dealing with them. For instance, materials from the book *The Unwanted European Refugees in the Twentieth Century* by Michael R. Marrus could put into stark relief the problems of ordinary people everywhere that come about by widespread misunderstanding of cultural differences. The author accents the terrible waste that misunderstanding of differences heaps upon the peoples of the world. This one book, and there are many others like it, accompanied by questions challenging students to think about why this happened and what should be done about it, might well be the starting point for a meaningful exploration of the problems and potentials of differing cultures in the world.

The same argument can be advanced here for including materials from the humanities in any serious study of cultures as were advanced earlier for the study of institutions. For example, brilliant commentaries on British society and social problems are afforded by such writers as William Shakespeare, Charles Dickens, George Bernard Shaw, the Brontë sisters, Aldous Huxley, and George Orwell. Equally useful commentaries on French culture are afforded by French writers such as Victor Hugo and Emile Zola. Similar works flowered from the pen of such German writers as Johann Wolfgang von Goethe and Thomas Mann and such Italian writers as Alessandro Manzoni.

Powerful accounts of Russian society are afforded by the writing of Fyodor Dostoevsky and Leo Tolstoy and more recently by Alexander Solzhenitsyn. Other useful words come from the pen of such Japanese writers as Yasunari Kawabata and Yukio Mishima, from the Senegalese, Leopold Senghor, and from South American poets Jorge Luis Borges and Pablo Neruda.

SOCIAL PROBLEMS

Social problems include the study in depth of one major social problem in each year of the social studies program, grades three through ten.[6] The purpose of the study of social problems is threefold. The first reason is to give young citizens an understanding about major compelling social problems, such as the worldwide environmental crises, the threat of nuclear war, the underemployment of human resources, and widespread poverty. It is to help students more clearly understand the issues at stake in the problems studied; to encourage them to see the interrelationships among such issues; and to provide them both with bodies of information that relate to the problem and with the opportunity to do some rigorous thinking about possible solutions.

A second reason for the study of a major social problem is to give students experience in dealing with such problems much as intelligent adults are expected to deal with them. They will then already know when they graduate into adulthood how to go about working with major social problems. They will not only be informed about major social problems but they will have already been enlisted in the effort of working out solutions to such problems.

A third and closely related reason for studying a major social problem each year, rather than at the end of the social studies program, is that such study will emphasize the relevance of other work under progress in the social studies. Students will be able to see more clearly why they are studying environmental, institutional, and cultural problems, and hopefully they will approach these strands in the curriculum with greater purpose. Such study will provide the glue that binds all parts of the social studies program together. It will no longer be quite so necessary to claim lamely that we are studying these subjects because we will need them someday when we are adults.

Because we believe so strongly that the ability to make intelligent decisions in the resolution of social problems is the ultimate goal of the social studies, and because we believe with Bruner, who said, "I have never seen anybody improve in the art and technique of inquiry by any means other than engaging in inquiry" (Bruner, 1965), that problem-solving ability is best learned by engaging in problem solving, we are led to the conclusion that problem solving, in all of its varieties, should be omnipresent in the social studies curriculum. We are also led further to conclude that the major social concerns of the society should be likewise omnipresent in the curriculum, for these are the concerns around which all of the curriculum will continually coalesce. These concerns feed into and are constantly fed by everything else we do in the curriculum. They are not matters to be left to some far distant future.

To meet, insofar as possible, all of these purposes, we propose that some one major social problem be studied for an extended period, in all of the depth that we can muster, on one occasion each year in each social studies classroom at every grade level in every school.

Great strength would accrue to such an effort if all classes could be engaged in the study at the same time, with the principal of the school serving as the leader of the study. Tremendous strength would be added to the study if other departments in the school, importantly science, language arts, and fine arts, could be enlisted in the study, as well as parents and the community at large. Full advantage should be taken of the adult resources in the community, such as adults with special expertise in the area being studied, adult periodical collections in public libraries and elsewhere, community groups with special interest in the area of concern, and public interest groups and citizens and parents willing to talk with youngsters about their concerns.

The study in depth each year of one major social problem should provide young citizens with the sobering experience of studying something in school about which the whole community as well as their teachers are genuinely concerned. We would hazard the guess that such an experience would set a serious tone for more thoughtful engagement by young citizens in all of their academic work, both within the social studies and outside.

PROBLEMS IN DECISION MAKING

The explosion of knowledge and the parallel explosion in the means of communication, together with an unsettling of values in the modern world, have heaped extraordinary responsibilities on citizens to be well informed and to know what values are at stake. Paradoxical as it may seem, it is actually more difficult today to know what is really true than it was fifty years ago when the quantity of knowledge available was much less and when the value choices to be made were far more simple and fewer in number.

The mushrooming of the means of communication has opened up tremendous opportunities to become better informed, yet simultaneously it has created tremendous possibilities of having our thoughts controlled by charlatans, politicians, religious leaders, and the representatives of special interests who try to control what we think by manipulating our opinions through the media. Thus Marcos in the Philippines, despite twenty years of the most unimaginably corrupt and brutal leadership, almost won reelection because he controlled the radio and the television stations, while his reform-minded opposition could only shout to the crowds within their hearing on street corners. To a considerable extent the media in the United States is controlled by the rich. The viewpoint of the poor has difficulty being heard.

Likewise, in the face of an unprecedented rate of change, traditional values are being called into question. The Civil Rights Movement which began in the 1960s is a case in point. What was seen as equitable treatment of blacks and other minorities became a very controversial matter. In some cases traditional values that we have held innocently in the past now seem to be in conflict, as, for instance, freedom of religion and the proposal to allow prayer in school. The number of such conflicts between values has multiplied many times in recent years. Citizens, pulled first one way and then another, frequently do not know what to believe or what to hold most valuable. Or they may easily fall victim to the oversimple answer and to the smooth talk of the unscrupulous.

These conditions impress upon us the need to help the young citizens of our democracy, whose opinions are supposed to be informed, well reasoned, and responsive to time-honored values, wade through the maze of information and conflicting value claims that are thrust upon them from every side, to help them learn to sort out the wheat from the chaff. Our purpose would not be to tell them what to think, but rather to help them develop the understanding and skill to decide for themselves what is and what is not credible.

Three groups of questions would guide this study. The first group, *epistemological*, would ask questions such as:

- What is knowledge? What does it mean to say that one knows?
- What is evidence? What is proof?
- Are there different ways of knowing?
- How does proof differ under different ways of knowing?
- Which way of knowing is most dependable?
- How can one determine the dependability of claims to knowledge of a scholar in a given field of study, a witness to an event, an expert in some line of endeavor, a textbook account, a proponent of some religious doctrine, a political speaker, a news report, an editorial, and so on? What is dependable evidence in each case?

The second group, *communications*, would ask such questions as:

- What are the various purposes of the media? To inform? To weigh alternatives? To persuade? To exhort?
- How can we judge the dependability of what we read, or hear, or are told in the newspaper, over the radio, over television, in a textbook, or in a political speech?

- How can one detect the use of media to distort or misrepresent the truth?
- In a political campaign how does one decide who and what to believe?

The third group, *values*, would raise such questions as:

- What do I value most? Are there good reasons for valuing highly each of the values dear to me?
- How can I know that my values are good values?
- Can I arrange my values from the most important to those of lesser importance? What do I do when two or more of my values seem to be in conflict?

Questions like these need to be raised from time to time in many subjects which students study in school—in science, mathematics, and language arts, as well as in the social studies. Good teaching directed toward asking such meaningful questions could hardly be conducted without awareness on the part of teachers and students of the nature of dependable knowledge and of the nature of evidence or proof. Memoriter teaching, which we reject, tends to sweep such questions under the rug. Students are supposed to remember predetermined and correct answers and are never to question why. They are simply supposed to believe what they are told.

But even in a curriculum that emphasizes questioning and thoughtful responses by students, there is still a special need to study the problem of knowing and valuing, independently and in depth, if students are to learn to cope with today's world of instant communication and a rapidly changing knowledge base.

Studies have indicated that children spend as much time each day watching television as they spend in school. It is recognized by many educators that television is a tremendous force in the child's learning, a force that may have either profoundly positive or profoundly negative consequences.[7] The student may become a critical viewer or a patsy to be exploited by anyone who has a good "Madison Avenue" line. Students need help with this problem, just as they need help in becoming more critical textbook readers and more discerning citizens.

The best of all worlds in this connection would be for the social studies department, in coordination with other departments in the school, who should be equally interested in developing more critical thinking, listening, reading, viewing, and valuing skills, to provide a jointly sponsored course in *knowing, communication,* and *valuing* to be offered approximately midway in the progress of students through the middle school.

CITIZENSHIP INTERNSHIP

A one-year, one-day-a-week internship in some useful social or civic enterprise would be a natural progression from meaningful experience in thinking about social problems to working to resolve them. The internship would be looked upon as a transition experience from neophyte to adult citizenship. Through the internship, young citizens upon graduation would already be involved in what might well become their life speciality as adult citizens. Useful volunteer work, without pay or credit, though required for graduation, would be sought with a service, political, or civic organization or with other interest groups. Internees would be supervised by a teacher in the school, possibly the same teacher who had arranged their internships, with whom they would also meet regularly to examine and appraise their experiences.

ELECTIVES

The purpose of the electives would be to afford the opportunity for students to study in some depth the methods by which social scientists and historians arrive at dependable knowledge about human affairs. Electives would include one-year courses in economics, political science, sociology, anthropology, and journalism. The emphasis would be placed on the nature of the discipline rather than on its findings, although the nature of a discipline might be illustrated by reference to some of its more important findings or key assumptions. Students would have the opportunity to engage in some laboratory practice in each discipline, such as writing a short historical account, conducting a simple sociological survey, studying a group as an anthropologist would study it, or reporting a significant event. All students would be expected and encouraged, but not required, to complete one such elective.

A DEMOCRATIC SCHOOL ENVIRONMENT

If commitment to democratic principles is to be an outcome of the education of citizens, it is of paramount importance that the school offer a good example of respect for democracy. There are two aspects to setting such a good example in the school setting. The most obvious is that the school itself must be governed democratically. We lose our case for democracy when students can easily perceive that the school itself is run autocratically. School rules, as with laws, should be fair and reasonable and students should be helped to understand the reasons for them. They should have a voice in their enactment. Governance should never be arbitrary or blatantly coercive. The school should never underestimate the willingness of students to participate in their own governance. As it should be in adult society, the rights of the minority in the school setting should be faithfully respected.

Democracy is also exemplified in the school by the respect shown by teachers for intellectual honesty. Democratic teaching should be carried on with full respect for the canons of scholarship. Furthermore, full respect must be given to the intelligence of students to think for themselves. Pressure tactics, being less than candid, talking down to students, or using the classroom to propagandize are all teaching methods completely out of character with democracy and must never be employed if students are to be expected to develop a deep commitment to democracy. Teachers must exhibit in their own behavior not only respect for the intelligence of students but also exhibit faith in the method of intelligence and reason.

9

Implementing the Curriculum

There are two aspects to the implementation of the curriculum outlined in the previous chapter: the development of an overall curriculum plan for a school or school system; and the development of plans for courses, subjects, or units within the overall plan.

THE IMPLEMENTATION OF THE OVERALL CURRICULUM

Traditional School Subjects as the Instrument of the Study of Problems

We debated the efficacy of two possible alternatives for the overall plan. The temptation was to reject entirely the traditional expository-memoriter curriculum with its heavy dependence on textbooks and start from scratch with selected content tailored to focus on important social problems. On sober thought, however, this alternative was rejected for a number of reasons. First, since each of the disciplines upon which the social studies are based has a field of inquiry separate and different from that of other disciplines, and since each has its own set of questions to ask and its own way of looking at data, disciplines are resistant to amalgamation. In studying a problem that falls primarily in the area of one discipline, more understanding seems to follow the simple process of comparing findings in one discipline with findings in another field. The interdependency of geographers and historians is a case in point. The views of writers of fiction and biography, which frequently clash with those of historians and economists, is another. In working with problems it is probably more important to understand why it is that people, even different scholars, hold different views of events than it is to know what is the current widely accepted view. Secondly, we were chastened by the recent experience of the "New Social Studies," which was summarily rejected by teachers despite the great promise it held for transforming the social studies from a meandering, thoughtless, memoriter process to one that was thoughtful and thought-provoking. It was rejected despite the gargantuan resources, both human and monetary, that were put into its development. It appears to have been rejected because it was too drastic a break with the past: teachers could not find themselves or the subjects they were used to teaching anywhere in the new social studies. Importantly, teachers who had always taught in the expository mode, just as they had been taught, were uncomfortable with the open-ended questioning that the "New Social Studies" required.

Our proposed curriculum would also nudge teachers toward more openness in questioning and in the answers sought, but we see our objectives, which are similar in some ways to those of the "New Social Studies," as being achieved, if not so perfectly, in the more conventional framework of the traditional social studies curriculum.

For example, the problems to be dealt with in the first three strands of our curriculum (environmental problems, institutional problems, and cultural problems,) bear a close correlation to the traditional subjects of geography, United States history, and world history. By utilizing these subjects somewhat differently than they are traditionally used, the objective held out for the first three strands of the proposed curriculum may be achieved. Taught differently, we believe these subjects can lead to a far greater understanding of these subjects than that ordinarily achieved by memoriter learning.

In choosing conventional school subjects as the setting for problem solving, we reject the idea that the scope and sequence of subjects covered, though of some importance, is the overwhelming problem of curriculum development. The case for scope and sequence is based on the doubtful assumption that if all the topics deemed important are covered, however superficially, the goals of the social studies are achieved. For that we would substitute the study of a few topics in depth, while highlighting other topics to the degree necessary. Looked at in this way, the content to be covered and the order in which it is to be covered is of less importance than is an in-depth treatment of selected topics in whatever order. This condition does not eliminate the necessity for making choices as to what problems shall be studied, but at least the pressure to cover everything is relieved.

For whatever reasons, the content of the social studies at each grade level has changed little over the years. Periodic efforts to change the scope and sequence of the curriculum, including that of the Task Force on Scope and Sequence (1984), have been little more than tinkering with the details of what has come to be called the traditional curriculum. We have chosen, therefore, to sidestep the controversy over scope and sequence and to accept the traditional curriculum with its courses in geography, United States history, world history and, in the early years, study of the expanding environment, as affording a sufficient, if not perfect, framework for the study in depth of important social problems.

We will expend our efforts instead on changing the nature of instruction in these subjects. This would mean a shift from an expository-memoriter treatment of whatever subject matter is being studied to one that draws attention to the problems embedded in the content of a discipline or subject area. It will also mean fostering serious student thinking about these problems. Teachers will need to learn how to identify the problems, both problems of fact and problems of public policy, embedded in the subject content they are teaching and they will need to learn how to use these problems as instruments of instruction.

It will be recognized, as we have pointed out in Chapter 8 above, that all serious students of a discipline like history or geography or, for that matter, students of the so-called hard sciences—physics, chemistry, or biology—think of their disciplines not so much as compendia of settled knowledge as repositories of unanswered questions. They see their discipline not only as a body of knowledge but even more importantly as a systematic way of thinking about and studying problems. The scholars in these disciplines are far more interested in finding answers to unresolved and, in some cases, as yet unrecognized problems than in recording and transmitting the little that is believed to be true. Thus, one of the greatest scholars of the West, the one who knew most about it, preferred to talk about his problems in dealing with the history of the West, problems of the meaning of this knowledge, rather than merely to dwell on the so-called facts (Paxson, 1936).

In this vein it is of course impossible to think of disciplines as ever being complete or final. Instead they are always open to new concatenations of knowledge and new findings and, as such, always tentative about any conclusions drawn. It is therefore an error to think of any discipline as merely knowledge to be transmitted to others. Geography and history, for example, if looked at in this way, are really each a cacophony of unanswered or partially answered questions and problems. For example, we have recently seen heated disputes among historians as to who discovered America, when, and why. Despite the terse way the subject is treated in history textbooks, the discovery of America is a very controversial subject among historians. Even the long-accepted credits to Christopher Columbus are now in dispute (Judge, 1986).

Might it not be better to get students right into the middle of this controversy than to pass off a few doubtful facts about discovery as the truth? Would not students, even young children, learn vastly more about discovery by reading about and being told in depth about some aspects of the controversy than by memorizing a few doubtful facts?

There is a very important debate raging at present over the exact meaning and the current meaning of the First Amendment of the Constitution of the United States. Might it not be more effective as a way of learning about the Bill of Rights to engage students directly in this debate?

It is of course impossible to study all potential problems in the depth necessary to support serious thought about the problem. Selecting a few of the most important and most manageable problem areas will be necessary. In order to provide context and a sense of progression, other content may be briefly reviewed without stopping to commit anything to memory. The memorization of vast quantities of factual material without focus on a problem or a question worth answering is a colossal waste of educational time. Facts memorized in this way are almost impossible to remember and are frequently outdated before there is any occasion to use them. In contrast, facts learned in the context of trying to answer an important question or problem are almost impossible to forget.

A further benefit of such learning is that any problem studied in depth will eventually relate quite naturally (since the whole universe is one universe) to many other, if not all, problems. Study in depth of one or a few problems is probably a more efficient and effective way to order the whole universe of facts than is the superficial coverage and memorization of great numbers of facts.

What we are asking of teachers and others concerned with social studies instruction is a change of attitude toward the subjects they teach, whatever these may be. We are asking that they honor the disciplines that underlie the subject as the investigative tools that they really are. We are asking that they abandon the notion that their job as teachers is to transmit the truth, however dubious, full-blown to children. We see this change of attitude as necessary to the preparation of citizens of a democracy who need to be able to think and make up their own minds about the problems facing society. In advancing this challenge, we are only asking that teachers become the scholars in their own field that they pretend to be.

Special Programs in the Curriculum

Turning to the remaining strands proposed (social problems, problems in decision making, internship, electives, and a democratic school environment), all require special arrangements, but none really interfere seriously with the traditional scope and sequence of the curriculum. Each is of such central importance in the preparation of citizens for a democracy that the special arrangements necessary are well worth the effort. We would confidently recommend that attention to the latter five strands will vastly improve the performance of students in the three subject-based strands.

THE STUDY OF SOME SOCIAL PROBLEMS. The study in depth of a major social problem would entail the setting aside of approximately two weeks in each school year, during which all the students enrolled in social studies classes in a school at all grade levels, in lieu of their regular classes, would study in depth, together with their teachers and parents, one important social problem. Quite aside from the knowledge gained about some significant social problem, this would give a tremendous boost to the idea that the social studies are really about something worthwhile after all, that they are useful for something, and that they represent subject matter about which adults—parents, teachers in other subjects as well as in the social studies, and the principal of the school—are all concerned. The boost to the morale of students and to teachers could hardly be measured. A likely improvement in all other work done in social studies classes could be expected.

CITIZEN INTERNSHIP. The internship requires that every student pursue a role in the life of the community by actually working on an extracurricular basis in some adult citizenship activity. It would replace no course presently taken in school. We would hope that students would continue the activity after graduation.

ELECTIVES. The electives would be different from the usual electives in two respects. First, the study would emphasize the nature of the discipline rather than its findings; that is, the study would inquire into the kinds of questions that scholars in the discipline ask themselves and it would inquire into the process used by scholars to investigate these questions. The principal change over the traditional curriculum that would be needed here is that teachers know their disciplines sufficiently well to deal with them critically.

Secondly, students would engage directly in a real laboratory experience. The objective would be for students to learn how to utilize a discipline as scholars utilize it in the thoughtful study of a social problem. This objective would replace the practice of using the tentative findings in a discipline to influence students toward particular and narrow points of view not justified by scholarly findings.

The study of economics, for example, would start by identifying some of the important problems or gray areas that economists are working on and about which they are frequently in disagreement. Statements of leading economists on some event of current economic importance could be compared and differences in opinion could be pursued. Students will quickly learn that there are about as many problems in the field of economics as answers and that there are a variety of ways of interpreting economic events depending on what one values most and how one is situated in life.

THE STUDY OF THE DECISION-MAKING PROCESS. The implementation of the proposed strand in "Decision Making" is a special case with very little precedent in schools, except possibly courses in logic, ethics, linguistics, and semantics, which are only rarely offered in high schools. This strand is an effort to respond to the problem of knowing what to believe in a complex technological society. The modern citizen is overwhelmed with messages, many of which are cleverly crafted to deceive rather than to inform. Television programming in general, and the Madison Avenue advertising images that accompany it in particular, threatens to destroy entirely more sober educational efforts to encourage critical thinking and decision making. While social studies teachers may correctly think of themselves as being on the front line in the effort to sort out the wheat from the chaff in this respect and to bring objectivity and reasonableness into the behavior of young citizens, the question of belief clearly is a problem toward a solution of which the whole school should dedicate itself. The most talented people in the school should be enlisted and supported in developing courses and programs that face up to this problem.

DEMOCRATIC ENVIRONMENT. The provision of a democratic environment in the school is taken for granted if the school is to have any part in developing democratic citizens. It is unlikely that a school run in an authoritarian manner can somehow inexplicably produce thinking, self-directing, democratic citizens. Furthermore, for a school to have its greatest impact on developing democratic behavior, such behavior must be favorably exemplified in all aspects of the school: in the way the school is administered, in how students are involved in the governance of the school, and in the way teachers are treated by the administration and by students. Probably most important of all is the way in which instruction is conducted in all classes of the school: Is the intelligence of students and their right to question and to know really respected by teachers? Is study real or is it just a game set up so that the teachers and other adults will always win? A school that is really serious about providing a democratic environment might well set up a committee composed of democratically selected students, teachers, parents, and administrators to study democracy in the school life, to prepare reports on democratic life in the school, and to make suggestions for its improvement.

THE IMPLEMENTATION OF THE GRADE
AND COURSE LEVEL CURRICULUM

Selecting Programs for Study

The implementation of a curriculum for democratic citizenship at the grade, subject, and unit level is primarily a matter of selecting major problems to be studied appropriate to that grade level and subject matter. Subsequently, it is a matter, first, of planning how the content afforded by that subject can be utilized to illuminate these problems and, second, of devising instructional strategies for achieving this end.

Subjects taught in school are conventionally defined by textbooks, which are usually organized to get children to remember facts and higher order generalizations in the more or less arbitrary order that scholars use in explicating a subject. This may bear little relationship to how children, or adults, for that matter, may use information in thinking about a problem. In studying a problem in depth it becomes necessary to skip around in the textbooks and to consult other sources to get all of the information that is needed to think about the problem. The textbook may well suggest problems for further study but other resources that treat some aspect of the problem in greater detail will almost certainly be needed. For instance, "rain forests," possibly mentioned in the geography textbook in connection with the study of Brazil or in connection with the study of climates, might well suggest a broader problem such as "the preservation of ecological balance on the earth." In turn, this might lead to a more flexible and searching way to utilize the textbook, as well as to a need for additional sources to flesh out the study of the problem. In this case articles such as that in *National Geographic* for January 1983 on "Rain Forests" (White, 1983) would be useful.

To continue in this general vein, it might be decided that "geography," whether it is called world, regional, or national geography, would be brought to focus on three problem areas, as follows: (1) How can we better utilize the variations in weather over the earth? (2) How can we better protect the fragile ecosystem of the earth? and (3) What should be done, if anything, to see that peoples of the earth eat better?

Each of these questions suggests a myriad of lesson questions, as well as ways of investigating these questions, which have the almost inevitable effect of freeing students from the need to memorize vast quantities of factual material in the unnatural order imposed by the textbook writers. It makes it possible, instead, to carry on inquiry naturally, as did the scholars who wrote the textbooks and as citizens generally would carry on investigating a real problem. It casts the student in the role of being, as Bruner put it, "the organizer of his own thoughts," a way of thinking which he says "is far more powerful" than is merely memorizing something (Bruner, 1965). To further illustrate the kinds of questions that are suggested in a study of the problem of how to protect the fragile ecosystem of the earth, the following come to mind:

○ What is an ecosystem?
○ Why is the ecosystem important to us?
○ Where on the earth is the ecosystem most under threat?
○ Is it possible to repair a threatened ecosystem?
○ How are endangered species related to the threat to the ecosystem?
○ Where on the earth is there the greatest threat to endangered species?
○ Where on the earth are useful things being done to protect the ecosystem?
○ Is it inevitable that some elements of the ecosystem will be destroyed while others survive or prosper?
○ Can an ecosystem repair itself?
○ What should be done, if anything, and by whom to repair the ecosystem?
○ Who should be responsible for protecting the ecosystem?

Also suggested by such a line of questioning are different ways of investigating the problem. For instance, in the very beginning before youngsters are burned out on memorizing geographic facts neatly classified into national, regional, and world geographies—as textbook writers persist in organizing them—a series of case studies might be instigated. Topics could include some of the following: rain forests in the Amazon and elsewhere; the imminent danger to all fish species from ingesting plastic waste; the threat of toxic waste to the groundwater supplies of the earth; the rapid depopulation of wild animals on the earth; growing shortages of space for people to live on the earth; hunger on the earth; desertification; the world's wetlands; the effect of pesticides on the ecological chain; the promise and the problems of high-tech agriculture; and many others. There are literally thousands of well-researched articles in such magazines as the *National Geographic, Smithsonian, Harper's,* and the *Atlantic* as well as hundreds of books and scholarly articles to support such case studies.

As an alternative, or possibly a supplement, to such case studies, classes could view and discuss documentary films or film strips, such as "A Swamp Ecosystem" (National Geographic Educational Services Film) or "Continents Adrift" (American Educational Films).

Such a series of studies would immediately immerse students into the very heart of geographic study. It would give every student the feeling of being an important participant in an important study. It would place resources, including the textbooks, in their proper place—as materials to be selectively utilized rather than merely remembered for some later unknown use. It would place geographic study in the only context in which it makes any sense, the context of the issues that face the peoples and lands of the entire earth.

In a somewhat similar vein, it could be decided to focus the study of United States history at upper grade levels on the study of a series of the institutional problems that have dominated various periods in our history. This kind of study may come as a welcome relief to students who are frequently required to repeat and refresh their memory of the same narration of our history usually three times over, with little gain in either mastering the facts or understanding them.

For example, the Revolutionary War period could be brought to focus on the problem of revolution. Such questions as the following could be explored: Under what conditions is a revolution justified? Did conditions in America in the late eighteenth century fulfill those conditions? Are there better ways than revolution for bringing about social change in society? Under what conditions, if any, should people disobey the law? Is it equally right or wrong for governments to break the law than for individuals to break the law?

Under this kind of questioning, not only will the revolution itself be more thoroughly understood and possibly reevaluated, but it will be seen that the same or similar questions are of great importance in contemporary society. The facts of history will not only be refreshed in the memories of students, but they will be put to use in thinking about real and important problems of our own day.

In like vein, the period of discovery and settlement could be focused on the treatment accorded to Native Americans and new immigrants to this country, with some effort to decide the justice or injustice of this treatment. The study might be extended to include successive waves of immigration and the present controversy over the regulations of immigrants, particularly from Mexico, into the United States.

The Civil War period could be studied to try to decide whether the anti-slavery movement was primarily an economic or a moral issue. Or students might be led to ponder whether the slavery issue could have been settled by compromise rather than by war. The study of the Civil War in this way would quite naturally bring into play the rich literature outside strictly historical treatment which relates to the Civil War and the anti-slavery movement.

Similarly, the period after the Civil War, the "Age of Big Business," could focus on the questions of whether or not business was fairly regulated, or whether labor was justly treated, or whether the public was fairly dealt with in this period. Such events as the "Haymarket Square Affair" or books by the so-called "Muckrakers" could be studied as points of departure for an in-depth study of some of the institutional problems, many not fully resolved to this day, that surrounded our development as an industrial nation. These are merely examples. Later periods in the history of the U.S. could be treated in a similar way.

World history may be studied in a similar way by identifying the major problems of world history that confront the peoples of the world. For instance, it would seem unconscionable, in light of the world situation today, to neglect a study in depth of the problems of how the contrasting cultures of the Arabic and Western worlds can be brought into some kind of peaceful coexistence. As a matter of fact, the serious study of world history might well start right here.[1]

It should be obvious that this is the kind of inquiry that requires resources, materials, books, and magazine articles, as well as thoughtful interpretations of events by contemporary scholars, that far exceed those possible in any textbook. It would require digging deep into a very few important questions and leaving aside the rest, at least for the time being. While the textbook will probably be useful, and can be consulted appropriately from time to time, we would hope that most students would be encouraged to read more broadly and to gather as much information as possible on the topic to be used in thinking about the topic rather than to be memorized.

To turn to the problem of the study of history at the lower grade levels: At this stage children are not sufficiently experienced to study in great depth comprehensive social problems of the kind illustrated above. They should receive straight narrative history as told by knowledgeable elders or even as it is presented in textbooks. We hope, however, that the textbooks used will be rich in detail, as indeed some United States history textbooks are, and that the emphasis on remembering a few facts from history will be abandoned in favor of the sheer pleasure of hearing the story, as told by the historian, biographer, or historical novelist, in all of its vivid detail. We believe that students will actually remember more and understand better what they read or hear if less attention is given to drilling in facts and more attention is given to telling a full and detailed story and to utilizing that story to think about some important, or even just interesting, questions.

Both remembering and understanding will be greatly facilitated if the story is frequently interrupted to raise questions about the story and discuss them—not factual questions but problems that have no correct answers. For example, about the period of exploration and settlement, it could be asked: What do you think about the conditions faced by Native Americans? What people in the age of exploration and settlement do you think got the best deal? Who the worst? Is there a better way that settlement could have been carried out? What person or persons do you admire most in this period? Who least?

A second way to introduce the problematic into the teaching of history at the lower grade levels is to confront children with alternative versions of well-known factual episodes and then to help them solve the riddle. Examples of such questions include: Who was really first in exploring the North American continent? Who fired the first shot at Concord? Were the soldiers in George Washington's army at Valley Forge good or bad soldiers? Was John Brown a patriot or a traitor? Very good cases can be made on all sides of these and many other interesting questions, and in discussing them even small children will begin to learn to question and not to take everything for granted. These are important attributes of democratic citizenship.

The Study in Depth of Selected Social Problems

It should be clear by now that we are thoroughly committed to a curriculum which focuses on the study of a few important social problems while merely highlighting or omitting entirely a large body of less important (at least for the moment) material. We are not entirely alone in taking this position. After making a comprehensive study of American high schools, T. S. Sizer concluded tersely that "less is more" (Sizer, 1984). We would say it another way: More about less is not only better, but is absolutely essential if our goal is to develop really substantive knowledge and thinking skills.

Fred M. Newmann, in a study originally reported to the Board of Directors of the National Council for the Social Studies on November 21,

1985, cites the penchant of the social studies to race through content as one of the most serious problems that confronts the field. "Racing through content," he says, "is useless. Students forget most of it in a few months." Citing a study by Glasser, Newmann says, "Students must spend sustained time in the comprehension and analyses of content to develop both knowledge and *thinking* skills. . . . The pressure to cover large amounts of material in a survey fashion must be resisted, and instead, few topics should be studied in greater depth" [emphasis added] (Newmann, 1986, p. 243). We would only add to this that the problem of whatever kind is the logical point on which to focus study in depth.

Neither are we alone among those who have developed models, and to some extent successfully employed them, for in-depth study of content. (A number of such models which the reader may want to consult are listed in the notes.)[2] Our proposal is to be distinguished from most of these in three respects, however. First, it would employ in-depth study for most of, if not the entire, curriculum and not to just a portion of it. Second, it would utilize the traditional subjects as a primary vehicle for organizing study. Third, the goal of any study in depth would be the attempted solution, or at least clarification, of a problem: a problem of fact, a problem of interpretation, a problem of value, a problem of public policy, or a combination of these.

INFORMATION SATURATION. From the very first, the topic and/or problem being studied should be saturated with information. Information should be collected from a wide range of sources, including textbooks, which may be read quickly but not memorized, journalistic accounts, biographies, diaries, official documents, scholarly interpretations, popular articles, and fiction. No special effort should be made to memorize anything. Serious students of events use large quantities of information but they do not waste time in memorizing anything. As the study of a topic is focused on a particular problem, the search for information should be continued and even intensified. This search should proceed up to and even beyond the moment the problem is resolved, if indeed it is resolved. As the problem is more clearly defined (for example, to focus the study of the Revolutionary War period on the problems of revolution), information gathering will become more research-like, honing in on answering the questions that are raised in studying that problem. For instance, was the revolution really justified? Was it necessary? Would we have been worse or better off today if it had never occurred? Under what conditions is a refusal to obey the law justified? Are the guerrillas who fight against military dictators throughout the world today like or unlike the patriots of the American Revolution? There is obviously no end to such investigations. The questions begin to suggest new information that is needed. It should also be obvious that such a focus on the problem of revolution takes study to a depth impossible if everything that is studied must be remembered. This is a program for dealing with quantities of facts, focused on answering real questions rather than on memorizing a few facts that by their very brevity are almost certain to be misleading.

IDENTIFYING THE PROBLEM. Students may be given the problem first off: "Under what circumstances is a refusal to obey the law justified?" or "Was the American Revolution justified?" Later, under very skillful questioning, students may learn to identify problems in the content for themselves. The teacher may ask, for instance, such leading questions as: "What do you see as the likenesses and/or differences between the American Revolution, the Civil War, and the Civil Rights Movement? What do you see as a problem which was common to all of them? In what way was the position in which a Minuteman found himself similar to or different from that of a soldier in the Confederate Army or a Civil Rights protester in the 1960s?" Or, at a later stage, students may be able to respond intelligently to the blunt inquiries: "What do you see as the most important problem posed by the American Revolution? What more would you like to know about it?" For instance, a student might ask: "Were all Americans patriots? Were there those in America who were opposed to the Revolution? Who were they, how many were there, and why did they oppose the Revolution? What part did radicals and rabble-rousers have in bringing the Revolution about? The press?" Or the teacher or some student might raise the query: "Was the Revolution more a movement for independence or for democracy?"

It is obvious that approached in this way a problem which was supposed to have narrowed study to a small field to be studied in depth has been exploded, so to speak, into a large field which includes almost everything worth talking about. The responsibility then, is to narrow down the scope of the problem to one, or a very few questions, that are manageable. It is good, however, to know that these questions are related to many others, possibly all the questions one could usefully raise about the United States.[3]

RESOLVING THE PROBLEM. Efforts should be made to reach some degree of consensus on the solution to the problem. This may of course prove to be impossible and in no case should it be insisted that a single answer must be agreed upon. To such questions as, "Was the American Revolution justified?" or "Under what circumstances, if any, should a people refuse to obey the law?" there may well be two or many sides, each with valid reasons that justify the answer given. Majority reports, minority reports, and even multiple reports may be in order, even after the opportunity to discuss the problem at length has been provided at every level in its study. It is really better to understand the complexity of a problem than to reach one final position. Such an outcome is far more consistent with democracy and contributes to student experience with diverse views—an inescapable quality of democratic life.

CONTINUITY AND VARIATION. The curriculum being proposed affords the opportunity for a wide variation in content while at the same time insuring that there will be no serious void in the content covered. Since the curriculum is readily adaptable to the traditional curriculum (or any variation of it, such as in the Task Force Proposal), the disciplines that are thought to be useful in the education of citizens will be fully utilized, thus insuring continuity in the curriculum. At the same time, the particular problems serving as the focus of study in any discipline at any time may vary widely, in order to take advantage of currency, relevance, interest, and even manageability of teacher and material resources. The study in depth of any problem, for whatever reason selected, has the effect of spreading out to touch other problems and will quite naturally fill in the voids in information that could occur. For instance, a meaningful understanding of contemporary institutions and their problems might quite reasonably follow from an in-depth study of the American Revolution or of the Constitutional period. However, it could conceivably develop quite as well from the in-depth study of the growth of U.S. industry. In either case the one would spread to encompass the other.

Teachers and school systems might therefore follow quite different paths in accordance with their own unique capabilities and resources to the same approximate end, that is, to the education of citizens who have deep insight into how our institutions and their problems came about. This kind of overlapping in the midst of wide variation would bind together the whole curriculum and at the same time reflect the way in which scholars and intelligent citizens think about our history, a process which the young citizen would hopefully come to emulate.

10

Reflective Teaching Practices

Reflective decision-making classrooms are settings where the thinking process is constantly nourished and where problems, ideas, and values, however controversial, can be freely examined. These conditions imply a particular orientation to teaching.

Reflective decision making requires teachers who are deeply committed to democratic principles and who see the development of informed, thoughtful, and democratic decision makers as their most significant professional responsibility. Without strong and authentic commitment, the goals of democratic education are likely to be seriously compromised. A reflective decision-making curriculum also implies respect for the idea that the thinking process can best be stimulated in an open classroom environment, where the exchange of ideas and dialogue, however controversial, contributes to intellectual growth, and where evidence, reason, and democratic values are seen as fundamental to decision making in a complex and democratic society. Only when teachers hold firm convictions about these values are their classroom goals and practices likely to genuinely represent the goals of reflective decision making for citizenship in a democracy.

In the reflective classroom, the teacher's role is to stimulate thinking, encourage dialogue, and guide students in evaluating the worth of ideas. The role of teachers becomes a facilitative one where teachers raise questions, foster doubt, present competing views, challenge the ideas of students, and promote rigorous and democratic dialogue. At the same time, the teacher must be informed with respect to the issues under discussion. This facilitative but goal-oriented role contrasts sharply with the authoritarian role that has often characterized classrooms. Moreover, covering content so that it may be memorized, limiting questions to those that require specified right answers, relying on a lecture-recitation mode, and emphasizing trivial facts without exploring significant ideas are practices that are not compatible with the reflective classroom. Neither the teacher nor the textbook serve as a major source of authority. In the reflective classroom, authority resides exclusively in evidence, reason, and democratic values. The teacher serves as a facilitator who stimulates intellectual dialogue and encourages students to be critical decision makers.

Thus, reflective decision making calls for a new and alternative teaching role that creates the conditions where serious thinking can take place. The shift away from a more conventional and authoritarian teaching role is a dramatic one. While this shift represents a difficult and challenging transition in how teachers think and in what they do, it is absolutely essential if democracy is to be nourished in the schools.

Two conditions are especially important to reflective teaching: creating a reflective classroom climate, and stimulating intellectual growth.

REFLECTIVE CLASSROOM CLIMATE

To the greatest extent possible, the reflective classroom needs to be democratic; that is, the climate must permit the participants to communicate easily in a supportive yet stimulating setting. Since reflective decision making involves the testing of ideas, students need to feel assured that when they share their ideas they will be treated with respect and that they will not be subjected to ridicule, sarcasm, or worst of all, ignored. However immature or limited a student's idea may be, teachers need to recognize that from the student's perspective, the idea is a reasonable one.

The reflective teacher has the responsibility for setting the norms for class discussion. Through their words and actions teachers need to emphasize that the classroom is a place where deeply significant questions are explored, where all views are worthy of examination, where each individual has worth, where listening to others is a vital part of discussions, and where the test of an idea resides in the reasons and evidence that support it. Teachers who respond to these concerns will provide students with direct experience in an authentically democratic process.

The following conditions can contribute to establishing a fitting classroom climate for a reflective curriculum.

An Open and Supportive Classroom Climate

Reflective teaching requires a setting that is open to all ideas and is, at the same time, purposeful (Massialas et al., 1975). In this setting students and teachers together pose and examine issues. No compulsion for the class to reach consensus exists. However, it is necessary for alternative solutions to be evident and for each of these solutions to be thoughtfully examined and evaluated.

Bridges (1979) provides further insight into the nature of openness as related to discussion. He suggests that a discussion must be open in the following ways:

> The matter is open to discussion
> The discussants are open-minded
> The discussion is open to all arguments
> The discussion is open to any person
> The time limit is open (not usually the case in the classroom)
> The learning outcomes are open, not predictable
> The purposes and practices of the discussion are out in the open, not covert
> The discussion is open-ended, not required to come to a single conclusion

Here, Bridges leads us to a deeper understanding of open discussion and provides educators with helpful guidelines that can foster genuinely open exchange of ideas.

Reflective classrooms should be settings where a student feels free to say, "I've heard that AIDS is a disease that is spreading very quickly. Someone called it an epidemic. Can we spend some time finding out about it and deciding what should be done?" Suggesting problems, new ideas, and taking unpopular positions should all be commonplace in the democratic classroom.

Listening

Listening to the ideas of others is fundamental to serious dialogue. Unfortunately, listening is not well demonstrated by teachers in many classrooms. Teachers are sometimes more concerned with what they are going to say next, with other students who may be losing interest, or with making hasty judgments than with what is being said. Furthermore, we know that in many classrooms teachers do most of the talking and students do most of the listening. If students come to feel that their ideas are not taken seriously, they are not likely to listen to each other or to the teacher. As Bridges (1979) has said, "Discussion . . . cannot take place . . . when students are afraid to speak fully; [when] teachers think student opinions are not worth listening to . . . or [when] people are not amenable to the influence of reason, evidence, or argument." Even more importantly, under these circumstances students are not as likely to participate. While listening is a necessary part of the teacher's behavior, listening needs to serve as a norm for student behavior as well.

Restating Student Ideas

One way to increase the chance that students will feel that their contributions are recognized is for teachers to paraphrase or summarize what a student has just said. Teachers can restate student ideas with such statements as, "I think I have the idea. Is this what you mean?" or "Marie has said that she thinks that a candidate who has already served in public office has more experience and therefore has one advantage over opponents who have not. Do the rest of you feel that previous experience with the office is an important consideration?" In this case, the teacher has recognized the student's contribution by asking the class to give it serious consideration.

Teachers need to guard against the tendency to evaluate comments made by students. Rather, every attempt should be made to understand clearly what the student is saying before making any kind of evaluation.

Johnson and Johnson (1975) suggest three skills that can help teachers to understand the student's message clearly. The first of these skills, paraphrasing, involves restating the student's statement in a manner that shows understanding of the student's frame of reference. For example: "Joan, you seem to be opposed to tightening our immigration policy and you feel that U.S. immigration policies should make it easier for all people to enter this country. Is that right?" The second skill involves describing the student's feelings. For example: "You really feel strongly about this, don't you?" The third skill involves paraphrasing what the student says until you both agree with the meaning of the message. Each of these skills can contribute to effective classroom communication and facilitate meaningful discussions and dialogue.

Restating student ideas represents a significant strategy for encouraging broadly based student expression in the classroom. This point has been underscored by research completed by Torney et al. (1975). This study compared students from ten nations and concluded that a classroom climate where expression of student ideas is encouraged is the most significant factor related to positive classroom outcomes.

Offering Competing Ideas

A challenge exists in creating a democratic classroom that is, on the one hand, comfortable and supportive but on the other intellectually challenging and open to competing views and controversial issues. Research findings by Ehman (1969, 1977) demonstrate that the use of controversial content contributes to positive student attitudes regarding citizen duty, political participation, and political efficacy (1969), as well as to political trust, social integration, and political interest (1977). While the study of controversial issues is central to education for democratic citizenship as set forth in this book, Ehman's studies underscore their value as facilitating a broad range of student attitudes essential to effective citizen participation.

Teachers need to recognize that it takes considerable courage, competence, and maturity for students to respond effectively when they are subjected to harsh criticism from other students or from the teacher. The effect of such a strategy is likely to overwhelm or alienate students. What the teacher can do is present a contrasting view in a detached way, for example with statements like: "I understand your point of view and the reasons why you support it but some people hold a different position. For example . . ." At the same time teachers need to avoid confronting students' views arbitrarily they must bear in mind that the reflective decision-making process loses its dynamism unless competing ideas are given full consideration. Teachers need to challenge student thinking when it is poorly supported or illogical, not just when they personally hold opposing views.

Humor

The use of humor can play an important role in easing the flow of classroom communication. While humor must not degenerate to the level of sarcasm or ridicule, it can focus on news events, public figures, or the foibles of the teacher himself, or even take the form of gentle teasing. The power of humor is that it contributes to a more relaxing and stimulating environment. Each teacher will have his or her own style of stimulating humor, but it is important to emphasize its role in facilitating dialogue.

The Teacher as a Model

The perception that students have of their teachers influences the quality of learning. The question here is: What personal qualities in the teacher help foster a reflective classroom? Fundamentally, the teacher has to exhibit those qualities entailed by the reflective decision-making process. This calls for acceptance of all ideas, even those ideas that the teacher personally finds distasteful. However, while acceptance and openness are essential, they are not sufficient. Teachers must also enjoy controversy and thrive on the intense exchange of ideas. If teachers demonstrate their enthusiasm for the ideas that students contribute, it is far more likely that their students will as well. Teachers also need to create conditions of fairness and equity. As much attention needs to be given to shy students as to ones who are assertive and confident, to the less popular as well as the more popular, to females as well as males, and to minority as well as majority students. Partiality has no place in the democratic classroom. Furthermore, teachers need to recognize that the decision-making process implies that right answers are difficult to come by and that their role is to stimulate thinking rather than to serve as a major authority on subject matter. An authoritarian posture, especially one that engenders fear rather than trust and respect, violates all the premises of reflective and democratic decision making. A study by Fowlkes (1976) demonstrated that the level of trust students had for their teachers was directly related to their general level of political trust. As a result, it seems that trust in the teacher is a necessary component of democratic schooling. Teachers also need to be willing to share their own doubts and ambiguities with students to demonstrate that perplexity is an integral part of a society where people govern themselves and to emphasize that no single individual has all the answers.

Is the teacher a concerned, thoughtful citizen? Is the teacher interested in public issues? Is he or she well read and informed on significant issues? Does the teacher become involved in public causes? These questions reflect our belief that teachers will be more effective if they serve as models of concerned and involved citizenship to their students. If students know that their teacher is active in community groups or political parties or belongs to social cause organizations, the teacher's credibility is considerably enhanced. Such consistency between a teacher's public life and his or her professional life underscores the teacher's authenticity and commitment, and students will easily perceive that classroom goals are congruent with the teacher's life as a citizen. Jaros and Cannon (1969) underscored that teachers serve as models of political values for students, who are likely to emulate them. In short, democratic teaching places high demands on teachers to behave as they would want their students to behave.

STIMULATING THE INTELLECT

Reflective decision making requires that teachers persistently stimulate thinking during the course of classroom dialogue. Stimulation can take the form of probing questions, presenting competing ideas and opinions, and facilitating the search for evidence.

In the discussion that follows we highlight essential aspects of teaching that are consistent with reflective decision making. This kind of curriculum does not lend itself to a set of prescribed steps that the teacher should follow, nor is there a single recipe or set of standard lessons that can be used. What we describe below are those unique aspects of reflective teaching that distinguish it from more conventional and more directive approaches.

Initially, teachers need to come to know their students, their circumstances, and their concerns. This knowledge is basic to relating instruction about social issues to the lives of the individuals involved. The following list identifies some different ways of identifying student concerns.

Open Forum Discussion

The purpose of such discussions is to uncover the interests and concerns of students. Here, students should be encouraged to talk about their hopes for the future and the social issues that concern them. To start such a discussion a teacher might distribute a list of several major issues, such as pollution, corruption, unemployment, environment, food and hunger, equal rights, nuclear war, and so forth, and ask students how each of these might affect their lives. Further, they might be asked to add to the list and to prioritize the issues. The ensuing discussion could center around student explanations about which issues are most important and why.

In a similar vein, classroom surveys could ask students to provide, in written form, background information about themselves, their goals, and the concerns they have about the future.

Out of School Events

Out of school events (a weekend camping excursion, a field trip) could be used by teachers to talk to students in less formal circumstances in order to gain additional insight into their interests and perspectives.

This kind of information-gathering can help teachers identify relevant subject matter. For example, a number of students might express concerns about their future employment, how they need to prepare for it, and what kinds of opportunities may be available. This concern could well provide a foundation for examining whether conditions in the state and nation support a promising future for their generation. Questions serving to organize class discussion might be: What can be done to stimulate the economic future of their state? What can be done to attract population? Industry?

Familiarity with the background and interests of students can also help the teacher relate topics under study directly to students' lives. If the topic under discussion is whether or not drafting young people into the armed services is a desirable practice, teachers can invite students who have brothers or sisters in the military to share their particular perspective. To be able to draw on the background of students strengthens the relevance of the discussion for all students in the class.

THE REFLECTIVE PROCESS

Identifying and Defining the Problem

We have already emphasized that problems selected for classroom study need to be related to the concerns of students. While problems can flow directly out of student experiences, such as "Why can't a special student lounge area be provided in our school?" or "Why can't we have a day off for a class picnic?" such problems are narrow in scope and are not likely to expand the student's view of domestic or international issues. At the same time, these problems, even though they are context-specific, can provide important learning opportunities. Students can try to generate reasons both for or against their position; they can interview others, collect evidence, and reach decisions; and they may even decide to take action. While problems of this sort can have educational value, it is important for teachers to present issues that apply more broadly and involve significant content. Therefore, teachers may identify a set of problems that relate to the subject being taught as well as to the interests of students. Since such issues will be broader in scope, teachers may guide the process of identifying the specific problem with materials especially designed to present alternative views of a particular issue. Two contrasting editorials or two contrasting cartoons can set the stage for identifying a specific problem. Poignant selections from television documentaries or dramas can serve the same purpose.

The use of "springboards" is especially advocated by Massialas et al. (1975). Springboards may be documents, photographs, charts or graphs that highlight significant information, magazine articles, music (especially protest songs), conflicting quotations, newspaper clippings, and the like. Springboards are used to highlight the essence of a controversy.

(graphs that highlight population decline in the state over the previous decade, quotations that represent both the pro and con sides of a current issue, and the lyrics to songs that protest the use of nuclear weapons can all serve to trigger questions that can lead to serious investigation of an issue.

Even though all students may view the same materials, they are likely to interpret them differently. After students identify the problems they perceive in the materials, they should be encouraged to give reasons why they believe their problem is an important one for study. In this context, it is important to have students grasp the notions that people define problems in different ways and that how the problem is defined usually reflects a person's biases and values.

Defining important terms is the task that accompanies identification of the problem. Defining terms helps to reduce ambiguity and to increase the chances that all students have a similar framework for discussing the problem. A question such as, "What can be done to reduce poverty?" forces a consideration of what is meant by "poverty" as well as what is meant by "reduce." The definition of poverty probably can not be easily answered by the students themselves. Rather some more authoritative or expert source should be considered. Though occasionally a dictionary may be helpful, in the case of a term like poverty it may be more helpful to examine the definitions used by the U.S. Census Bureau or contained in a sociological reference. A small committee of students can assume responsibility for obtaining this information. The members of the class will then have to decide which definition best fits their purpose.

Another example can be found in the question: "Were Japanese-Americans unfairly treated during World War II?" After presenting students with alternative views of the treatment of Japanese-Americans, teachers need to challenge students to think about the meaning of the term "unfairly." In this situation, what does "unfairly" *really* mean? Does it mean that these people received punishment they did not deserve? Or does it mean that in comparison to other groups these Japanese-Americans were more harshly treated? Or both? The teacher needs to involve the whole class in wrestling with the definition before the issue can be more fully explored.

The Use of Probing Questions

Earlier, we presented several categories of probing questions designed to stimulate the level of intellectual exchange. Definitional questions, evidential questions, policy questions, value questions, and speculative questions are all intended to cause the student to reach well beyond the level of recall and memory and to reflect and examine issues that are controversial and do not have predetermined answers. For example:

- What does censorship really mean? *(Definitional Question)*
- Can proof be found to illustrate that censorship exists in our society? *(Evidential Question)*
- Should interest groups be allowed to remove books from a public library? A school library? *(Policy Question)*
- Which is more important—free speech or preserving the dignity of particular groups of people? *(Value Question)*
- What might have happened if the First Amendment to the Constitution (freedom of speech) had not been included in the Bill of Rights? *(Speculative Question)*

All of these kinds of questions have a dynamic, vigorous quality. None can be easily answered, all require serious thought, and the answers to most of them will have a tentative quality.

In spite of the desirability of probing questions to trigger critical thinking, research indicates that about 60% of the questions teachers ask require students to recall facts, about 20% require student to think, and the remaining 20% are procedural (Gall, 1984).

Probing questions must become the stock-in-trade of teachers who support a reflective decision-making curriculum. The pattern described above must be substantially altered. Probing questions permeate all aspects of the process and need to become an inherent part of every teacher's repertoire. Without the persistent use of probing questions, the goals of reflective process will not be realized.

Identifying Value Assumptions

What values will be used to decide what should be done about the problem under discussion? Should the decision be one that is least costly, that shows respect for the individual, that creates equitable conditions, or that preserves basic freedoms? The possibilities will vary with the nature of a particular problem. If the problem concerns pollution, salient values may be related to costs for both industries and taxpayers as well as to concern for protecting the health and appearance of the community. Prior to considering alternatives and consequences, it is important to identify guiding values in a preliminary way and to select among competing values. However, it must be recognized that these values may be modified as the problem receives further examination.

Identifying Alternatives and Predicting Consequences

Knowledge plays a significant role both in generating alternatives and in identifying consequences. It is here that students engage in research. It is also at this stage that it seems useful to organize several small groups of students to broaden the base of class participation. More students are likely to participate in small groups than in total class discussions. In order to generate alternatives and consequences, students need to gather information from a variety of sources. While the teacher may select one or two initial articles to lay a foundation, students need to identify other sources of information that they need. While conventional library sources will be helpful, students may also survey knowledgeable adults, invite one or more experts to class, or suggest an appropriate film or field trip. After collecting data that leads to the identification of alternatives and their consequences, each group can summarize the alternatives and consequences they have identified. These results are then shared with the entire class so that the broadest possible range of options can be available to each group. At this point, it is important that the teacher examine the alternatives that students have identified to make certain they represent all points of view. If they are one-sided, the teacher has a responsibility to identify competing ideas that have not been included.

Alternatives in a decision-making context play a role similar to hypotheses in a scientific investigation. The implications of an alternative and the consequences to which it leads need to be supported with evidence and logic (Cassidy & Kurfman, 1977). The following statement serves as an illustration: "If the old library is torn down, the neighborhood surrounding it will deteriorate." The prediction that the neighborhood will deteriorate requires evidence before it can be accepted as a valid consequence. As we have already mentioned, students can obtain evidence from a variety of sources, but it is especially critical that they evaluate the worth of the evidence. Such questions as the following are appropriate in guiding such an evaluation:

- Where did you get your information?
- Why do you think the source is reliable?
- Are there competing sources?
- Are there others who agree with the source you used?
- Does the author have a personal reason for making this claim?
- How did your source reach this conclusion?

From time to time, teachers may find it useful to play devil's advocate, albeit in a supportive and constructive way, to see if the evidence students have presented can withstand challenge. Moreover, throughout the process of identifying alternatives and consequences, teachers need to caution students not to reach decisions too early. Rather, they need to first listen to all the possibilities with as open a mind as possible.

Examining consequences also involves establishing a logical relationship with the values one hopes to realize—that is, asking whether the consequences of a particular alternative will contribute to the desired set of values. For example, if the neighborhood deteriorates and the area around the old town library becomes less attractive or more susceptible to crime, these conditions will erode the quality of life for others who own businesses or live in that area. One could therefore argue that tearing down the library ignores the welfare of the people in this area and thereby contradicts the value of human dignity or respect for others. In a reflective classroom teachers need to involve students in exploring the relationship between the consequences of their alternatives and the values they have identified.

Reaching and Justifying a Decision

After an issue has been examined carefully, the process of reaching a decision can become even more difficult. The need for more knowledge and an increased awareness that the situation is difficult and the choices not clear are conditions similar to those facing citizens. At this point students need to rank-order the alternatives and justify their decisions by identifying the strongest possible reasons and evidence to support their choice. In addition, they need to provide reasons as well as evidence for rejecting alternatives. The classroom discussion that follows should be a rigorous and challenging one where both the teacher and students listen to all arguments and feel free to challenge each other's positions. During the discussion the teacher can and should raise probing questions, some of which should encourage students to focus on the relationship of their decisions to democratic values. However, in a democratic classroom, there should be no effort to prescribe a single right answer to complex value-laden questions. If the process of reflective decision making has been carefully followed, students will reach their own conclusions and challenge one another's arguments. Neither classroom consensus nor compliance with the teacher's decisions is desirable or appropriate.

The Appendix to this book contains a checklist for reflective teaching that was adapted from Jadallah (1985). Such a list can be useful to teachers in examining the extent to which their teaching practices correspond with the principles of reflective decision making.

The essence of the reflective process has perhaps best been captured by Alan Griffin (1942):

> The reflective examination of any proposition tends to develop skill in the use of the [reflective] method. The reflective examination of a belief to which one is committed tends to develop a reliance on reflection as a method of securing truth. But if we are headed in the direction of enabling the student at some time to choose his way of life, to make his decision as between democracy and one or another of the available competing authoritarianisms, we need to act positively in terms of that purpose.
>
> For this reason, it is necessary to include in addition to what has been said, three additional principles:
>
> 1. So far as possible, any belief under examination should be placed in clear opposition to other beliefs in the culture which are or appear to be inconsistent with it.
>
> 2. So far as possible, students should be brought to see conflicts among their beliefs as exemplifying familiar controversial issues.
>
> 3. So far as possible, subject matter drawn from those areas which are most sharply controversial within our culture should be deliberately preferred over equally evidential but relatively less highly charged subject matter.
>
> The repeated phrase, "so far as possible" is meant to call attention to the fact that every procedure suggested above is problematic, in that it may incur the violent opposition of powerful groups. We have, however, reached the point where refusal to make the distinction between democracy and authoritarianism clear is even more dangerous. Even at some risk, we must seize the limited chance we still have to build for a world fit for free men to live in. (pp. 193–194)

11

Assessing Learning
for Democratic Citizenship

In this chapter, we are interested in identifying student assessment strategies for classrooms that implement the goals of reflective decision making in a democracy.

At the outset we would like to share our perspectives about the relationship between a problem-solving curriculum and the process of student assessment. When contrasted with more conventional curriculum goals, this relationship is especially complex and challenging.

First of all, in the context of problem solving, knowledge, intellectual skills, and values are necessarily intertwined. Unlike curricula that emphasize memorization, this curriculum, which involves students in making decisions about the compelling problems that citizens face, cannot easily isolate or separate knowledge from thinking and reasoning. After all, our goal is not the mere acquisition of knowledge but rather the application and evaluation of knowledge in the service of solving citizen issues.

The following example should illustrate the point. Let us suppose that a class has studied the treatment of Chinese immigrants during the Railroad Era with the purpose of deciding whether the Chinese were exploited in ways not befitting a democracy. Which of the following facts would merit inclusion on a conventional test?

- By the year 1860, approximately 35,000 Chinese immigrants had entered the U.S.
- Chinese laborers worked for the Central Pacific Railroad. To cut through the Sierra Nevadas, it was necessary for them to build tunnels through solid granite.

○ The railroad builders needed cheap labor to make a profit.

Many additional "facts" could be added to this list. However, from the standpoint of a problem-solving curriculum, our answer is that not one of these facts, nor all three of them taken together, is essential. In this kind of curriculum, the question we wish to answer is not whether students can recall specified facts, but how effectively these students can evaluate relevant facts and relate them to decisions that need to be made in a democratic context. Included here is the extent to which students recognize the role that values play in selecting facts and, conversely, the role facts play in influencing values. For this kind of assessment recall or true-false questions that assess student memory will not suffice.

Suppose, on the other hand, students are asked to respond to the following tasks, which embody content as well as intellectual skills.

○ Some people argue that Chinese immigrants were exploited by railroad builders in ways not befitting a democracy. Do you agree? Draw upon our study of this issue and provide relevant evidence and reasoning to support your position.
○ Now that you have defended your position, state the opposing position and summon all the relevant evidence you can to support it.

This two-part assignment reflects the interrelationship between knowledge, intellectual skills, and values which is an integral part of dealing with social issues in a democracy. It is reasonable to expect that different students will use different facts to support their respective positions, and while their facts should necessarily be accurate, several students may submit strong responses without relying on the *same* facts. To call for a single set of facts is to ignore conditions faced by even our most informed citizens who neither have all the facts at their command nor use the same facts to arrive at decisions. To require knowledge of the same set of facts from all students is to contradict the way even the most sophisticated citizen functions. More importantly, requiring such uniformity, achieved through memorization and rote learning, denies the intellectual rigor entailed by a problem-solving curriculum.

Secondly, if such a curriculum is implemented appropriately, students will play a significant role in shaping the nature of classroom content and discourse. Certainly teachers will influence the general parameters of what is studied. Teachers may specify the topics to be studied in a general way (Westward Expansion, Checks and Balances, and so forth) and may also identify the intellectual processes that will be emphasized; but the specific way the content is structured, the questions that will be explored, and the way these questions will be investigated will be negotiated in classroom discussions where students are active participants in the deliberations. Therefore, while assessment procedures must be guided by the overall goals of a problem-solving curriculum, at the same time student assessment cannot be solely determined by the teacher in advance of instruction. The questions raised by students and the nature of classroom interaction must be represented as well. Consequently, the strategies used to assess learning outcomes need to represent the overreaching goals of the curriculum as well as the classroom events that transpired in the course of the unit.

In effect, both teachers and students need to be reminded of the goal that guides a problem-solving curriculum. Stated simply, the goal of such a curriculum is to foster the development of thoughtful and informed citizens who can make decisions in a democratic context that recognizes the tension between self-interest and the common good.

Thirdly, a problem-solving curriculum embraces the tension that exists between two distinct, and sometimes competing, educational goals. One of these goals has as its aim the fulfillment of the individual and the development of personal autonomy and independence to the greatest extent possible. The other goal is cast in terms of contributing to society. The proposed curriculum speaks to both of these goals. (The discussion of socialization and countersocialization presented in Chapter 3 explored this matter more fully). In its emphasis on the development of intellectual skills, this curriculum seeks to expand the power of all individuals to think for themselves, to form their own attitudes, to make their own decisions, and to act on their own convictions. Simultaneously, it strives to strengthen social responsibility, a commitment to the social good, and democratic values. This tension between empowering the individual and strengthening societal commitments is openly and explicitly recognized in this curriculum. Consequently, the process of determining assessment strategies also reflects this tension. On the one hand, we want to find out if students develop as individuals who can play an active and meaningful role in decisions that citizens make. On the other hand, school or state requirements mandate that students receive grades, study certain topics, and demonstrate certain skills that represent societal expectations.[1] Any assessment for the proposed curriculum will need to respond to both of these goals.

IMPLICATIONS FOR ASSESSMENT

The complexity and scope of the goals of the proposed curriculum, the involvement of students in the process of learning, and the presence of the tension between individual fulfillment and the social good have some apparent implications for the process of assessing student learning. Three of these implications follow.

Beyond Testing for Memory

A problem-solving curriculum combines the ideas related to social issues and conditions (content) with an intellectual and values dimension (process) to develop higher level thinking and decision-making skills. Far too often educators have relied exclusively on paper and pencil tests that focus on a limited context to assess student learning. These conventional assessment strategies typically require students to take tests that emphasize the memorization of dates, events, and individuals. Questions such as the following are commonplace on tests given to students:

- Which side fired the first shot in the Civil War?
- What happened at the Battle of Saratoga?
- What was the year of the Stock Market Crash?

These questions represent trivial learning of virtually no significance to the lives of citizens. Such limited knowledge does little to empower citizens to address complex and controversial public issues. The questions listed above do not tap higher level intellectual abilities. The major point we wish to underscore is that memorization of this kind of information is of little use and that assessment needs to include alternative strategies in order to assess higher level thinking abilities and the understanding of social conditions and issues adequately.

Problem-solving Curriculum

Assessing knowledge that students have learned to use, the extent of their reasoned respect for democracy, and their intellectual and political skills are all entailed by this curriculum. Assessing student progress with respect to these several components is a central responsibility of teachers. The assessment procedures to be used may be explored with students and even influenced by them. However, in the last analysis, teachers must insure that these components are effectively represented in the assessment strategy.

Collaboration Between Students and Teachers

Since this curriculum calls for teacher-student negotiations regarding the selection of content and learning experiences, it would be a contradiction to impose assessment techniques that are externally determined without also permitting students to participate as fully as possible in the determination of these assessment strategies. As assessment procedures are negotiated, both students and teachers will address the tension that exists in a curriculum that seeks to serve both the individual and society, one that fosters individuality and independence, while at the same time strengthening social cohesiveness and social responsibility.

Each of these implications challenges conventional assessment practices. Furthermore, we are fully aware that these implications call for an alternative orientation to assessment as well as for different roles for both students and teachers. Nonetheless, we wish to stress that the goals of this curriculum will be negated unless the process of assessment is as consistent as possible with the democratic principles that undergird curriculum. The content and procedures used for any kind of student assessment communicate, to teachers and students alike, what is really valued, what pays off, and what one needs to do to be successful. An assessment process that is externally determined (by either teachers and/or commercial test publishers), one that emphasizes memorization of factual information, or one that is designed on an a priori basis without student involvement communicates a message that is contradictory to the participatory values involved. In effect, the message conveyed is that what is important is remembering those facts that teachers (or commercial test publishers) deem desirable, that the teacher is still the sole external authority whose standards are the only ones that count, and that the intellectual exchange of the classroom is not particularly significant.

We have emphasized that teacher-student collaboration is just as important in the process of assessment as it is in the planning and implementing of instruction. However, we also recognize that teacher-student negotiations are subject to limitations. For example, students are not free to decide whether assessment will take place or not. For that matter, neither are teachers. In addition, neither students nor teachers can responsibly suggest spurious or frivolous kinds of assessment. Collaborative discussions need to be entered into in a serious and responsible manner by both teachers and students. These limitations do not diminish the value of collaborative assessment. Rather, they help to define the context in which collective agreements can be reached. By participating in the shaping of the assessment process, students are given greater control over what happens to them and are able to exercise greater responsibility with respect to their own learning. Conversely, if teachers impose assessment procedures unilaterally, they deny the opportunity for shared responsibility and foster an authoritarian rather than a democratic relationship with students. Such procedures make it clear to students that compliance with authority is still the order of the day. Further, such practices create a climate in which democratic problem-solving becomes as arbitrary and authoritarian as practices that might be found in dictatorial political systems.

ASSESSING STUDENT PROGRESS

The goals of the curriculum must guide the assessment process. In this case we are concerned with goals related to (1) knowledge and intellectual skills, (2) student commitment to democracy, (3) group and political skills, and (4) student attitudes toward public issues and citizen participation.

Knowledge and Intellectual Skills

In this curriculum students should be able to differentiate relevant from irrelevant knowledge, demonstrate their ability to place facts in a meaningful context, and assess the validity of factual claims. Knowledge may be drawn from the following areas: environmental studies, institutional studies, cultural studies, social problems, epistemology, communications, and values.

At the same time students should be able to make effective use of reason and evidence to support decisions about significant topics and issues. The skills that follow combine both substantive knowledge and intellectual process and values.

1. Being able to size up a problem and identify the central conflict or the main issue, including the underlying values that are at stake.
2. Being able to select information that is relevant to the problem and to relate it logically to proposed solutions.
3. Being able to judge the reliability of various sources of information, including firsthand experience and research-based information.
4. Being able to see a problem in its broadest possible context including the value considerations involved.
5. Being able to build a scenario of likely consequences regarding any proposed solution to a problem.
6. Being able to make reasoned judgments where the evidence is conflicting or where there is conflict between desired values.

Since knowledge cannot be separated from intellectual processes in a problem-solving curriculum, these goals represent the essence of the pro-

posed curriculum. In classrooms, particular topics or issues will be selected for study. Topics such as Westward Expansion, the U.S. Congress,
or the Cultures of the Middle East might be explored. Or issues such as
World Hunger, Environmental Pollution, or the Expansion of Civil Rights
might be pursued. Once a topic or issue has been determined, the students and their teacher will identify the central questions that they wish
to pursue. For purposes of illustration, let us assume that a class studying Westward Expansion has agreed to explore these three questions:

- Were Chinese immigrants, who provided the manual labor for
  building the Transcontinental Railroad, exploited?
- What could have been done to relieve this situation?
- Could the tensions between Native Americans and the U.S. Government have been minimized during the last half of the nineteenth
  century?

Students will need to turn to several sources to find evidence about
whether exploitation of Chinese immigrants did indeed take place. They
will appraise these sources in terms of validity and examine them from
several points of view. They will report on their findings in class, discuss
them, and reach their own decisions about the best answer to the question. Most importantly, they should be able to defend their decisions in
a manner that demonstrates their full use of reason and evidence. To design appropriate assessment strategies, we face the challenge of representing this dynamic intellectual process as well as the substantive
knowledge that students have gained in this unit of study.

We now suggest the following strategies.

STUDENT PROJECTS.   Student projects can take the form of, among
others: (1) a written essay or paper, (2) an oral presentation, (3) a debate,
(4) a photographic essay, (5) a slide-tape presentation, or (6) a dramatization. Other ideas for student projects can be generated by students and
teachers. Such projects are a particularly useful means of appraising student progress because they involve both knowledge and intellectual skills.
Most importantly, these projects should involve students in the exploration of serious questions and their search for answers should involve examination of multiple sources. These are not projects where a student
merely turns to an encyclopedia or some other single source. Rather, the
project must demonstrate an active search for truth, harnessing and evaluating evidence from a variety of sources in the presentation of defensible conclusions.

For example, let us suppose that for the purposes of assessment students debate the issue, "Resolved that Chinese immigrants were exploited in the building of the Transcontinental Railroad." The use of a debate format permits students to demonstrate that they can draw upon relevant knowledge, evaluate their sources of information, and defend a position in a way that is supported by reason and evidence. In the context of the debate they will encounter challenges to their position and have an opportunity to demonstrate their capacity to respond to these challenges. Furthermore, the debate format, along with the criteria for evaluating student performance, can be determined through the combined efforts of teacher and students.

Both the students and the teacher should be involved in appraising student projects. The teacher need not, and should not, be the sole authority in determining the worth of the project. After a project is presented, both the teacher and the students can evaluate the project using criteria such as those in Figure 11.1. In addition to rating the project, they can use the space provided to explain their ratings and make suggestions for improvement. In the interests of all students, the evaluation done by students should be completed anonymously. This assessment activity can culminate in a class dialogue, in which students are encouraged to examine their strengths and weaknesses.

While this assessment strategy is more complex than administering a teacher-made test, it holds the potential for contributing much more to student learning. Its use can foster reflection about the problem-solving process. In other words, it serves to increase student awareness of the abilities involved in being a reflective citizen. Furthermore, it involves students in a peer review process. It honors the individuality of students, while at the same time expanding their perspectives about the nature of serious thinking. Finally, it removes the teacher from the role of an ultimate authority to whose standards all must comply and gives the students, whose work is being assessed, a broader base of feedback that will necessarily be more comprehensive than that provided by a single source.

CLASSROOM DIALOGUE. The quality of classroom discussions represents the grist of teaching and learning in a problem-solving curriculum. Whether students contribute ideas, raise thoughtful questions, and give reasons and use evidence to support their ideas can be observed in day-to-day classroom discourse. There is no need to wait for the scheduling of a major test. Over time, it is in the context of classroom participation that students reveal the strength of their intellectual abilities. Classroom dialogue is so salient to the goals of this curriculum that every effort needs to be made to appraise its quality.

Figure 11.1 Criteria: Student Project

Does this project do very well, adequately, or poorly in:

1. Representing student understanding of the issues related to Chinese railroad workers?

2. Revealing that the student took a stand with respect to the appropriate treatment of Chinese railroad workers?

3. Presenting reasons to defend the position(s) taken?

4. Demonstrating understanding of alternative positions and their supporting evidence?

5. Indicating that students are both able and willing to seriously consider opposing views?

6. Indicating that the student recognizes his or her own bias?

Classroom dialogue can be appraised by the teacher, by a selected student acting as observer, by a teacher colleague, or by any combination of students and teachers. Student observation permits students to become more acutely aware of the factors that contribute to a valuable intellectual exchange. At periodic intervals the teacher may interrupt classroom dialogue and involve students in an appraisal of how well they are performing. Are we supporting our ideas with evidence? Are we listening to each other? Are we on topic or off on a tangent? Such questions as these involve students in an examination of their ability to participate in reflective discussions. Another teacher (a colleague invited to visit class) can help the teacher diagnose the strengths and weaknesses of class discussions. In addition, by listening critically to student responses, another teacher can infer intellectual abilities of the students. Another teacher can provide a fresh perspective that classroom participants might otherwise ignore. Therefore, using all of these evaluators is likely to be more beneficial than using any one of them.

The criteria for evaluating classroom dialogue are similar to those for evaluating a student project. While these criteria need to be agreed to by both the teacher and the students, the following questions should provide a starting point for appraising teacher-student discussions:

- What proportion of students participate in class discussions?
- Do those who do not participate appear to be intellectually engaged?

- Do students listen to each other?
- Do they ask clarifying questions?
- Do they challenge each other's points of view?
- Do they probe for clear definitions and explanations?
- Do they support their ideas with evidence and reason?
- Do students appear to be relatively free of teacher domination?
- Does the discussion remain focused on the major questions?
- Can students relate the question under study to other situations?

In appraising classroom dialogue, we are especially interested in the growth of students' intellectual ability and the quality of their participation over time. Consequently, appraising classroom dialogue periodically is desirable. A reasonable schedule would provide for such appraisal once a month or once every six weeks. A videotape recorder could serve the useful purpose of permitting both teachers and students to carefully assess a particular classroom discussion. Furthermore, a videotape would allow a closer analysis of each student's participation over time and provide external feedback to all students as well as the teacher about the collective performance of the class.

OPEN-ENDED ESSAY TEST QUESTIONS. Paper and pencil tests, whether commercially developed or teacher-made, are likely to represent limited learning outcomes. Such tests most often emphasize factual information or stipulated definitions that do not represent the broader goals of such a curriculum as previously stated. However, some paper and pencil exercises can be useful.

Open-ended questions can be used for testing. Such questions permit divergent student responses and can provide evidence about the ability of students to function at higher intellectual levels. Some examples follow:

- Do you agree with the following statement: Racism towards people of color was a major factor in the conditions faced by the Chinese immigrants? Explain the reasons for your conclusion.
- Suppose that you were a member of Congress in 1881. A bill has been proposed to ban further Chinese immigration. How would you have voted? Defend your position with reasons and evidence.
- If an effort were made today to ban any particular group of people from immigrating to the U.S., would you support it? Defend your answer.

Each of these questions allows students to reveal their understanding of the issue and to demonstrate their thinking abilities. Obviously, the responses to these questions will take different forms and will be difficult to appraise.

In a manner similar to the procedures suggested for student projects, the teacher along with students can determine both the pool of questions and the criteria for appraisal. Responses can be evaluated by using the following criteria as the basis for a rating scale.

1. Does it demonstrate the student's understanding of knowledge relevant to the issue?
2. Does it reflect the student's position on the issue?
3. Does it present reasons for the position taken?
4. Does it present evidence to support the position taken?
5. Does it reflect the student's awareness of competing sources of evidence?
6. Does it reflect the student's awareness of the values inherent in the positions advocated?

The kinds of test questions suggested here are consistent with the goals of a problem-solving curriculum. Further, both the design and evaluation of such questions can be done by both the students and the teacher and can reflect both of their perspectives. Even the process of appraisal can involve students. Students can exchange papers and rate each other's work. Subsequently, a rating by the teacher can take place. Again, students can benefit from a broader base of input and the teacher need not serve as the sole authority.

It needs to be emphasized that each of these assessment strategies represents both objective and subjective elements. The criteria for appraisal, which are openly and collectively arrived at, make the standards clear to everyone. This condition reflects the objective dimension of assessment. However, the process of applying the criteria and making a judgment is much more subjective. All raters are guided by the same criteria but they will bring different perspectives and different levels of sophistication to the task. Some educators might argue that this process is too subjective to meet the canons of evaluation. However, from our vantage point, the strategies suggested here are comparable to the way many citizen judgments are made. Furthermore, the appraisal of abstract ideas and higher level intellectual abilities does not easily lend itself to objectivity. While it is possible to construct appropriate multiple-choice tests, it is not feasible or practical for students and teachers to collectively design such instruments. The tension between objectivity and subjectivity that is inherent in our suggested strategies parallels the manner in which ideas are judged in any public setting.

Finally, it should be noted that in the last few years the New Jersey Task Force on Thinking has, in a qualified way, identified three tests that may be of interest to teachers who wish to assess general reasoning skills.[2]

- The New Jersey Test of Reasoning Skills (available from: 1APC Test Division, Montclair State College, Upper Montclair, NJ 07043)
- The Cornell Critical Thinking Test, Level X (available from: University of Illinois Press, Box 5081, Station A, Champaign, IL 61820)
- The Whimbey Analytical Skills Inventory (available from: Franklin Institute Press, Box 2266, Philadelphia, PA 19103)

A Reasoned Commitment to Democracy

This goal represents a value, both in terms of content and process. Values are inherently difficult to assess. Direct questions that probe students for their opinions are not likely to be productive since the respondent is likely to know what answers are expected. However, careful observation of student behavior, particularly during class discussions, offers a more useful way to determine whether students reveal values that are consistent with democratic principles and whether they hold their values in a reasoned way. Questions such as the following can be helpful to the observations made by the teacher:

- Does the student's behavior demonstrate respect for all of his or her fellow students? (This behavior may take the form of listening to others, acknowledging competing views, asking clarifying questions of other students, and the like.)
- Do the arguments advanced by the student demonstrate a respect for democratic values such as respect for the dignity and worth of each individual, equality of opportunity, minority rights, and freedom of expression, religion, and the press?
- Using reason and evidence, can the student support the values that he or she holds?
- Does the student seriously consider competing points of view?

Each of these questions calls for careful judgments. The teacher needs to carefully examine evidence derived from what students do and say prior to drawing conclusions (and then, only tentative ones) about their values. To a considerable extent, the judgment made will be a subjective quality. While subjectivity can never be entirely removed from human judgment, teachers need to make every effort to make these judgments equitably for all students. Furthermore, these judgments about student values have no place in the grade that a student receives. To use these judgments about

the students' commitment to democracy for grading purposes would negate an important premise of a problem-solving curriculum that permits
students to reach their own conclusions about value judgments. Rather,
the observations suggested above provide feedback to both students and
the teacher about whether students are demonstrating a reasoned commitment to democratic values. This feedback can become the basis for
student interviews where the observations are examined and discussed on
a one-to-one basis.

Political and Group Skills

In this discussion we are concerned with the appraisal of political as well as group skills. In terms of political skills, we have drawn
on some of the citizen action competencies identified by Newmann, Bertoccie, and Landsness (1977). These competencies evaluate the ability of
citizens to communicate effectively, interpret data, describe the political-
legal decision-making process, justify personal devices on controversial
public issues, apply principles of justice, and work cooperatively. These
skills substantially overlap with those of our earlier discussion related to
assessment of knowledge and intellectual skills. At the same time they include group skills, which will be discussed subsequently.

Political skills will receive particular attention in the Internship component of the program. Teacher and peer evaluations of written and oral
reports, such as those described earlier, continue to represent the basic
form of assessment. However, student logs, in which each student is asked
to describe and reflect on community-based experiences, represent another important assessment tool. Here, students are asked to share and
interpret their experiences. The log is, in effect, a way for all students to
make meaning of their internship. At the same time it is a vehicle for
teachers to examine what students learn and how they interpret what they
learn.

The assessment of group skills is often overlooked, although group
settings provide the context for making many public decisions. Indeed,
the effectiveness of citizens is directly related to their ability to function
effectively as members of groups. Appraisal of student progress should
give attention to this important aspect of citizen behavior.

Guided observations by students, the classroom teacher, and an external observer are the most useful approaches for assessing student
growth with respect to group skills. The following questions suggest possible points of focus for observing student groups. However, to the greatest extent possible, the guidelines for such observations need to be
developed collaboratively by students and teachers.

1. *Extent of Participation*: Who participates? Who does not? Do a majority of students participate in group discussions? Do some dominate while others remain passive?

2. *Quality of Participation*: Is the student exchange of ideas entered into enthusiastically, reluctantly, or not at all? Are the contributions of students relevant or tangential?

3. *Listening*: Do students carefully listen to each other? Do they seek clarification of ideas presented by other members of the group? Do their comments build on the contributions of others? Do they demonstrate interest in the perspectives taken by others? Do they show a willingness to consider all ideas—even unconventional ones?

4. *Communication Skills*: Do students present their ideas clearly? Do they illustrate their ideas with relevant examples? Do they give explanations for their ideas? Do they defend the positions they take with evidence or reason?

5. *Autonomy*: Do students demonstrate independent thinking? Can they independently appraise ideas in the face of group pressures for agreement? Do they demonstrate a capacity to defend a reasonable position independently of group pressure or criticism?

While group skills can be conceptualized in many ways, the questions presented above serve as a starting point for analysis. The information obtained by careful observation can foster student growth and provide teachers with a deeper analysis of their students and classrooms. On the basis of such knowledge, classroom environments can be strengthened so that they more effectively respond to the goals of a problem-solving curriculum.

Attitudes Toward Civic Education

Whatever the subject matter of the curriculum may be, educators are usually concerned with the attitudes that students develop toward that subject. Teachers of reading hope that their students will not only learn to read, but that they will enjoy reading and develop a habit of reading throughout their lifetimes. Similarly, educators concerned with preparing citizens who can understand, analyze, and make decisions about social issues hope that their students will want to continue to learn more about these matters and that they will apply these intellectual skills in their personal as well as their public lives. Such attitudes represent an inescapable by-product of authentic learning. But whatever subject is taught, we can be sure that students will develop attitudes toward that subject, the topics that they studied, and the classroom experiences they had.

In this curriculum, we are particularly interested in whether students express interest in:

- Knowing about social issues?
- Participating in social issues discussions?
- Clarifying their ideas about an issue?
- Defending their ideas in a public forum?

Too often, assessment strategies do not include plans for assessing attitudes toward the subject matter. Yet teachers can benefit from knowing more about the kinds of attitudes that students are forming. Regardless of how well students are meeting the explicit goals of the curriculum, if their learning does not generate a positive attitude toward being an informed citizen, if students find the instruction uninteresting or tedious (as students of conventional social studies often do), little has been accomplished.

Three approaches to assessment may be useful here. Careful teacher observation of student interactions and behaviors, student interviews, and student surveys all can provide helpful indicators about student attitudes.

Whether students participate in classroom discussions or projects enthusiastically, half-heartedly, or not at all probably provides the strongest clue about the attitudes they hold. Over time, what students say and do (or for that matter, do not do) provides insights to perceptive teachers about how students feel about their subject. Observation of students can be strengthened by asking a colleague to serve as an impartial observer of student interaction. This procedure can yield perspectives the classroom teacher may not have considered. Such observations may focus on the following kinds of questions:

- Do students seem to be involved?
- Do they appear interested?
- Do most of them participate in class discussion?
- Do they ask probing questions?
- Do they give detailed explanations?
- Do they initiate ideas or topics for the class to consider?
- Do they share relevant experiences of their own with the class?
- Do students reveal that they have energetically searched for information through newspaper clippings and additional readings?
- Do they ask about additional readings?
- Do they express interest in attending related events in the school or community? Watching relevant television programs?
- Do they discuss social issues with their friends and parents?
- Do they engage in community activities outside the school setting?

These questions are only illustrative. The main purpose of this suggested list of questions is to examine the degree of interest expressed by students.

Student interviews can also be helpful. One-on-one discussions between teachers and students can free students to discuss feelings they may not express in the presence of their peers. They may be more honest and may offer more constructive suggestions in an interview setting. Interviewing students also demonstrates that teachers are genuinely interested in their students as individuals and not just as members of the classroom group. Such interviews will be more effective if the teachers and students have developed relationships that are open, intellectually honest, and supportive. Further, if the teacher takes the suggestions of students seriously and responds to them in overt ways in the classroom, students will recognize that the interview setting is a meaningful one that deserves to be taken seriously.

Surveys of student attitudes are still another way to appraise student attitudes toward the subject. Teachers can develop a set of appropriate questions (similar to those identified under Student Observations above) and ask students to respond to them anonymously in writing. Surveys will not reveal as much detail as interviews, nor will it be as possible to assess the intensity of student responses. Nonetheless, a periodic student survey can yield useful information about student perspectives.

Implementing any of these approaches communicates to students that teachers care about what is being learned and are willing to provide an opportunity for student expression that is all too often ignored. Further, student feedback can directly benefit teachers to the extent that students make useful suggestions for improving the quality of their classrooms.

SUMMARY

This chapter has treated four components of appraising student growth with respect to reflective decision making: (1) knowledge and intellectual goals, (2) student commitment to democracy, (3) group and political skills, and (4) attitudes toward public issues and citizen participation. For assessment to be comprehensive and to provide useful feedback to teachers and students, each of these four components needs to be represented in the assessment of student progress with respect to the goals of a problem-solving curriculum.

Furthermore, in addition to the assessment strategies that have been described, we also recommend the use of follow-up studies that survey or interview students after they have graduated. This strategy can provide strong indications about the impact that the curriculum has made on their lives as citizens and provide useful information that identifies the strengths and weaknesses of such a program. Such questions as the following might be asked.

- Do you keep up with community and national issues?
- Are you active in community affairs?
- Do you subscribe to news magazines?
- Are you registered to vote?
- Did you vote in the last election?
- Have you followed the discussion related to protectionism, the national debt, or other current issues?
- Do you belong to any civic groups?

These questions represent a starting point. We wish to emphasize that follow-up studies should try to establish the extent to which graduates of the program are informed, responsible, and active citizens.

Clearly, the assessment strategies identified in this chapter are not exhaustive. However, they are all consistent with the principles of reflective decision making. First, they represent both the content and the intellectual processes involved in reflective decision making and deemphasize memorization of specific information. Secondly, they respond to specific classroom activities that students have experienced and are not determined prior to instruction. Thirdly, they are collectively negotiated by the teacher and student, so that the teacher is not the sole authority.

The assessment strategies suggested in this chapter depart markedly from conventional practice. Nonetheless, these strategies represent our best response to appraising student progress for a curriculum that fosters higher level understandings and intellectual skills. At a time when accessibility to computers can increase the ease of scoring more objective, multiple-choice tests, it may seem arrogant and even old-fashioned to suggest the use of assessment strategies that are more subjective and less amenable to computer efficiency. However, in our view, the goals of the proposed curriculum offer substantial hope for enhancing citizen competence in a democracy. The learning tasks involved are complex, conflict-laden, and sometimes abstract. We are persuaded that this curriculum can produce more knowledgeable, more thoughtful, and more committed citizens. It follows that the appraisal of citizen learning cannot be cast in simple, concrete terms. Like the curriculum itself, its assessment is demanding and challenging. Most importantly, the assessment process must mirror curriculum goals. To maintain conventional assessment practices with a curriculum that challenges the reach of students and teachers is not only to contradict but to negate the potential embedded in democratic education.

Epilogue

At the end of the eighties we have completed a book whose thesis continues to be central to our professional lives. This thesis recognizes the critical role that citizens must play if democracy and self-governance are to flourish and prosper.

Yet, as we review the conditions that now confront both this society and the planet, we are awed by the array of issues facing today's citizens. At the present time, the following issues are receiving media attention:

- The sale of arms to Iran and its threat to the President's credibility
- The viability of arms control negotiations and their relationship to the survival of the planet
- The continuing specter of racial violence as three black men were assailed by a gang of white youths in Queens, New York
- Recent immigration legislation that offers amnesty to illegal aliens who entered the United States prior to January 1, 1982
- A plea for a Clean Soil Act that would mandate a comprehensive study of the nation's soil and the impact of soil contamination on health

Clearly, the examples above are not by any means exhaustive. However, they are sufficient to lead us to these salient questions. How many of our citizens care about these issues? How many of us are informed enough to take a reasoned position on these matters? How many of us know how to become informed? How many of us can read a newspaper critically? Watch television critically? How many of us are willing to take a stand? How many are motivated to assume responsibility and take action to improve conditions surrounding a particular issue? Much to our dismay, we are persuaded that very, very few citizens hold such capabilities and predispositions.

Some might claim that citizen disinterest and citizen apathy do not constitute cause for alarm. After all, since we elect our government officials, the citizen still retains control. To the contrary, we are compelled to argue that voters who are both intelligent and informed are, without a doubt, no more than a paltry few. Even the total number of voters is declining. Indeed, the consequences of apathy and disinterest directly affect the quality of self-governance and democratic life. By voluntarily giving up responsibility to others and not holding those who actually make decisions accountable, citizens render themselves powerless and demonstrate that as a people we are unwilling to assume the responsibilities that attend self-governance.

The issues stated above augur a host of changes that will affect many aspects of our lives. What ethical standards should govern the Presidency? How open should our immigration policy be? What is the relationship between expanded industrialization and soil pollution? How do we judge whether and when technology has positive or negative effects? Can racism be reduced or eliminated?

Many sectors of our lives are involved: industry, labor, technology, health, relationships among peoples and nations are but a few. Furthermore, education and schooling are not exempt.

One cannot help wondering what issues will face citizens a year from now or a decade from now. And we also cannot help wondering how those responsible for the schools and their curricula will respond. To do nothing and thus reaffirm the status quo is not a promising alternative. If we are genuinely committed to a democratic citizenry, thoughtful and deliberate educational change is not only in order, it is a mandate.

In this book we have advanced a set of ideas about the nature of the social studies for citizens of a democracy. The curriculum that we propose emphasizes the crucial importance of expanding the intellectual powers of citizens as they study significant problems of the past, present, and future. In this context, we argue that students can and must experience the dynamics and complexities associated with decisions that citizens make. Or, to state it differently, we have tried to make the case that one learns to engage in citizen decision making by actually making such decisions. Therefore, we have taken issue with current practices that emphasize rote memory of textbook knowledge and instruction in the lecture mode. Taken together, such practices foster neither intellectual growth nor the understanding of significant historical or contemporary issues that plague this democracy and the entire planet. Current practices are far too authoritarian and far too simplistic to achieve such ends. We do not claim that this kind of shift in the nature of social studies education is an easy one. Indeed, it is most challenging. However, we are convinced that it is an important, even an essential one, if democracy is to be significant for the next generation of citizens and if, in turn, graduates of the public schools are to be able to make viable contributions to its strength and vitality.

The changes entailed by this curriculum are many. Among them are more democratic roles for teachers and students, an extensive and diverse set of materials for learning, and more attention to student discussions that are intense with intellectual challenge. Some may argue the change is too drastic, and perhaps too inconvenient. Our response is that not to change, not to teach in ways that stimulate the intellect of future citizens, not to confront them with significant issues is to sell democracy short. For unless students are vigorously prepared for democratic life, we can expect citizens who are likely to be passive, acquiescent, uninformed, and incapable of meeting the challenge of self-governance. Democracy will then lose by default. The risks and costs of maintaining the status quo are too high. We cannot afford *not* to change if we believe that democracy is indeed the last best hope for human beings on this earth.

APPENDIX

NOTES

REFERENCES

INDEX

ABOUT THE AUTHORS

A Reflective Teaching Observation Instrument

This checklist is derived and adapted from Edward Jadallah, *The Development of a Reflective Teaching Instrument*, Columbus, Ohio: Ohio State University, 1984 (unpublished doctoral dissertation).

The checklist can be useful to teachers as they examine the degree to which their teaching styles correspond with the principles of reflective teaching.

REFLECTIVE TEACHING PROCESS

Identifying a Problem

To what extent does the teacher:

1. *Ask divergent questions to identify a problem?*

    The teacher asks questions that confront students with problem situations. Divergent questions allow for a variety of answers. The teacher does not seek a single "right" answer, only plausible and sometimes best responses. The teacher may ask, for example: How might the U.S. improve relations with the Soviet Union? What would you predict would happen in Central America if Congress denies military aid to Nicaragua? What effect will the dispute between Iran and Iraq have on the U.S. economy?

2. *Use materials to introduce conflicting data?*

    The teacher uses newspapers, books, magazines, pictures, recordings, artifacts, or other means that guide students to identify or discover a problem. For example, the teacher may read aloud two conflicting editorials on the subject of the new drunk driving laws.

The teacher may show pictures that illustrate impoverished and wealthy lifestyles within the same city.

3. *Ask probing questions that identify inconsistencies or contradictions in the beliefs, opinions, or ideas of students?*

The teacher, after listening to students express a belief, asks a question focusing on other beliefs that may be consistent with or contradict the first belief. For example, the teacher may hear students concur that, "Any form of censorship is unconstitutional and it is the government's responsibility to protect our freedom of speech." The teacher then asks the students, "Do you feel it is all right to spend tax dollars to provide police protection for the American Nazi Party to hold a rally in Skokie, Illinois?" Students who disagree with tax monies spent in this manner, or who don't feel that Nazis should be allowed in America, are forced to reevaluate the first belief. Thus, a problem is identified for investigation.

4. *Ask students to state the problem/question in their own words?*

The teacher, after initiating a problematic situation, asks probing questions to help students narrow the focus of the investigation. For example, the teacher might ask, "What do you see as a problem? Why do you feel this is a problem? Can you phrase this problem as a question? What are some specific questions that you think need to be answered in order to solve this problem?"

5. *Ask students to define ambiguous or new terms to help make the problem or question clear and precise?*

The teacher asks questions about specific terms that may need to be defined and clarified so that the problem or question is clearly understood by all students. For example, if the problem/question to be investigated was, "What effects has technology had on American lifestyles?" the meaning of "technology" and "lifestyles" may need to be precisely defined in the context of the investigation. The teacher could ask, "What kind of technology are we talking about? What do you mean by lifestyles? Are you referring to our present lifestyles, or those in the future or past?"

Developing Hypotheses

To what extent does the teacher:

6. *Present students with a hypothesis to test?*

The teacher foregoes having students identify a problem and instead gives them a predetermined hypothesis that they can test against evidence. For example, the teacher might read a quote from a book, newspaper, or magazine and ask students to support or refute with evidence.

7. *Ask divergent questions to solicit hypotheses?*

The teacher asks questions that require students to offer an opinion or hypothesis about possible solutions to a problem/question. Student responses are usually based on past learning or personal experiences. For example, the teacher may ask questions like: What are some possible causes of the Viet Nam War? What effect might the present cold war have on world peace? What foreign policy could be expected from Jesse Jackson?

8. *Present data and then ask questions to solicit hypotheses?*

The teacher presents newspapers, books, magazines, pictures, recordings, word lists, diaries, or other data sources that can be used to generate hypotheses. The teacher then asks questions that require students to make inferences, predictions, and classifications or to state relationships. This may be done on an individual basis or in small or large group sessions.

The questions asked by the teacher may be phrased in the following manner: What do these pictures indicate about life in China? Based on these newspaper articles, who do you think will win the Democratic nomination? What time period are this music and art work from? Why did Benjamin Franklin write this comment in his diary?

9. *Ask probing questions to help students identify and locate sources that could be used to generate hypotheses?*

The teacher, after having students identify and clarify a problem/question, asks them questions that will guide them to sources that relate to the problem/question. For example, a teacher may ask, "Where could we find more information about the American Indian? How could the Museum of History help us find out more about American Indians? Can you think of other resources or places that would provide us with information? What kind of information do we need to find in order to answer our problem/questions?"

10. *Provide time for students to gather sources and formulate hypotheses?*

The teacher, once students have identified reasonable and accessible sources, encourages students to locate these sources and investigate them for hypotheses related to the problem/question. For example, the teacher may allow students to gather information in a library or browse through materials that are already provided in the classroom.

Testing Hypotheses

To what extent does the teacher:

11. *Ask students to suggest possible evidence that may support or refute their hypotheses?*

    The teacher, once students have formulated clearly defined hypotheses, asks them to determine what kind of evidence they would expect to exist if their hypotheses were true and if their hypotheses were false. For example, the teacher may ask, "What evidence would you need to find that will help prove the hypotheses that most early American Indians were farmers? What evidence would suggest that most early American Indians were not farmers?"

12. *Ask probing questions to help students identify and locate sources that could be used to generate evidence?*

    The teacher, after having students identify supportive and non-supportive evidence, will ask them questions that will guide them to sources that relate to the evidence they are looking for. For example, a teacher may ask, "Where could we find evidence about the occupations held by early American Indians. What kind of books might we refer to? Can you think of other sources or places that might tell us about early American Indian occupations?"

13. *Provide time for students to locate sources and gather evidence?*

    The teacher, once students have identified reasonable and accessible sources, allows them to locate these sources and investigate them for evidence related to the hypotheses being tested. For example, the teacher may allow students to conduct a survey, interview people, gather information in a library, or use materials that are already provided in the classroom.

14. *Present data and then ask questions that require students to test their hypotheses?*

    The teacher presents data sources that can be used to generate evidence that supports and/or refutes the hypotheses. The teacher then asks questions that require students to identify supportive and non-supportive evidence, evaluate the validity of the evidence and its source, and state relationships between the evidence and the hypotheses. For example, the teacher may say, "Read this letter written by Benjamin Franklin. Can you find evidence that supports or refutes our hypothesis about slavery in Colonial America? Do you think the information contained in this letter is accurate? How can we be sure? Based on the evidence you've cited so far, what can you tell me about the accuracy of our hypothesis?"

15. *Ask probing questions which lead students to evaluate the validity of the evidence they have collected?*

The teacher, once students have collected evidence to support or refute their hypotheses, may ask them to prove that the evidence collected is factual, not just opinions, biases, or assumptions. For example, the teacher may ask, "What other sources have you found that support this evidence? Have you compared and contrasted this evidence with other sources? What did you find out? Is this evidence current? Who wrote it? When was it written and why? Is your evidence consistent?"

16. *Ask questions that require students to relate the evidence to the hypotheses being tested?*

The teacher will ask students how the evidence they have collected either supports or refutes the hypotheses being tested. For example, the teacher may ask, "What evidence did you find that provides support for the hypothesis that early American Indians were farmers? Why do you think that this evidence actually proves that they were farmers? What evidence did you find that might refute our hypotheses?"

Developing Conclusions

To what extent does the teacher:

17. *Ask questions that require students to state conclusions concerning the initial problem/question based upon the valid and invalid hypotheses they have tested?*

The teacher, after students have tested their hypotheses, will ask divergent and evaluative questions to guide students in developing conclusions. For example, the teacher may ask, "What hypotheses provided an accurate description about the negative effects technology has had on American lifestyles? What evidence do you have that supports this conclusion? What can we definitely state about the effects technology has had on American lifestyles?"

Applying Conclusions to New Data

To what extent does the teacher:

18. *Present new data and ask students to find evidence that supports or refutes their conclusions?*

The teacher introduces new data that is relevant to the initial problem/question but has not been used by students to develop their conclusions. The teacher will ask the students how the new data either supports or refutes their conclusions. For example, the teacher may introduce two medical journals and ask, "What evidence can you find that provides support for the conclusion that advanced technology has increased our life expectancy?

CLASSROOM CLIMATE

Facilitating an Open Discussion

To what extent does the teacher:

1. *Arrange chairs in seminar or small-group style?*
   The teacher asks students to arrange their chairs in a circle or semicircle so that communication between students and the teacher will be face-to-face, or the teacher has already done so.
2. *Direct student-to-student interaction?*
   The teacher asks students to comment on each other's opinions and ideas. For example, the teacher may say, "John said that Abraham Lincoln used the issue of slavery merely to further his political career. He, in John's opinion, was a political opportunist. How do the rest of you feel about this statement?
3. *Direct the discussion to many students, not just a few?*
   The teacher asks questions and solicits opinion from a wide variety of students to ensure that a few students do not monopolize the discussion.
4. *Talk briefly and then stop so that he or she does not monopolize the discussion?*
   The teacher makes most explanations, reviews, and responses to students' questions or comments brief and to the point. He or she deliberately pauses and provides time for students to respond and ask questions.
   The teacher may directly solicit comments and questions from students, or may pause for a while and give some nonverbal cue to students indicating they are invited to begin discussion.
5. *Allow time for students to reflect on the topic being discussed?*
   The teacher deliberately pauses after important comments or questions to allow students time to think. The teacher may say to students, "Let's stop and think about this for a while," or "This requires serious consideration. Let's think before we make any hasty judgments."

6. *Point out what is relevant and not relevant to the discussion?*

The teacher deliberately draws the attention of students to those aspects of the discussion that are important and relevant and courteously draws attention away from irrelevant discussion. The teacher may say, for example, "That is a very important observation. Let's pursue it further." In the case of an irrelevant comment, the teacher may say, "That is an interesting comment, but let's redirect our attention to the main topic."

Empathy and Acceptance

To what extent does the teacher:

7. *Give examples that relate to what the student is saying?*

The teacher describes or explains a similar instance related to what a student has just described or explained.

8. *Listen attentively and without interrupting while students express their ideas, opinions, and questions?*

The teacher pays close attention to what students are saying and provides nonverbal cues like nodding his head and maintaining eye contact to encourage continuation of expression.

9. *Provide students with corrective feedback in a nonthreatening manner?*

The teacher uses data to help students discover that what they are saying may be wrong. Rather than presenting himself or herself as the authority on the subject, the teacher directs students to data sources that contradict what the student is saying. The teacher then asks students to explain the contradiction. This allows students to retain the integrity of changing their own minds and keeps the quest of knowledge in a spirit of true reflective thinking.

10. *Make remarks which indicate that the students' comments are appreciated, accepted, and subject to analysis?*

The teacher provides students with positive feedback when they participate in discussions and at the same time facilitates a critique or analysis of their comments. The teacher might say, for example, "Thanks for that interesting observation. You seem to have done a lot of reading on the subject. Let's examine how your ideas compare with others in this class and the authorities in the field."

11. *Redirect the focus of discussion when student appears to be uncomfortable or self-conscious?*

The teacher, on observing a student's nervous reaction to a question or comment, provides the student with an option not to answer the question or not offer a comment. The teacher may say, for example, "Think about it for a while and I'll get back to you," or the teacher might direct a general question to the whole class, "What do the rest of you think about . . . ?"

Establishing and Maintaining Rapport with Students

To what extent does the teacher:

12. *Make nonthreatening humorous remarks when relevant?*
    The teacher eases the tension of a discussion or relaxes students prior to a discussion with some humorous anecdote.
13. *Address individual students by their names with friendly mannerisms such as smiles, approving nods, pats on the back, and so forth?*
    The teacher conveys to the students through verbal and nonverbal signs that they are liked and that their participation in class is respected and appreciated.

This checklist covers the major aspects of reflection and emphasizes the use of probing questions as imperative to the entire process of reflective thought.

Notes

CHAPTER 1

1. A detailed analysis of how recurring wars place a strain on the maintenance of free democratic institutions may be found in Barnes (1942, chaps. 9–10).

2. For a thorough and thought-provoking treatment of the present state of democracy in our society and of the intellectual difficulties experienced by citizens applying democratic principles to particulars, see Broudy (1981).

CHAPTER 2

1. For a comprehensive development of the diverse and in some ways private nature of citizenship see Anderson (1979, chap. 10).

2. We acknowledge the dependence of this section of Chapter 2 on the article by Broudy, Smith, and Burnett (1964), from which parts of this chapter are a liberal adaptation. The reader may want to consult the earlier work.

3. A basic work on the method of democratic problem solving was published in 1943. Its authors, Kenneth D. Benne, George E. Axtelle, B. Othanel Smith, and R. Bruce Raup were original and incisive thinkers about the problem of how citizens of a democracy are to make decisions regarding practical problems that confront them. The reader may want to consult this original work.

4. For a somewhat more traditional statement of skills to be taught in the social studies, see The National Council for the Social Studies, *Essentials of the Social Studies* (1980).

CHAPTER 4

1. See Fitzgerald (1979) and Miller and Rose (1983) for a more complete development of this claim.

2. See Myrdahl (1944) Vol. 2, Appendix 2, for an exhaustive treatment of the effect of hidden valuation on the scientific study of history.

3. For a thorough analysis of the complexity of a practical problem in an open, ongoing society see Longstreet (1977, 1982).

CHAPTER 6

1. Sigel (1984) emphasizes the compatibility between Piagetian ideas and Heinz Werner's orthogenetic principle, which involves such processes as differentiation, integration, reintegration, and dedifferentiation of experience.

CHAPTER 7

1. See a somewhat humorous article depicting the ideational dilemma facing economists who can hardly agree on anything and whose predictions of economic development are notoriously amiss in *Newsweek*, February 4, 1985, pp. 60–61, under the title "What Good Are Economists?"

2. The recent plight of *Harper's*, one of the most venerable and respected journals of public opinion, may be cited as one example. Other respected journals of public criticism which are so hard pressed to stay alive that they seek donations from their friends include the *Nation*, the *New Republic*, and the *Progressive*.

3. It was reported in *Newsweek*, August 26, 1985, p. 42, that the popular TV show "Entertainment Tonight" has an average nightly audience greater than the combined audiences of "The CBS Morning News," "The Today Show," and "Good Morning America."

4. Taken from the Report of the *Federal Election Commission*, January 8, 1985.

5. Ibid.

6. An example may be found in the President's speech to 14,000 students at North Carolina State University as reported in *Time*, September 16, 1985, p. 29, when he said, "Do you want America's tax plan—a fair share for *everyone*?"

7. Based on a reading of the full text of his speech as reported in *The New York Times*, November 15, 1985, p. 8.

CHAPTER 8

1. Support for the in-depth study of a few topics over the necessarily superficial coverage of many topics is lent by the following authors: Whitehead, (1929, pp. 1–2) who warned of the uselessness and, above all, the harmful effects of "inert ideas, that is, ideas that are received into the mind without being utilized or tested or thrown into fresh combinations"; Myrdahl (1944, pp. 1052–1053), who observed that to narrate history straight without stopping to consider the as-

sumptions, implied or explicit, and the qualifiers chosen by the historians and without considering other scholarly versions of the events being described is tantamount to indoctrination; Richard H. Brown, historian at the Newberry Library, Director of the Amherst Project, who published a number of units in which he demonstrated the feasibility of studying a few significant episodes by what he called "postholing," studying these issues in depth as an alternative to the survey course in United States history. Many of the projects in the New Social Studies movement were based on the principle of in-depth study of a relatively small number of topics; recently Newmann (1986) recognized the replacement of coverage with in-depth study as a primary need in the field.

2. The argument for the use of the hypothetical mode over the expository in the study of social content was most succinctly presented by Jerome Bruner (1965, pp. 81–96). This idea was largely responsible for spawning the whole "New Social Studies" movement.

3. The authors were greatly influenced in their choice of strands by the ideas of Broudy, Smith, and Burnett (1964, pp. 159–274) who suggested a classification of knowledge for purposes of instruction similar in some respects to the one being proposed in this work.

4. According to Peter Drucker, in an article written for a forthcoming issue of *Foreign Affairs* (reported in *Time Magazine*, April 7, 1986, p. 48), there is no longer a problem of the number of people to be fed outstripping the food supply. The problem lies rather in the economy of financial flow. This illustrates how quickly social problems may change.

5. An entire issue of the *Center Magazine* has been devoted to the problem of intelligence and secrecy in an open society; see Vol. XIX, No. 2, March/April 1986.

6. The authors were somewhat influenced in proposing this strand by Broudy, Smith, and Burnett (1964, pp. 231–243). A similar proposal was made in this work. The seminal work on thinking about a social problem is by Raup, Axtelle, Benne, and Smith (1943).

7. In two recent books, Neil Postman (1979, 1982) has pointed out the deleterious effects of mass media in the education of children.

CHAPTER 9

1. Suggestions for possible problems around which world history could be studied are to be found in Fenton (1969).

2. Among those who have proposed models for study in depth are Oliver and Shaver (1966), Fenton (1966), R. H. Brown (1966), Hunt and Metcalf (1955), and Martorella (1976).

A number of courses and units have been developed that exemplify in-depth study. See Oliver and Newmann (1967), for unit booklets, each providing the materials for the study in depth of a vital issue in American history, and Fenton (1970). Especially noteworthy is the Fenton series *A History of the United States*

(1970; revised, 1975). See also *High School Geography Project* (1974); *Man: A Course of Study* (1969); and Brown and Halsey (1965).

3. Heavy reliance in this section is placed on Oliver and Newmann. *The American Revolution*, Public Issues Series (1972). On several occasions, we have taught various adaptations of this series to high school students.

CHAPTER 11

1. While we fully recognize that grading is an established practice in schools, we wish to point out that assigning letter grades to students in classes that foster problem solving runs counter to developing independent, autonomous citizens who can make their own decisions about a variety of matters—including their own progress in a given course. The learning involved in such courses is complex, and this condition contributes to arbitrary judgments about what kind of effort deserves an A, a B, and so forth. The situation is slightly improved if teachers and students collaboratively arrive at criteria for assigning grades. However, the assessment strategies presented in this chapter have as their purpose providing feedback to teachers and students and are not related to the assignment of letter grades.

2. For more complete information see Morante and Ulesky (1984).

References

Association of American Geographers (1969). *The high school geography project* (Boulder, CO). New York: Macmillan.

Anderson, L. (1979). *School and citizenship in the global age.* Bloomington, IN: Social Studies Development Center.

Apple, M. J. (1982). *Education and power.* Boston: Routledge & Kegan Paul.

Ault, R. (1977) *Children's cognitive development.* New York: Oxford University Press.

Barnes, H. E. (1942). *Social institutions.* New York: Prentice-Hall.

Barth, J., & Shermis, S. (1979). Defining social problems. *Theory and Practice in Social Education, 7*(1), 1–19.

Becker, C. L. (1936). *Everyman his own historian.* New York: F. S. Crofts & Co.

Benne, K. D., Axtelle, G. E., Smith, B. O., & Raup, B. (1943). *The improvement of practical intelligence.* New York: Harper and Brothers.

Beyer, B. K. (1977). *Inquiry in the social studies classroom.* Columbus, OH: Charles E. Merrill.

Beyer, B. (1984). Improving thinking skills—Practical approaches. *Phi Delta Kappan, 85*(8), 556–560.

Bidna, D. B., Greenburg, M. S., & Spitz, J. H. (1982). *We the people: A history of the United States.* Lexington, MA: D. C. Heath.

Bowles, S. (1972, June). Getting nowhere: Programmed class stagnation. *Society, 9,* 42–45.

Bridges, D. (1979). *Education, democracy and discussion.* Windsor, England: Nelson Publishing.

Broudy, H. S. (1981). *Truth and credibility: The citizen's dilemma.* New York: Longmans.

Broudy, H. S., Smith, B. O., & Burnett, J. R. (1964). *Democracy and excellence in American secondary education.* Chicago: Rand McNally.

Brown, L. R., Chandler, W. U., Flavin, C., Pollock, C., Postel, S., Starke, L., & Wolf, E. C. (1986). *State of the world.* New York: W. W. Norton.

Brown, R. H. (1966, October 15). History and the new social studies. *Saturday Review*, pp. 80–81, 92.

Brown, R. H., & Halsey, V. R. (1965). *New dimensions in American history*. Boston: D. C. Heath.

Brown, R. H., & Halsey, V. R. (Eds.). (1970, 1972). *The Amherst project*. Menlo Park, CA: Addison-Wesley.

Bruner, J. S. (1962). *The process of education*. Cambridge, MA: Harvard University Press.

Bruner, J. S. (1965). *On knowing: Essays for the left hand*. New York: Atheneum.

Bruner, J. S. (1972). Culture, politics & pedagogy. In Ronald Shinn (Ed.), *Culture & the school* (pp. 42–53). Scranton, PA: Intext Educational Publishers.

Bryce, J. (1921). *Modern democracies*. New York: Macmillan.

California State Department of Education. (1921). *California social studies framework*. Sacramento: California State Department of Education.

Cassidy, E. W., & Kurfman, D. G. (1977). Decision-making as purpose and process. In D. G. Kurfman (Ed.), *Developing decision-making skills* (NCSS 47th Yearbook, pp. 1–26). Washington, DC: National Council for the Social Studies.

Cogan, J. J., & Schneider, D. O. (1983). *Perspectives on Japan: A guide for teachers* (NCSS Bulletin No. 69). Washington, DC: National Council for the Social Studies.

Cohen, M. N. (1947). *The meaning of human history*. Lasalle, IL: Open Court Publishing.

Commager, H. S. (1966). Should the historian make moral judgment? *American Heritage, 17,* 26–27, 87–93.

Cronkite, W. (1983, February 19). TV audience overexposed, underinformed. *The (New Orleans) Times-Picayune/States Item*, Section 1, p. 14.

Dewey, J. (1922). *Democracy and education*. New York: Macmillan.

Dewey, J. (1933). *How we think*. Boston: D. C. Heath.

Ehman, L. (1969) An analysis of the relationship of selected educational variables with the political socialization of high school students. *American Educational Research Journal, 6*(4), 559–580.

Ehman, L. (1977). Research on social studies curriculum and instruction: Values. In F. P. Hunkins (Ed.), *Review of research in social studies education, 1970–1975* (Bulletin 49, pp. 55–95). Washington, DC: National Council for the Social Studies.

Elliott, D. L., Nagel, K. C., & Woodward, A. (1985). Do textbooks belong in elementary schools? *Educational Leadership, 42*(7), 22–26.

Engle, S. H. (1982, Fall). Alan Griffin (1907–1964). *Journal of Thought, 17,* 45–54.

Engle, S. H. (1986). Late night thoughts about the new social studies. *Social Education, 50,* 20–30.

Essentials of the social studies. (1980). Washington, DC: The National Council for the Social Studies.

Fenton, E. F. (1966). *Teaching the new social studies: An inductive approach*. New York: Holt, Rinehart & Winston.

Fenton, E. F. (1967). *The new social studies*. New York: Holt, Rinehart & Winston.

Fenton, E. F. (Ed.). (1969). *32 problems in world history*. Glenview, IL: Scott, Foresman.

Fenton, E. F. (Ed.). (1970). *The Americans: A history of the United States*. New York: Holt, Rinehart & Winston.

Festinger, L. (1957). *A theory of cognitive dissonance*. Stanford, CA: Stanford University Press.

Festinger, L. (1964). *Conflict, decision and dissonance*. Stanford, CA: Stanford University Press.

Fitzgerald, F. (1979: Feb. 26; March 5; March 12). Rewriting American history. *New Yorker*, pp. 41–77; 40–91; 48–106.

Forbes, R. H. (1976). *National assessment of educational progress: Education for citizenship* (Citizenship/Social Studies Report No. 07-CS-01). Washington, DC: National Center for Education Statistics.

Fowlkes, D. (1976). *Classroom climate and political socialization*. Paper presented at the annual meeting of the American Political Science Association, Chicago, September, 1976.

Gall, M. (1984). Synthesis of research on teachers' questioning. *Educational Leadership, 42*(3), 40–47.

Goodlad, J. (1983). A study of schooling: Some findings and hypotheses. *Phi Delta Kappan, 64*(7), 465–470.

Griffin, A. F. (1942). *A philosophical approach to the subject matter preparation of teachers of history*. Unpublished dissertation, Ohio State University, Columbus, OH.

Handlin, O. (1961, September). Live students and dead education in high school. *The Atlantic*, pp. 29–34.

Hill, C. (1983). History and culture. In *The Random House encyclopedia* (pp. 944–1431). New York: Random House.

Hill, W. F. (1953). *Learning: A survey of psychological interpretations*. San Francisco: Chandler.

Hunt, M. P., and Metcalf, L. E. (1955). *Teaching high school social studies*. New York: Harper & Brothers.

Hutchins. R. M. (1982, March/April). The aims of a democratic society. *Center Magazine*, back cover.

Jadallah, E. (1985). *The development of a reflective teaching instrument*. Unpublished doctoral dissertation, Ohio State University, Columbus, OH.

Jaros, D., & Cannon, B. (1969). Transmitting basic political values: The role of the educational system. *The School Review, 77*, 94–107.

Johann, R. O. (1965). Authority and responsibility. In J. C. Murray (Ed.), *Freedom and man* (pp. 141–151). New York: P. J. Kenedy & Sons.

Johnson, D. W., & Johnson, F. P. (1975). *Joining together: Group theory and skills*. Englewood Cliffs, NJ: Prentice-Hall.

Johnson, H. (1940). *Teaching of history*. New York: Macmillan.

Judge, J. (1986). Our search for the true Columbus landfall. *National Geographic, 170*, 565–566.

Larrabee, H. A. (1945). *Reliable knowledge*. Boston: Houghton Mifflin.

Lewin, K. (1936). *Principles of topological psychology*. New York: McGraw-Hill.

Longstreet, W. S. (1977). Decision making: The new social studies. In *Decision making: The heart of social studies instruction revisited* (Occasional Papers No. 1). Bloomington, IN: Indiana University, Social Studies Development Center.

Longstreet, W. S. (1982, Winter). Action research: A paradigm. *Educational Forum, 46,* 135–158.

Man: A course of study. (1969). Cambridge, MA: Educational Development Center.

Martorella, P. H. (1976). *Elementary social studies as a learning system.* New York: Harper and Row.

Martorella, P. H. (1985). *Elementary social studies.* Boston: Little, Brown.

Massialas, B. G. (Ed.). (1963). The Indiana experiments in inquiry: Social studies. *Bulletin of the School of Education* (Indiana University), *39*(3), entire issue.

Massialas, B. G., Sprague, N. F., & Hurst, J. B. (1975). *Social issues: Coping in an age of crisis.* Englewood Cliffs, NJ: Prentice-Hall.

Matthews, D. (1985). Civic intelligence. *Social Education, 49,* 678–681.

Miles, M. (1971). *Annie and the old one.* Boston: Little, Brown.

Miller, S., & Rose, S. (1983, Spring). The great depression: A textbook case of problems with American history textbooks. *Theory and research in social education, 11,* 25–39.

Molnar, A. (1983, May). Are the issues studied in school the important issues facing mankind? *Social Education, 47,* 305–307.

Morante, E. A., & Ulesky, A. (1984). Assessment of reasoning abilities. *Educational Leadership, 42,* 71–74.

Murray, J. C. (1964). *Challenges to democracy: A tenth anniversary symposium of the Fund for the Republic.* New York: Praeger.

Myrdahl, G. (1944). *An American dilemma* (Vols. 1 & 2). New York: Harper & Brothers.

Nagel, E. (1961). *The structure of science.* New York: Harcourt, Brace & World.

Newmann, F. M. (1986). Priorities for the future: Toward a common agenda. *Social Education, 50*(4), 240–250.

Newmann, F. M., Bertoccie, A., & Landsness, R. M. (1977). *Skills in citizen action.* Madison, WI: Citizen Participation Curriculum Project.

Niebuhr, R. (1971, July/August). Democracy's distinction and danger. *Center Magazine,* pp. 1–4.

Ogburn, W. F. (1922). *Social change.* New York: B. W. Huebach.

Oliver, D. W., & Newmann, F. M. (1967). *Public Issues Series* (Harvard Social Studies Project). Columbus, OH: Xerox Corp.

Oliver, D. W., & Shaver, J. P. (1966). *Teaching public issues in the high school.* Boston: Houghton Mifflin.

Parallel passages: Contrasting views from Japanese and United States textbooks. (1983). Bloomington, IN: Social Studies Development Center.

Paxson, F. (1936, Summer). Lecture notes, History of the West. University of Wisconsin, Madison.

Pohl, F. J. (1986). *The new Columbus.* Rochester, NY: Security Dupont.

Postman, N. (1979). *Teaching as a conserving activity.* New York: Delacorte Press.

Postman, N. (1982). *The disappearance of childhood*. New York: Delacorte Press.

Reich, R. (1983). *The next American frontier*. New York: Time Books.

Remmers, H. H. (1957). *The American teenager*. Indianapolis, IN: Bobbs-Merrill.

Rugg, H. (1921, October). On reconstructing the social studies curriculum. *The Historical Outlook, 12*, 249–52.

Selman, R. L. (1980). *The growth of interpersonal understanding*. New York: Academic Press.

Senesh, L. (1966). *Organizing a curriculum around social science concepts*. West Lafayette, IN: Social Science Education Consortium.

Shaver, J. P., Davis, O. L., & Helburn, S. (1979). The status of social studies education: Impressions from three NSF studies, *Social Education, 43*, 150–153.

Sigel, I. E. (1984). A constructivist perspective for teaching thinking. *Educational Leadership, 42*(3), 18–21.

Sizer, T. S. (1984). *Horace's compromise: The dilemma of the American high school*. Boston: Houghton Mifflin.

Stake, R. E., & Easley, J. A., Jr. (1978). *Case studies in science education. Vol. 2: Design, overview and findings*. (University of Illinois, Urbana: Center for Instructional Research and Curriculum Evaluation). Washington, DC: National Science Foundation.

Starr, P. (1971). The edge of social science. *Harvard Educational Review, 44*, 393–415.

Superka, D. P., Hawke, S., & Morrisette, I. (1980). The current and future status of the studies. *Social Education, 44*, 362–369.

Taba, H. (1967). *Teacher's handbook for elementary social studies*. Reading, MA: Addison-Wesley.

Task Force on Scope and Sequence. (1984). In search of a scope and sequence for social studies. *Social Education, 48*, 249–262.

Thurow, L. C. (1985, November). "Big trade-off" debunked: The efficiency of a fair economy. *The Washington Monthly, 17*, 47–54.

Torney, J., Oppenheim, A., & Farnen, R. (1975). *Civic education in ten countries*. New York: John Wiley & Sons.

Wesley, E. B. (1937). *Teaching social studies in high school*. Boston: D. C. Heath.

White, P. J. (1983). Rain forests. *National Geographic, 163*, 46–48.

Whitehead, A. N. (1929). *The aims of education*. London: Collier Macmillan.

Zuriff, G. E. (1985). *Behaviorism: A conceptual reconstruction*. New York: Columbia University Press.

Index

About the Authors

SHIRLEY H. ENGLE is Professor Emeritus of Education at Indiana University, where he also served as Associate Dean of the Graduate School. He earned a bachelor's degree and master's, both in education, at the University of Illinois, and then taught in the Illinois public schools for 14 years before returning to the university for his Ph.D. His distinguished career has included a term as president of the National Council for the Social Studies and a long list of publications. He continues to be actively involved in efforts to improve social studies education and frequently presents papers and lectures on the subject.

ANNA S. OCHOA is Director of Undergraduate Studies at Indiana University, where she previously was a member of the Social Studies Education faculty. A Wayne State University graduate, she earned an M.A. in history at the University of Michigan and a Ph.D. in curriculum studies at the University of Washington. She is a past president of the National Council for the Social Studies and has published extensively in the field of social studies education.